Votes for Delaware Women

To Tricia,

Best wishes,

Anne M. Boylan

Cultural Studies of Delaware and the Eastern Shore

Votes for Delaware Women

Anne M. Boylan

University of Delaware Press
Newark

University of Delaware Press

© 2021 by Anne M. Boylan
All right reserved

First published 2021

ISBN 978-1-64453-206-5 (hardback)
ISBN 978-1-64453-207-2 (pb)
ISBN 978-1-64453-208-9 (ebook)

Library of Congress Cataloging-in-Publicastion Data is available for this title.

Distributed worldwide by Rutgers University Press

Printed in the United States of America on acid-free paper

For the Next Generation:
Ree, Jo, and John

Contents

Figures and Tables

Abbreviations

AERA	American Equal Rights Association
AWSA	American Woman Suffrage Association
CU	Congressional Union for Woman Suffrage (later, NWP)
DAR	Daughters of the American Revolution
DESA	Delaware Equal Suffrage Association
EE	Wilmington *Every Evening*
EJ	Wilmington *Evening Journal*
ERA	Equal Rights Amendment
GFWC	General Federation of Women's Clubs
HWS	*History of Woman Suffrage*
MN	Wilmington *Morning News*
NAACP	National Association for the Advancement of Colored People
NACW	National Association of Colored Women
NAWSA	National American Woman Suffrage Association
NWP	National Woman's Party
NWSA	National Woman Suffrage Association
OBD	*Online Biographical Dictionary of the Woman Suffrage Movement in the United States*
WCTU	Woman's Christian Temperance Union
YWCA	Young Women's Christian Association

Acknowledgments

For starting me on the journey that led me to write this book, I owe a debt of gratitude to Tom Dublin of Binghamton University. When he asked me to coordinate the research and writing of Delaware suffragist biographies for the planned *Online Biographical Dictionary of the Woman Suffrage Movement in the United States*, he sent an intriguing breeze my way. Before long, my little boat's sails were filling with the questions and ideas that led this book to its eventual destination. The work of the students, teachers, librarians, curators, and writers who contributed to the online biographical project provided crucial ballast; I thank them all. I also wish to acknowledge the valuable research assistance provided by the staffs of local institutions, particularly: the Delaware Historical Society; the Delaware Public Archives; the University of Delaware Library, Museums and Press; the University of Delaware Library's Special Collections Department; and the University of Delaware Archives.

Grateful thanks are due to Rebecca Johnson Melvin in the University of Delaware Library Special Collections for alerting me to sources I might not otherwise have consulted, and for guiding me as we created an exhibit based on those (and other) materials. In addition, archivists and librarians at the Library of Congress and the Belmont-Paul Women's Equality National Monument, home of the National Woman's Party, provided helpful guidance and speedy responses to my inquiries. Connie Cooper deserves her own shout-out for willingly tutoring me in all aspects of Delaware history, answering my questions, sharing her research, and taking time for tea and conversation at Sinclair's Café. My colleague Carol E. Hoffecker wrote the first major scholarly article on Delaware's suffrage struggle. I remain indebted to her for both her scholarship and her mentorship. Invited lectures at the University of Delaware and the Delaware Public Archives provided opportunities to share my research and hone my arguments. At the University of Delaware Press, Julia Oestreich edited the manuscript and guided it through the publication process with efficiency and precision. Her enthusiasm for the project from start to finish buoyed my spirits. Two readers for the press provided helpful suggestions.

As always, my family and friends smoothed the research and writing process through their care and support. My friend and colleague Margaret Stetz, with her keen interest in the book and her passion for feminist scholarship, has been an inspiration throughout. Bridget Boylan looked over the manuscript with an astute reader's eye, and Peter Kolchin read every word, offering reliably trenchant suggestions. He and the rest of our extended clan were consistent sources of encouragement, ideas, distraction, laughter, and love.

Votes for Delaware Women

Introduction

During the spring and early summer of 1920, all political eyes were on Delaware. The Nineteenth Amendment to the U.S. Constitution was one state short of being ratified. The amendment, which guaranteed that "the right of citizens of the United States to vote" could not be "denied or abridged by the United States or by any State on account of sex," had passed both houses of Congress by the required two-thirds vote. A second section empowered Congress to enforce the amendment "by appropriate legislation." Once the necessary three-quarters of the states approved it, the decades-long struggle for "votes for women" would conclude in triumph. By March 22, thirty-five states had ratified the amendment. Delaware, which took pride in having been the first state to ratify the U.S. Constitution in 1787, had lost the opportunity to be the first to support the woman suffrage amendment because the General Assembly was not in session when Congress approved it. Now, with the pro-suffrage governor having called the legislature into special session, Delaware could provide the final vote for ratification.

From March until June 2, an epic struggle played itself out in the state's capital city, Dover. As historian Carol E. Hoffecker put it in her article "Delaware's Woman Suffrage Campaign," for a brief time "the little state controlled the political future of millions of women." During those crucial weeks, suffragists and anti-suffragists descended upon Dover or took to newspaper columns in an effort to sway legislators' votes. Their ranks included national suffrage leaders, officials of the Delaware National

Woman's Party (NWP), members of the Delaware branch of the National American Woman Suffrage Association (NAWSA), founders of the African American Equal Suffrage Study Club, anti-suffragists, and even the president of the provisional Irish revolutionary government, who was in Delaware to raise money for the cause of Irish independence.

In the end, Delaware's General Assembly never got to "yes." Although the Senate voted to ratify in May, on June 2, the members of the House adjourned after refusing to take a final vote. It was another heroic struggle, this time in Tennessee, that brought a successful end to the decades-long struggle for women's full suffrage. On August 18, 1920, that state's legislature approved ratification of the Nineteenth Amendment. When the U.S. Secretary of State certified the process on August 26, 1920, now commemorated as Women's Equality Day, the amendment became part of the Constitution. Only in 1923, when it was no longer necessary, did Delaware legislators ratify it.[1]

Delaware's suffrage story is both dramatic and consequential. It embodies many of the contradictions that have characterized the state's history. In the words of writer, teacher, and suffragist Alice Dunbar-Nelson, Delaware was "a Jewel of Inconsistencies."[2] A slave state that remained with the Union during the Civil War, Delaware would not emancipate its small slave population until the Thirteenth Amendment's ratification in 1865. The state legislature refused to ratify that and the other Reconstruction amendments until 1901. It was also a state that, in its 1897 constitution, embraced segregation in schools and other facilities yet eliminated a poll tax that had disfranchised African American men. Finally, it was a state whose population in its northernmost county (of three) looked northward, toward Pennsylvania, while inhabitants in its southernmost county looked south and west toward Maryland and Virginia. Delaware was all these things and more. Of the former slave states, it was the only one where the Republican Party enjoyed serious electoral and legislative strength, beginning in the late 1880s and continuing well into the twentieth century.[3]

Its suffrage story begins in 1869, when women's rights advocate Thomas Garrett chaired the state's first suffrage convention. The story also includes the work of Wilmington-born Mary Ann Shadd Cary, a newspaper editor and lawyer who championed African American women's voting rights in the early 1870s. And it encompasses visits to the state by such luminaries as Elizabeth Cady Stanton and Susan B. Anthony, who, along with Greenwood's Mary Ann Sorden Stuart, testified before the legislature in 1881, seeking to amend the state constitution to provide equal suffrage to women. With the founding of the Delaware Equal Suffrage Association (DESA) in 1895, Delaware had a statewide organization dedicated to the cause of women's enfranchisement. Newport's Martha Churchman Cranston was there from the beginning. Cranston, who served as the group's president until 1915, came to be termed "the Susan B. Anthony of Delaware."[4]

From the 1890s to the 1910s, Delaware's suffragists pursued both state and federal constitutional amendments, putting most of their energy into securing a state amendment. In 1897, Georgetown's Margaret White Houston, Wilmington's Emalea Pusey Warner, and others came to the state constitutional convention with pro-suffrage petitions signed by over three thousand Delawareans. The new constitution should drop the provision that only men could vote, they argued. The convention members demurred. In 1898, a national Equal Suffrage Convention brought a new generation of suffrage leaders—Carrie Chapman Catt and Anna Howard Shaw—to Wilmington to rally local advocates for their cause. At legislative session after legislative session, Delaware suffragists continued their attempts to amend the new state constitution to remove the word "male" from the list of voter qualifications.[5]

By the 1910s, a shift in focus to the national level, to a push for a federal amendment, pulled a new, younger, more diverse, and more fractious group of proponents into the coalition of suffrage advocates. In the parlance of the day, they were "New Women." But the shift created bitter contests over strategy and tactics. Those who favored patient, time-consuming grassroots organizing, petitioning, educating, speechifying, and lobbying coalesced around the Delaware Equal Suffrage Association. Members of the newly formed Congressional Union (renamed the National Woman's Party in 1916) insisted upon militant actions designed to call attention to the cause, including, eventually, White House picketing and "watch fire" protests. Of the seven Delaware National Woman's Party devotees who were jailed after being arrested for demanding the right to vote, Wilmington's Annie Melvin Arniel was perhaps the most militant; arrested eight times, she served a total of 103 days.[6]

Although tactical contests took place largely between the state's two white suffrage associations, African American suffragists were vocal and visible in their activism, hosting lectures and regularly publishing pro-suffrage pieces in local newspapers. In a segregated state, they often found themselves targets of racially inflammatory claims about African Americans' unfitness to be voters. Nevertheless, they persisted, joining together in a Wilmington Equal Suffrage Club in 1914 as well as in a wide variety of church groups, women's clubs, the "number 2 unions" of the Woman's Christian Temperance Union (WCTU), and the civil rights organization the National Association for the Advancement of Colored People (NAACP). Through these organizations, they made diplomatic overtures to white suffragists, consistently advocated for a broad platform of racial justice (of which the right to vote was a significant component), defended their names against the calumnies of white critics, and established their claims to suffrage and equal rights. Like African American suffragists elsewhere, they never advocated simply for votes for women, but participated in a larger, ongoing freedom struggle.[7]

True to Alice Dunbar-Nelson's sobriquet, Delaware's suffrage story was complex and contradictory. There were women on both sides of the issue, with anti-suffragists Emily Bissell and Mary Wilson Thompson testifying before Congress and the state legislature that women did not want voting rights, and that suffrage would add to their burdens. There were Republicans and Democrats on both sides, too. Within Delaware's prominent families, such as the Bayards and the du Ponts, the suffrage issue was a source of division and conflict. Florence Bayard Hilles, perhaps the most visible of Delaware's militants, was allied within the National Woman's Party with Josephine Anderson du Pont and Alice du Pont Ortiz. The opposition included her brother Thomas F. Bayard, Jr. and his wife, Elizabeth du Pont Bayard, Alice Ortiz's sister. In some instances, there was no predicting an individual's position. On the face of it, Bissell, with her full-time career and deep commitment to social service work, might have predictably been a suffragist. Yet she was not, and indeed became the state's best-known advocate of the position that women did not want the vote and would not use it if they won it.

By 1920, women had full suffrage in fifteen of the forty-eight states and Alaska Territory, as well as limited, "presidential" suffrage in thirteen other states. In 1893, New Zealand became the first country to fully enfranchise its female citizens, and by 1920, there was a robust international suffrage movement. Yet winning a federal amendment to the U.S. Constitution was by no means easy or inevitable. For decades, the prospect of permitting women to vote appeared radical in the extreme.

Because full suffrage would make women into full citizens, it seemed to opponents to offer a nightmarish future in which women and men—and womanhood and manhood—would themselves be fundamentally remade. How else to explain the appeal of anti-suffrage claims that, if suffrage were enacted, the American family would be destroyed, traditional gender roles shattered, children abandoned, and men emasculated?[8] The perceived radicalism of the demand for voting rights rendered the struggle long and difficult. Suffragists petitioned, lectured, marched, picketed, protested, lobbied, testified, organized, got arrested, engaged in hunger strikes, won and lost key legislative votes, then regrouped and began again.[9] In Delaware, a combination of racial and class issues, particularly political leaders' assumptions about how African American women might vote, partisan bitterness, concerns over taxation and schooling in a segregated state, legislative gerrymandering, political intrigue, and the enduring legacy of rural-urban and North-South divisions doomed the effort to make it the final state to ratify the Nineteenth Amendment.

The struggle to guarantee women's voting rights did not end in 1920. Both Black and white women voters organized, registered, and voted. Delaware's African American women voters in particular dedicated themselves to pressing Congress to enforce the Nineteenth (and the Fifteenth) Amendment in the states of the former Confederacy, where, in the name of white supremacy and states' rights, the voting rights of African Americans—both women and men—were being egregiously violated. Not until 1965, when Congress passed the Voting Rights Act, were their concerns finally vindicated. Efforts to secure and guarantee other rights to women, including legal, economic, civil, educational, sexual, and personal rights, continued long after 1920 as well. In the 1970s, Delaware's General Assembly was one of thirty-five (of the required thirty-eight) states to ratify the proposed Equal Rights Amendment to the U.S. Constitution, an amendment that sought to guarantee "equality of rights under the law" regardless of sex. Despite massive organizing efforts, that amendment failed to win enough states for ratification. But in Delaware in 2019, the state constitution was amended to include a state Equal Rights Amendment.[10]

This book tells the story of Delawareans' journey toward the goal of "votes for women," with all the bumps along the way and the baggage that advocates—and opponents—carried with them. Despite laborious struggles, in the end, the state's suffragists did not succeed in winning either a change to the state constitution's definition of voters or timely ratification of the Nineteenth Amendment. Unlike tales of suffrage referenda won (in California in 1911; Kansas in 1912; and New York in 1917) or dramatic legislative victories hinging on one vote (as in Tennessee in 1920), it recounts a more complicated history of repeated effort followed by dismal defeat. In that, Delaware's suffrage history is perhaps more typical of the suffrage story writ large than its final triumph suggests. For winning full suffrage involved almost as many defeats as victories, and the final victory was by no means inevitable. Moreover, even after 1920, as long as the Nineteenth Amendment's guarantees remained unenforced with any consistency, women could be denied access to voting rights, not on the basis of sex alone, but on other intersecting social categories, including race, nativity, marriage, and, where poll taxes were imposed, economic class.[11]

Beyond its elements of typicality, the Delaware case also commands attention for its unusual aspects. Most notably, the efficacy of African American suffrage organizing in Delaware set it apart from what occurred in other border states as well as in the ex-Confederate states. To be sure, across the country, North, South, and West, Black suffragists were united in the strength and depth of their commitment to voting rights, including the restoration of Black men's suffrage in the disfranchising states. They regularly pressed for congressional enforcement of the Fourteenth and Fifteenth Amendments. But Delaware's 1897 constitution meant that African American men participated in the electoral process, and at least in Wilmington, won political office. (Suffragist Fannie Hopkins Hamilton's brother, John O. Hopkins, sat on the city council from 1913 until 1945.)[12] These circumstances provided African American suffragists with a solid footing in which to anchor their lobbying efforts and made it possible to build a bridge with the leadership of the state's small National Woman's Party branch, to do some interracial alliance-building. That bridge was a shaky structure that all but collapsed during the ratification debate in 1920, yet its very existence defied the usual segregated blueprint for activism and rendered Delaware's suffrage story less predictable than it might otherwise have been.

Votes for Delaware Women also includes the stories of some of the major actors in the state's suffrage struggle. My ability to include biographical material on the state's suffrage leaders has been substantially aided by an ambitious crowdsourcing project, initiated by Professors Thomas Dublin and Kathryn Kish Sklar of Binghamton University and facilitated by the work of volunteers who researched and wrote biographical sketches for publication in the *Online Biographical Dictionary of the Woman Suffrage Movement in the United States*.[13] Readers will find in Appendix A a list of the names of over sixty Delaware suffrage leaders whose biographies are included in the *Dictionary*. Their stories provide texture and context to the broader history I relate here. In some cases, they change the accepted narrative; in all cases, they enable me to recount the history with nuance and an awareness of the influence of individual personalities.

Drawing upon the biographies of a diverse array of suffragists, along with a wealth of archival sources, digitized local newspapers, and organizational records, this book situates Delaware's experience within the vast scholarship on women's rights and women's suffrage generally, and within the broad context of national (and international) struggles for women's voting rights. I intend the book to be accessible both to scholars and to an interested general readership. To that end, I avoid lengthy content endnotes, but provide full references to primary source research as well to interpretive works by historians. The bibliography lists all sources consulted. It is my hope that scholars will have no difficulty following the historiographical context for my narrative while general readers will pursue any research leads that intrigue them.

CHAPTER 1

Beginnings

The history of woman suffrage in Delaware begins in the 1860s, when two individuals later awarded the label of "pioneers," Mary Ann Sorden Stuart and Thomas Garrett, first began to agitate about the issue. In the immediate aftermath of the Civil War, as Congress and the states amended the U.S. Constitution to redefine citizenship and citizens' rights, Stuart and Garrett made the case for women's full citizenship through suffrage. Born in 1828, Stuart, who had grown up in the tiny community of Greenwood in rural Sussex County, was the daughter of landowners and a landowner herself; her father had served in the Delaware State Senate as a Democrat. By 1870, she was a widow with five children, managing family properties in Dover and Greenwood, and chafing against the restrictions on women's legal status that she encountered. Pennsylvania-born Thomas Garrett had lived in Wilmington since the early 1820s, establishing a successful mercantile business and, more important, becoming a key figure in the Underground Railroad. Along with other radical Quakers, he lived his commitments to human rights and pacifism, taking personal risks in order to assist some 2700 enslaved people on their journeys to freedom, and serving as vice-president of national woman's rights conventions in 1859 and 1860.[1]

In the aftermath of a failed attempt to enfranchise women through the Fourteenth and Fifteenth Amendments (1868–1870), the two pioneers took different paths toward their common goal. In 1869, Garrett presided over a suffrage convention in Wilmington designed to establish a state organization affiliated with the newly organized American Woman Suffrage Association (AWSA). The association's founders and leaders, Lucy Stone and her husband Henry B. Blackwell, attended and addressed both the 1869 convention and a larger gathering in 1870. Garrett died soon thereafter, but Delaware's AWSA affiliate carried on his work. For her part, Stuart joined a rival organization, the National Woman Suffrage Association (NWSA), serving for two decades as its active representative in Delaware. In that capacity, she spoke before a congressional committee, worked with NWSA founders Elizabeth Cady Stanton and Susan B. Anthony, and personally lobbied for changes to the state's laws regarding women's economic rights, particularly the rights of married women. She died in 1893, not long after the AWSA and NWSA agreed to end their rivalry and unite. Believing that cooperation was preferable to competition, in 1890, the two organizations formed the National American Woman Suffrage Association (NAWSA).

The 1890s witnessed new energy and focus in the suffrage movement on the state-level as well. The creation of the Delaware Equal Suffrage Association (DESA) in 1895 as an affiliate of NAWSA signaled the change. Between 1895 and 1914, DESA served as a home base for Delaware's suffragists, or to be more precise, its white suffragists. Under its auspices, they regularly engaged in public agitation designed to secure statewide suffrage for women, while also chipping away at existing laws that constrained women's economic and legal status. At the same time, African American Delawareans were developing their own activist networks, through churches, schools, neighborhood and community institutions, and local affiliates of national organizations. By 1914, that institutional web included a suffrage organization, the Equal Suffrage Study Club. When marchers in Wilmington's first large-scale suffrage parade took their places in line that year, both white and Black advocates of women's full voting rights had decades of organizing and lobbying experience at their disposal. They would need it for the challenges ahead.[2]

Background: 1869–1896

Well before the formation of the Delaware Equal Suffrage Association in December 1895, women's rights activists in the state and in the United States had a history of agitating for a wide range of rights. In the 1830s and 1840s, demands for legal rights, occasionally including suffrage, arrived regularly at state constitutional conventions and legislative bodies. A few state-level victories ensued, particularly the passage of married women's property acts, protecting the real property—including slaves— that wives brought into marriage. Woman's rights conventions, held first in the summer of 1848 at Seneca Falls and Rochester, New York, quickly became the most visible mechanism for organizing and mobilizing to advance the rights cause. National conventions, such as the ones in which Thomas Garrett served, began in 1850 and continued to be held annually until just before the outbreak of the Civil War in 1861. By 1869, however, when Garrett chaired the first suffrage convention in Wilmington, the historical context had changed. Suffrage, which had previously been one among many rights being sought—educational, legal, economic, sexual, professional, personal—now acquired priority status. It became the one right that seemed to promise a path to achieving others, and the one that the largest number of women and men would support. A shift in terminology signaled the change: whereas Garrett had attended *woman's rights* conventions, and after 1866, meetings of the American *Equal Rights* Association, the 1869 Wilmington meeting was dedicated to woman *suffrage*.[3]

The enactment of the Fourteenth and Fifteenth Amendments precipitated this shift. In the aftermath of the Civil War, the emancipation of four million Americans from enslavement and the ratification of the Thirteenth Amendment (1865), the succeeding constitutional measures sought to define the rights held by all citizens, regardless of "race, color, or previous condition of servitude." If, as the Fourteenth Amendment stated, "all persons born or naturalized in the United States" were citizens of the United States and of the state in which they resided, then the question arose: was the right to vote a right of adult citizenship? One provision of the amendment, by pressing the former Confederate states to enfranchise African American men, using the terms "male inhabitants" and "male citizens," seemed to close off any gender-neutral answer to the question. The Fifteenth Amendment, referring to "the right of citizens . . . to vote," cemented the Fourteenth Amendment's guarantees of full citizenship to male citizens—in principle, at least.

Both amendments sparked serious divisions among ardent advocates of racial and gender equality. Within the American Equal Rights Association (AERA), an organization founded in 1866 by abolitionists and women's rights advocates, there were fierce and wounding debates over whether the group should endorse the amendments or hold out for universal suffrage without regard to gender. Some members, such as Frederick Douglass, were convinced that suffrage for African American men, most of them former slaves like himself, would be doomed if it were coupled with a demand for woman suffrage. Others, such as Douglass's allies Elizabeth Cady Stanton and Susan B. Anthony, felt that the urgency of the moment could win suffrage for all and that "equal rights" had to be interpreted broadly and universally. In the end, the organization and its members split over the matter. In the aftermath, suffrage assumed a new priority within the array of rights that advocates sought. The titles of the two national organizations that succeeded the AERA told that story: the American Woman Suffrage Association, led by Stone and Blackwell, and the National Woman Suffrage Association, headed by Stanton and Anthony.[4]

Of the two, the NWSA had the higher profile in Delaware, largely due to Mary Ann Sorden Stuart's energy, indomitability, fierce dedication to the cause, and ability to generate publicity. Delawareans who affiliated with the AWSA, including Thomas Garrett, Dr. John Cameron, Isabella Hendry Cameron, Samuel D. Forbes, and Dr. Mary Homer York Heald were never quite as visible suffragists as was Stuart. Moreover, Garrett's death in 1871 deprived the AWSA group of its most prominent—and beloved—foot soldier. Scotland-born Isabella Cameron was gone by 1885, as was Mary Heald. John Cameron died in 1896, his reputation scarred by a malpractice suit in which he was accused of performing an abortion on an unmarried domestic servant. It did not matter that he had agreed to the procedure "at her earnest solicitation," or that she suffered no ill consequences; abortion was a felony in Delaware, punishable by prison time. Individual AWSA supporters, such as the Camerons, had worked with Stuart and the NWSA in some successful efforts to amend Delaware's laws on married women's rights. Those small successes convinced them that suffrage was the key to full adult citizenship status. "Give woman the ballot," wrote John Cameron in 1870, "and she at once becomes a responsible citizen."[5] In other words, as long as state law continued to treat women in general and wives in particular as men's incompetent inferiors, they would never achieve equal citizenship. Suffrage offered the promise of that achievement.

In lobbying the legislature for such issues as the right of a married woman to make her own will, and at each passing election, Mary Ann

Stuart saw women's lack of access to the right to vote as evidence of their obvious second-class status. Such a deprivation of equal citizenship was particularly galling to individuals like her, whose possession of property, education, and social status—combined with racial identification—encouraged their almost unthinking conviction that they and women like them were entitled to suffrage. As Stuart put it in an 1878 speech to a congressional committee, during which she described her "colored man servant" as ignorant of basic voting procedures: "The negroes (sic) are a race inferior, you must admit, to your daughters, and yet that race has the ballot."[6]

Her comments were no aberration, particularly her assumption that "your daughters" were white and "negroes" were men. In the aftermath of Reconstruction, such racially charged sentiments found their way into the mainstream suffrage movement. Perhaps most notoriously, Elizabeth Cady Stanton, in her critiques of an "aristocracy based on sex alone," routinely employed soulless, ethnocentric language in her advocacy of women's rights and woman suffrage. Comparisons between male voters as "Patrick and Sambo and Hans and Yung Tung" representing "the dregs of China, Germany, England, Ireland, and Africa" and disfranchised women as "the daughters of Adams, Jefferson, and Patrick Henry" revealed her racial and class assumptions. In adopting similar arguments, Stuart often—but not always—joined Stanton in brushing aside the concerns of African American women, thereby altering the grounds upon which women's rights advocates stood.[7]

That alteration would have surprised Thomas Garrett. In his day, abolitionism and woman's rights were two sides of a common struggle for human equality. After all, the woman's rights movement had emerged in the 1840s from the crusade to end slavery. Once emancipation was won, achieving racial justice seemed, logically, to require "Equal Rights to All," including "the right and duty of women to claim and use the ballot," as Stanton framed it in 1866. African Americans in particular needed the vote, argued Frances Ellen Watkins Harper, for "justice is not fulfilled so long as woman is unequal before the law." Suffrage was not "immediately going to cure all the ills of life"; still, "much as white women need the ballot, colored women need it more." But, in the context of the "political realities" of the 1860s, Black male suffrage seemed achievable only if cleaved from the principle of universal adult suffrage. In defending that principle "on unabashedly racist grounds," as historian

Lori Ginzberg has noted, Stanton and those who followed her lead took a path with "profound implications for the character, reputation, and constituency of the woman's rights movement" in later years.[8] In her passion for women's rights, Stuart more than once trod that road as well.

With the Reconstruction Amendments folded into the Constitution, suffragists like Stuart had to decide where to focus their energies. Should they seek a new constitutional amendment enfranchising women, or employ a state-by-state strategy? (Wyoming Territory enfranchised women in 1869, Utah in 1870.) For a brief period between 1869 and 1873, NWSA adherents rolled out a novel national approach to woman suffrage, one they termed a "New Departure." Put simply, it claimed that the Fourteenth Amendment had implicitly enfranchised women because women were citizens enjoying the amendment's guarantee of equal protection under the law. Initially proposed by Missouri suffragists Virginia and Francis Minor, the idea received endorsement from, among others, Stuart and another Delaware-born suffragist, journalist Mary Ann Shadd Cary. Between 1868 and 1873, hundreds of African American and white women registered to vote, attempted to register to vote, voted, or attempted to vote. In Washington, D.C., where Shadd Cary attended Howard University Law School, she and sixty-three other District women failed in their attempt to register to vote; in 1874, Shadd Cary swore out a statement, then had it notarized, arguing that her attempt to register had been wrongfully denied. Others had a different experience. In Rochester, New York, Susan B. Anthony and fourteen other women registered, voted, and then were arrested for illegal voting in the 1872 national elections. In Missouri, the St. Louis registrar, Reese Happersett, refused Virginia Minor's request to register to vote. She and her husband filed a lawsuit against Happersett, which went all the way to the Supreme Court. When the Court unanimously rejected the "New Departure" in 1875, it affirmed that women were citizens, but that the states (not the federal government) set voter qualifications.[9]

With the door shut to any new departures, NWSA and AWSA took different routes toward the overarching goal of full suffrage. Stuart's NWSA centralized its labors in one place, New York, and in two people, Stanton and Anthony. It restricted leadership roles to women alone, and, while pressing Congress for a new amendment to the Constitution, endorsed state- and territory-level enfranchisement plans. Its short-lived newspaper, *The Revolution* (1868–1870), adopted a full-throated women's rights platform, championing women's economic rights and wives' rights within marriage, including, most controversially, the right to divorce. "Men, their Rights and Nothing More; Women, their Rights and Nothing Less," proclaimed the newspaper's masthead. The AWSA, to whose annual conventions Delawarean John Cameron often traveled, was a federated organization with auxiliaries in states and territories. Led by both women and men, the group had its base in Boston, where its long-lived newspaper, *The Woman's Journal* (founded 1870), pronounced the group "devoted to the interests of woman, to her educational, industrial, legal and political equality and especially to her right of suffrage." Fearing hostility from anti-suffragists who charged suffragists with being anti-marriage, the AWSA stayed away from such thorny issues as easier access to divorce. Its suffrage strategy was largely state-focused, and included support for partial suffrage, such as women's right to vote only on local questions, often pertaining to school issues, mayoral elections, or municipal cleanups.[10]

Delawareans split their loyalties between the two national groups, with their different strategies for winning the franchise. Still, during the decades after 1869, suffragists from both camps occasionally worked together. That comity was particularly evident when opportunities arose to rewrite the state's laws relating to women's economic and civil personhood—laws that were, even by the standards of the time, exceedingly retrograde. Between 1869 and 1897, responding to lobbying by individuals like Stuart and to organized pressure from women's groups, the legislature passed laws that enabled wives to own property separately from their husbands as well as exempted that property from a husband's debts, allowed them to make their own wills, required employers to provide seats and then "comfortable toilet rooms" for women workers in stores and factories, authorized the state's Chief Justice Charles B. Lore, an advocate for gender and racial justice, to appoint a woman as factory inspector, appointed a woman matron to the Wilmington police station, implemented a "bastardy law" requiring unmarried fathers to pay small sums for their children's support, permitted the arrest and jailing of husbands for non-support of wives and children, and raised the age of consent for girls from seven to fifteen and then to eighteen, largely as a mechanism to facilitate statutory rape prosecutions. On occasion, the state responded to suffragists' arguments by bestowing limited suffrage on taxpaying women. Knowing that she could both vote and run as a candidate for Wilmington's school board, in 1895, the pioneering physician Dr. Josephine White De Lacour mounted a vigorous campaign but lost. (Only forty-two of the city's women taxpayers—of whom there were a total of perhaps one thousand—cast ballots.) Newport's Ella Weldin Johnson won numerous elections for school commissioner, serving from 1909 until 1921. Only four towns permitted women to vote for town commissioners.[11]

These victories seemed small indeed to women like Stuart, whose simmering anger at their exclusion from full citizenship sometimes boiled over. "I have, by my own individual efforts, by the use of hard-earned money, gone to our legislature time after time," she wrote in the *History of Woman Suffrage*, an NWSA publication, "and have had this law and that law passed for the benefit of women; and the same little ship of State has sailed on." She paid her taxes under protest, she told the 1878 U.S. Senate committee at which she insulted African American men voters, "and if I live twenty years longer, I shall pay them under protest every time." She did not live another twenty years, but in 1881, along with Stanton and Anthony, she addressed a joint session of the Delaware legislature in an effort to have the state constitution amended to strike the word "male" from the description of voter qualifications. Interestingly, as first submitted, Stuart's proposal would have replaced the phrase "free white male citizen" in the state constitution with the radical words "every citizen male or female," doing away with restrictions on African American voting. (By 1888, she was freely castigating *all* of Delaware's male voters as drunken louts and praising African American women's civic and entrepreneurial spirit.) While some local newspapers mocked Stuart, Stanton, and Anthony, particularly by commenting on their personal appearance, at least one acknowledged Stanton's ability to speak "clearly, persuasively, [and] impressively." Their proposed 1881 amendment died in committee.[12]

In her own self-presentation, Stuart was a lone figure in an unforgiving landscape. The terrain on which women's rights advocates attempted to scratch out victories "for the benefit of women" was indeed forbidding, yet during her lifetime, a thicket of suffrage allies and supporters grew. In 1884, for instance, when Stuart traveled to Newark to attend a lecture by Belva Lockwood, "the Woman's Rights candidate for President," the venue was Delaware College, which had been co-educational (though for white students only) since 1872. The lecture's sponsors, the

Young Ladies Pestalozzi Literary Society, comprised of an energetic group of women students of the college, debated woman suffrage, published a literary magazine, and felt free to berate their state's legislators as "narrow-minded and pig-headed" for doing little to improve the state's "shamefully inadequate schools." When a student editorialist remarked that "the spirit of Woman's Rights appears to have pervaded the Pestalozzi Society," it was not a compliment. Nevertheless, Lockwood's appearance, at which the College's president, William H. Purnell, escorted her to the stage, was evidence that Delaware's suffrage environment was becoming less arid. In 1888, the state's Woman's Christian Temperance Union (WCTU), following the national organization's official endorsement of suffrage, created a franchise department, headed by Martha Churchman Cranston of Newport, who would soon be dubbed "the Susan B. Anthony of Delaware." The Grange, with deep roots in the state's farming communities and a history of accepting women members, joined the suffrage bandwagon too.[13]

If Delaware remained a difficult environment for women's rights and suffrage activism, Stuart's home county, Sussex, seemed particularly problematic. Yet even in New Castle County, where white women's educational prospects appeared bright, the trustees of Delaware College decided in 1885 to end their "experiment" in co-education after thirteen years, prompting the publication of a scathing pamphlet by the Pestalozzi Society. Should "unreasonable prejudice be allowed to dictate the policy of a State Institution of learning?" they asked. Apparently so. They pledged to "await with confidence the sober second thoughts to right this injustice."[14] Until then, women seeking to attend a degree-granting college or university would have to go out of state.[15] The 1891 opening of the Dover-based co-educational State College for Colored Students provided opportunities for African American women to seek baccalaureate degrees in a few subjects, as well as teaching certification via a three-year "Normal Course."[16]

A Movement: 1896–1914

Suffragists inaugurated a new era in Delaware suffrage history in December 1895 and January 1896. A new state constitution was to be crafted; delegates would begin meeting in December 1896. Seeing an opportunity, local organizers including Cranston, already well known for her temperance advocacy, Emma Worrell, a beloved Wilmington teacher, Chief Justice Lore and his daughter Emma, and Margaret Kent planned to seize it. After all, as a speaker at their initial suffrage convention argued in December 1895, if Delaware women were "compelled to wait for congressional action," they would not cast a vote for "a long time." State-level enfranchisement was substantially more promising. All they had to do was convince the constitution's drafters to strike from the voter qualifications clause "that little objectionable word 'male.'" Led by the newly formed Wilmington Equal Suffrage Club, which at twenty-five members was the state's largest suffrage organization, and prodded by facilitators from NAWSA, the organizers created a statewide federation, the Delaware Equal Suffrage Association. (Six clubs formed the initial assemblage: four in New Castle County, and one each in Kent and Sussex Counties.) By May 1896, there were seventeen suffrage clubs in the organization, and by the time of its first annual convention that December, members had secured almost three thousand signatures on a suffrage petition ready to be submitted to the constitutional convention.[17]

At the constitutional convention itself, in January 1897, suffragists were allotted two hours to make their case. Martha Churchman Cranston presented the petition, noted that the state Grange had recently endorsed equal suffrage, and introduced speakers from all three counties. Wilmingtonians Emalea Pusey Warner and Worrell made their pleas largely on the basis of justice. Women, Worrell stated, wish only to "stand in all things equal before the law" with men, "equally sharing in its privileges, as we do with its exactions as citizens." After all, women paid taxes, owned property, held jobs, and yet had "no vote to say what the law shall be" to which they were subject. "We believe in suffrage as the great right of the people," she concluded, "as people, not as classes." Margaret White Houston of Sussex County used her time to answer, point by point, various anti-suffrage contentions about the dangers of suffrage. "Equal suffrage is coming," she predicted; to refuse women the right to vote was to attempt to "command the waves to recede only to see the tide steadily coming in." Delaware, "the little Diamond State," she reminded her listeners, "was first to adopt the Constitution; . . . let her be first of her Eastern sisters to enfranchise the woman." Speaking last, NAWSA organizer Carrie Chapman Catt recounted the positive experiences of the suffrage states and set forth clear, logical arguments, but was thoroughly dismayed when not one of the convention delegates asked the women a single question. Instead, the men simply offered "our thanks to the ladies" for the "propriety, elegance, and power" of their presentations. The convention then moved on to other matters.[18]

Even before the suffragists took their seats, the delegates had already heard from a New York association opposed to woman suffrage. After the proposal went down to defeat,[19] the women found anti-suffrage arguments repeated in local newspaper coverage. "Women Will Not Vote: Delaware's Constitution Makers Believe they are Better at Home than at the Polls," read one headline.[20] Delaware women, the reporter claimed, "are opposed to the imposition of this new right or duty upon them"; suffrage "would destroy the harmony of the home." Besides, "those least qualified would take advantage of the right," especially women of "the colored race." Indeed, Black men "are vastly superior" to Black women "in intelligence [knowledge] especially so far as political matters are concerned." (The new constitution removed an 1872 poll tax that had been an unscalable barrier to African American men's voting, while gerrymandering General Assembly seats in a way that substantially reduced the voting power of urban districts.)[21] However contradictory such arguments were—women shouldn't vote and didn't want to vote, except for Black women, who would vote as soon as it became possible—they permeated discussions of suffrage at the turn of the twentieth century.

The five women who spoke in favor of suffrage at the convention certainly did want the vote, believed women should have that right, and were comfortable in the "harmony" of their own homes. To them, suffrage was, first and foremost, a matter of simple justice. As Emma Worrell later put it, the Equal Suffrage Association committed itself to "the one inflexible idea of woman's human and equal right with man to life and all its duties, pleasures and responsibilities."[22] Some also framed suffrage as a means of extending the values of "the home" into the economic and social realms, while enabling women to shape the economic and social conditions that affected their homes. Could they be good wives and mothers, they argued, if they were unable to influence the external conditions, whether public health matters such as sewage disposal and disease control or regulatory policies such as tuberculin testing of milk cows, which affected their families' health and well-being? Conversely, might not the ways in which women kept their own homes clean and tidy be applicable to the management of cities? What was a mayor's job but "municipal housekeeping"? Delaware suffragists interlaced arguments about the injustice of women's lack of voting rights with claims to their deeper sense of morality, employing one or both of these arguments as they fit particular situations. Temperance devotees such as Cranston and Houston particularly advocated the ballot as a means to "home protection," the rubric under which the WCTU endorsed suffrage. But outrage over vote-deprived women's second-class citizenship status, sometimes framed in racial and class terms, remained another constant theme in the efforts of the state's white suffrage activists.[23]

In their own lives, too, the women of the Equal Suffrage Association offered rebukes to those who envisioned "the harmony of the home" as destroyed when wives, mothers, and daughters dared to demand the right to choose their leaders. When she appeared before the men writing Delaware's new constitution, Georgetown's Margaret Houston was thirty-three years old and the mother of three young children, aged eight, six, and two. With the support of her lawyer husband, Robert Griffith Houston, and the aid of domestic help (the Houstons usually had two or three live-in African American servants), Margaret combined family care with activism in temperance and women's club work as well as in suffrage efforts. Emma Worrell, some thirty years her senior, was a teacher and Quaker leader. A suffragist since the 1860s, she was devoted both to her family of origin and to her Quaker family, traveling to Philadelphia on occasion to participate in the Friends' Yearly Meeting. Quaker principles of social justice, peace, and equality consistently animated her life. Emalea Pusey Warner, Worrell's dear friend and former pupil, aged forty-five in 1897, never shed the training she had received at Worrell's school and in a family of Friends, though she now worshipped at Wilmington's First Unitarian Church. Her own family life was rich and busy. Married in a Friends ceremony in 1873 to Alfred D. Warner, president of his family's shipping firm, she enjoyed the comfortable home that his wealth secured and, with the benefit of live-in help, cared for her four surviving children.

In other aspects of their lives, too, these women were rather typical of their white middle-class suffrage colleagues. All were well educated, but none possessed the college degrees that some of their younger colleagues—termed "New Women" in popular media—were pursuing as women's colleges grew in number and prestige. Houston had graduated from the Normal Department of the Academy of Newark in 1887 but after her 1888 marriage had put aside any plans for teaching. (Delaware school boards required women teachers to resign upon marriage.) Like so many women of their class and education, these women channeled their energy and skill into women's clubs and organizations, as well as into their (Protestant) churches. In 1889, Worrell and Warner had been charter members of the Wilmington New Century Club, and in 1903, Houston founded and became the first president of the Georgetown New Century Club that, in turn, joined the state federation, founded in 1898. Together, state federations affiliated themselves with the General Federation of Women's Clubs (GFWC), at whose biennial national conferences delegates could meet and exchange ideas with each other.

Officially, and despite the enthusiastic suffrage advocacy of clubwomen like Warner and Houston, the Delaware Federation of Women's Clubs, like the General Federation, avoided taking any official position on woman suffrage. The issue was simply too divisive, the Federation believed. Club members and officers preferred to work together on matters of common interest, such as children's welfare, women's access to higher education, conditions that working women and girls faced, civic beautification and improvement, and cultural enhancement. Introducing divisive political questions into club work would, they feared, destroy the clubs' effectiveness. But of course, as many a clubwoman discovered, even an attempt to fund a local library necessarily embroiled members in public policy and politics, while also teaching them more than a few lessons about the latter.[24]

Then, too, the Delaware Federation knew and worked with Emily Bissell, a social settlement and public health reformer, and the author of numerous pieces of short fiction under the pseudonym "Priscilla Leonard," who was fast becoming nationally known for her anti-suffrage positions. Early in 1900, she presented her arguments in Washington, D.C., to both House and Senate suffrage committees, reiterating some of the views that Delaware's constitutional convention delegates had heard in 1897, including that most women "do not want the ballot," that, in the small number of underpopulated states where women had the right to vote, "the results are negative," and that the suffrage movement promoted "sex antagonism," not "sex harmony." Adding her own perspective, one that she would continue to espouse throughout successive national and state debates, and that reflected the political access she enjoyed because of her social position, she averred that, "I have never yet been ensituated that I could see where a vote could help me."[25]

Although both suffrage and anti-suffrage members found a place within the women's club Federation's fold, Delaware's Federation, like the vast majority of its counterparts, excluded African American women. To be sure, there were women's associations, such as the WCTU and the Young Women's Christian Association (YWCA), that took tentative steps toward cross-racial cooperation by accepting both Black and white affiliates, but they did so almost uniformly by creating racially separate units. The national YWCA, for example, employed a "rigidly segregated structure" that required Black YWCAs to participate only under the "stewardship" of white associations. Although it offered the "possibility of interracial cooperation among women," at the turn of the twentieth century, realizing that possibility remained in the Y's future. In this era, Delaware had no Black YWCA. The WCTU, at the time the largest women's organization in the United States, pursued a much broader reform agenda than did the YWCA, encompassing not only temperance but also educational innovations, "social purity" (a single standard of sexual behavior), censorship, and suffrage. Through its Department of Work among Colored People, the WCTU fostered African American women's leadership opportunities and encouraged joint efforts across the color line, although Black temperance leaders preferred not to label their branches "colored," and instead simply termed them "No. 2" unions. Still, the secondary designation reflected the accommodation that the WCTU made to racial segregation. Women's right to vote may have been a divisive issue within white associational circles, but the forces arrayed against any hint of joining hands and resources with African American women were considerably more powerful.[26]

Delaware's small coterie of middle-class Black women, forming their own groups, built résumés not unlike those of many white counterparts: they acquired degrees from institutions of higher learning, created clubs and associations, provided the volunteer workforce for local African American churches, championed girls' educational and work opportunities, and spoke out on public policy issues, including suffrage. They represented "New Negro Womanhood." In June 1895, as Delaware's white suffragists were putting together their city and state organizations, Blanche Williams, a Wisconsin-born graduate of Howard University and now a Wilmington teacher, watched as seven pupils received their high school diplomas from the Howard School in Wilmington, the only school in the state providing a full four-year secondary education program to African American students. A "debate on woman suffrage" and an address by educator and Oberlin College graduate Mary Church Terrell of Washington, D.C., were key features of the commencement exercises. Soon, Williams had married Dr. J.B. Stubbs, a graduate of the Howard University Medical School, and as required by Board of Education rules, resigned her teaching post. She turned to church and community activism and social work, and in 1910, while raising three children, she helped found the Federation of Christian Workers, which by 1916 became the cornerstone of the Delaware Federation of Colored Women's Clubs, with Blanche Williams Stubbs as its first president.[27]

During those years, Stubbs's associational and church circles included Alice Ruth Moore Dunbar, a Louisiana-born writer and teacher and graduate of Straight College in New Orleans, who moved to Wilmington in 1902 and began a career as a literature teacher at the Howard School. When still single, Alice Moore had served as a delegate and then Recording Secretary for the National Association of Colored Women's (NACW) first and second conferences. After her marriage to the poet Paul Laurence Dunbar, she moved to Washington, D.C., where her next-door neighbor was Mary Church Terrell, the NACW's first president. Paul was a besotted husband; he was also unfaithful and abusive. Refusing to endure any more harm, Alice left him. In Wilmington, which became her home for the next three decades, she joined Stubbs and others in clubs and organizations supporting a variety of projects within the city's African American neighborhoods. These included establishing schools and other educational and cultural opportunities for children, building two homes for "aged colored" persons (the Layton Home and the Sarah Ann White Home), facilitating visits by notable African American intellectuals, holding Emancipation Day celebrations at local churches, and creating a network of religious, social service, and political institutions established for, and largely run by, African Americans.[28]

The conditions that Wilmington's middle-class African American woman suffragists faced in segregated Delaware rendered their concerns and activism, and the terms in which they framed their work, substantially broader than those of their white counterparts. In addition to advocating for their communities, they were obliged to defend themselves against both ancient libels concerning Black women's sexuality and intellect, and incessant threats to the rights that African Americans had won during Reconstruction. When they spoke of woman suffrage,

Figure 1. Alice Ruth Moore Dunbar, c. 1900. Alice
Dunbar-Nelson liked this photo's representation
of her youthful self and used it regularly for
publications and publicity. Credit: Alice Dunbar-
Nelson Papers, University of Delaware Library,
Museums and Press

then, their language was commonly that of *universal* or *equal* suffrage.
With the disfranchisement of African American men proceeding rapidly across the former Confederate states after 1890, African American
suffragists committed themselves to championing both their men's
voting rights with demands for congressional enforcement of the Fourteenth and Fifteenth Amendments, and the expansion of those rights to
all women.[29]

Equally, if not more on their minds was the spread of white-insti-
gated racial violence, including sexual violence, particularly visible

in the practice of lynching. Depictions of Black men as "beasts" or "fiends," usually accompanying claims that they raped white women, were commonplace in Wilmington newspapers. Such representations justified lynching as an extra-judicial practice invoked to bypass the legal system and deliver swift "justice" for the female accuser. Yet, as Ida B. Wells pointedly noted, white men accused of raping Black women and girls seldom even faced arrest, let alone indictment or prosecution. The brutal lynching of a local man, George White, in June 1903 in front of a mob of four to five thousand New Castle County spectators, most of whom had been directed to the Price's Corner site by advance notice, brought the topic directly into Delaware's homes. Fear for their sons, husbands, brothers, and other male relatives made the topic personally terrifying for African American suffragists. Moreover, voices calling to undo the 1897 state constitution's expansion of African American men's voting rights became louder and more insistent in the aftermath of George White's horrible fate. For Black suffragists, the relationship between the right to vote and what the WCTU termed "home protection" resonated with acuity. To protect their homes, they made anti-lynching work a priority and sought both their own voting rights and the restoration of Black men's suffrage wherever it had been suppressed.[30]

In the expansiveness of their approach to suffrage, Delaware's middle-class African American women, like others across the country, responded to the circumstances of segregation, white supremacist violence, and disfranchisement in three ways. First, in the ways they lived and (selectively) shared knowledge about their experiences, they sought to demonstrate the respectability of their homes, persons, families, churches, and community institutions. What historians have termed a "politics of respectability" directly addressed the crude sexual stereotyping and the demeaning racial assumptions these women and their families faced every day. Second, they garnered resources for their communities' needs by strategically positioning themselves as ambassadors to white women and white women's groups. And third, they emphasized that they suffered denial of their rights on the basis of both race and gender. They asserted themselves, in the language of the day, as "race women" and "citizen-women," knowledgeable about, capable of, and entitled to full participation both with Black men and with white women in addressing the great challenges of their era.[31]

Teachers were "citizen-women" par excellence, possessing as they did intellectual accomplishments, middle-class status, knowledge, and skill at navigating the treacherous shoals of segregation. Among the founders of Wilmington's African American suffrage club was a cluster of Howard School teachers or former teachers. Most lived near each other on East Tenth (students dubbed it "Teachers' Row") and Eleventh Streets between King and Walnut Streets in Wilmington, walking distance from the school. A middle-class enclave, the neighborhood was affordable and healthier than the rest of the city's East Side. In the words of one former resident, it "was quiet and shaded; . . . there were porches and hedge-bordered patches of front yards, and deep back yards with grape arbors and flowers." Located uphill from the swampy, industrial lowlands where poorer neighbors were increasingly crammed together into substandard housing, the enclave had an anchor in Edwina Kruse, the Howard School's formidable principal, whose home at 206 East Tenth Street was the site of genteel parties and receptions for students graduating from the high school. Although Kruse did not join the suffrage club, at its organizing meeting her friend and boarder, Alice Gertrude Baldwin, head of the school's teacher training program, "made a spirited address" supporting suffrage. The meeting took place next door to Kruse's, in Emma Gibson Sykes's living room. Sykes was a graduate of the Howard School, a friend and protégé of Kruse, and after her marriage continued to teach as a substitute and at Howard's night school. Also present at the organizing meeting were: geography teacher Caroline Williams, a graduate of the Westfield, Massachusetts, Normal School, who lived at 202 East Tenth Street; Nellie B. Nicholson, mathematics teacher and graduate of Pembroke College of Brown University, who boarded with Williams; domestic arts teacher Helen Wormley Anderson, whom Kruse had recruited to the Howard School faculty; teacher-turned-social worker Blanche Williams Stubbs; and dressmaker Fannie Hopkins Hamilton, who offered night school classes while conducting a separate apparel making establishment in the city. Together, these women commanded the social and economic capital necessary for combating the rights deprivations they faced regularly.[32]

At the center of the Howard School cluster was the Wilmington Equal Suffrage Club's president, Alice Moore Dunbar, who lived on French Street, around the corner from her dear friend "Krusie." By the time the group formed, she was well known to Black and white Wilmingtonians alike for her prowess as a poet and writer and for her chosen role as keeper of Paul Laurence Dunbar's flame after his death in 1906. By that time, too, she had positioned herself as a source of knowledge about Wilmington's African American residents and the conditions they faced under racial segregation. In a series of investigative articles published in the city's Sunday newspaper early in 1914, Dunbar provided vivid descriptions of the alleys and shacks in which Wilmington's poor Blacks lived while paying more, proportionally, for housing than white urbanites and suffering the dreadful health effects of poor sanitation and crowded conditions. (The matter came painfully home to her when a beloved niece died of tuberculosis in 1921.) Using a strategy employed by labor unions and consumer advocates, and without mincing her words, Dunbar warned her white neighbors of the dangers they might face when they were "jostled upon the streets and public conveyances" or "employ[ed] as [their] servants" individuals living in such conditions. "The common house fly, which knows no prejudice, and draws no distinction or color line" she wrote, "deposits . . . germs . . . upon the food and clothing alike of both rich and poor, high and low, whites and [N]egroes."[33]

Dunbar and others investigating these conditions realized that ameliorating them would take more resources than those available to the Black churches, clubs, and institutions that dotted the neighborhood. In the full series of articles, Dunbar appealed to white philanthropists, male and female alike, and city officials to join in seeking solutions. For her part, Stubbs's strategic outreach to white women stressed their common commitments to their Christian faith and to the value of temperance. Although she and her physician husband attended the African American St. Matthew's Episcopal Church, as head of the Federation of Christian Workers (an affiliate of the NACW) she ventured into the white Methodist churches where the local WCTU branch usually met. In a 1911 address, pronounced "valuable" by her listeners, she closed "with a plea to the white women to help their colored sisters towards better ways of living." Balancing that plea with praise for a white social worker who was doing "good work . . . among the colored people of the community," she floated an idea that her Black colleagues had long discussed: the state needed a "colored girls' industrial school" comparable to the existing industrial school for white girls.

The following year, an invited "report" of "work among colored people" was more pointed. Confidently predicting that "the next decade will witness a decided decrease in [Wilmington's] criminal and dependent white citizens," due to the proliferation of community institutions such as settlement houses and YMCAs, Stubbs asked, "what inducements or opportunities are being offered the [N]egro boys and girls to make them better and more useful citizens?" Appealing to "the generosity of public-spirited citizens of Wilmington," she laid out the work that her federation had accomplished as an exemplar of the "true comradeship" that Christian temperance workers believed they shared across racial lines.[34] Through such diplomatic outreach to white Delaware churchwomen and clubwomen, individuals like Stubbs sought to garner resources for community activities and institutions that were currently beyond the collective purses of African Americans. Like Dunbar, she was able to be, at the same time, a "race woman" and an exemplar of the sort of respectable "colored" woman whom white clubwomen might be willing to accept as a guest at their meetings.[35]

The fruits of such outreach became evident in the establishment of an African American social settlement in Wilmington. In 1911, Stubbs's Federation of Christian Workers, hoping to bring a community center to the East Side, rented a house (at Eighth and Buttonwood) and began offering programs. Although it helped the Federation's budget when the existing Thomas Garrett Kindergarten moved into the facility, paying rent to the Federation, it very quickly became clear that the house was "unsuitable." Eager to create a permanent social settlement, the Federation of Christian Workers began a fundraising campaign for a "suitable" building in a better location. Naming the institution "the Thomas Garrett Settlement House" in honor of the man who "did so much to promote the welfare of the colored people" and who remained a revered figure in the city, the Federation members invited a white advisory board to "act with them" in the campaign. Heading the list of advisory board members was Helen Garrett, Thomas Garrett's granddaughter; another white Quaker, Frederick Bringhurst, became both the advisory board's treasurer and a key donor to the new institution. The settlement's corporate board of directors, however, was comprised of African Americans alone, headed by the Stubbses and including Alice Dunbar. When the settlement opened at Seventh and Walnut Streets in January 1914, Blanche Stubbs, now the institution's executive director, gave an address on Thomas Garrett's life, following through on her pledge to Helen Garrett that "I shall not let his memory die as long as I am able to teach children to cherish and revere one of the greatest of God's nobility." The settlement house quickly became a community gathering place, providing a variety of services focused particularly on children's needs; in the evenings, groups as diverse as sewing classes and a Bible society utilized its spaces.[36]

With the Garrett Settlement established on a sound footing, another element in an interconnected network of African American women's activism took form. Since the turn of the century, middle-class women had worked together in a variety of community improvement and service institutions. In 1914, the creation of the Equal Suffrage Study Club and the Wilmington chapter of the NAACP added direct political activism to education and uplift as significant priorities of network members. The Equal Suffrage Study Club, founded in March, and comprised entirely of African American women, initially announced in local newspapers that the members would merely seek to "become better informed on the subject" through "a campaign of education." But surely that was a strategic smoke screen designed to quiet the fears of white readers regarding Black suffragists' ambitions. Soon enough, the club's women marched in Wilmington's May 2 suffrage parade, and in early June, they announced a series of lectures on both suffrage and "questions of municipal, state, national, and international interest," the first of which considered "The World Wide Woman Movement and What it Means To The Negro." Given that Dunbar was the club's president, it seems logical to conclude that the lecture's focus reflected her understanding of the ways that race and gender intertwined to shape Black women's lives and activism. And with businesswoman Fannie Hopkins Hamilton serving as the club's treasurer, the group had a direct tie to Wilmington's only African American elected official, her brother John O. Hopkins.[37]

Wilmington's NAACP branch, organized in November, was both biracial and gender integrated. Once again, Dunbar was a key figure, as she and Edwina Kruse had initiated the process of creating the local branch two years earlier and Dunbar had addressed the national NAACP annual conference in Baltimore earlier in 1914. The group's officers and executive committee included a few white allies, such as clubwoman and suffragist Gertrude Fulton Nields, a member of the city's First Unitarian Church, where Alice Gertrude Baldwin (soon to become the branch's long-term secretary) also worshipped. More significantly, the founding membership was about sixty percent female and included a substantial cohort of suffragists—not only Dunbar and Baldwin, but also Stubbs, Emma Gibson Sykes, Mary J. Johnson Woodlen, Caroline B. Williams, Helen Wormley Anderson, and Nellie B. Nicholson. All told, these were nine of the fourteen women who had founded the suffrage club in March. Their overlapping commitments to both organizations represented a familiar pattern in the lives of middle-class African American women, and marked them as "New Negro women" through and through. Over the next decade, the Wilmington NAACP branch would champion women's voting, address segregation in housing and in courtrooms, attempt to get the city to hire at least one African American police officer, protest against screenings of the film *Birth of a Nation* and against the use of public space for Ku Klux Klan meetings, and compel Wilmington's prosecutor to take to a grand jury the case of white man who had raped his African American employee.[38]

The separate networks that characterized African American and white Delawareans in their quests for suffrage had parallels at the national level. During the 1890s, the growing coterie of white Southern suffragists in NAWSA's ranks, boosting its numbers and resources, convinced more than one NAWSA leader to abandon its principle of seeking universal suffrage. Between 1899, when the national conference program committee permitted Kentuckian Laura Clay to argue from the podium that African American women's concerns were not those of the organization, and 1903, when white supremacist Southern suffragists convinced the group to meet in segregated New Orleans, African American suffragists found their presence and their concerns shunted aside. A "Southern Strategy" gained support among white suffragists, a strategy that simply accepted the ongoing disfranchisement of African American men and assumed that "woman suffrage" in the former Confederate states would in fact be white women's suffrage. "The enfranchisement of women," intoned Mississippian Belle Kearney at NAWSA's segregated 1903 meeting, "would insure immediate and durable white supremacy." Concurrently, in response to a New Orleans newspaper editorial about "the race question," the group's leadership agreed that "each State" could, once it had enfranchised women, determine "what other qualifications" women voters would need to meet in order to be eligible to vote. Chief among those qualifications were the very literacy tests and poll taxes being used to bypass the Fifteenth Amendment and "insure white supremacy."[39]

As NAWSA's membership changed, so too did its leadership. By 1906, when Susan B. Anthony died (Stanton having predeceased her in 1902),

the generation that had championed women's rights and woman suffrage during the Reconstruction and post-Reconstruction eras was gone.
Carrie Chapman Catt replaced Anthony as the president of NAWSA in
1900; in 1904, Anna Howard Shaw, a noted orator and ordained Methodist minister, took the reins. Both had visited Wilmington to speak at
the 1898 National Equal Suffrage Convention. For twelve years, Shaw
"led [its] transformation from a struggling voluntary association," in the
words of her biographer, "to a professional organization . . . with sala-
ried executive workers and a sophisticated publicity department." She
also capitulated to the demands of Southern white NAWSA members,
agreeing on one occasion that African American men's voting rights had
made "former slaves the political masters of their former mistresses,"
although later, she welcomed African American Fannie Barrier Williams to a speaking role at the 1907 convention and quashed an effort
by Southern white suffragists to create a whites-only NAWSA affiliate
in the Southern states. Like others in NAWSA's leadership, Shaw reck-
oned with the challenge of expanding voting rights to women at a time
when men's rights to the franchise were contracting due to the wave of
disfranchising laws initiated in the 1890s. In the Jim Crow era, both in
Delaware and at the national level, anyone seeking white suffragists who
gave full-throated support to Black suffragists' aspirations might as well
have been looking for snow in June.[40]

Conclusion

Between 1895 and 1914, Delaware's suffragists amassed organizational strength and organizing experience, and created networks of support for their cause. Through local and state women's clubs, affiliations
with national associations, church connections, and their own suffrage-
focused efforts, they reshaped a landscape that had, during the 1897 effort
to amend the state constitution, looked particularly bleak. Victories for
women's rights as a whole, including the rights of married women, constituted one bright patch. The educational rights of white girls flowered
when, after a years-long effort, suffragists active in the Delaware Federation of Women's Clubs achieved a major goal: state funding for a Wom-
en's College "coordinate" with the (all-male) Delaware College, located
in Newark. It had taken years of patient organizing and lobbying, but it
had also provided suffragists and clubwomen with invaluable experience

Figure 2. By 1913, "Votes for Women" was enough of
a slogan that advertisers used it to sell products like
breakfast cereal. Credit: Wilmington *Evening Journal*,
March 6, 1913, 3.

in the political realm. If there was one individual who could claim major
credit for the achievement, it was Emalea Pusey Warner, who mobilized
clubwomen and male allies across the state into a pressure group that, in
the end, the General Assembly could not resist. Delaware Women's College welcomed its first entering class in fall 1914. As Warner wrote to the
college's founding dean, Winifred Robinson, the opening constituted "a
new day for little Delaware" and wrote "a fresh page . . . in our history."
The state's "shamefully inadequate schools" that some college student
predecessors had decried in 1884 might now acquire well-trained white
teachers.[41] Activists like Warner could also claim a few wins for the suffrage cause, such as municipal suffrage in some towns and voting rights
on school issues—for taxpaying women.

By 1914, too, the topic of suffrage itself was considerably more on Delawareans' minds and lips than it had been in 1895. "Votes for Women"
read a large advertisement in one of Wilmington's daily papers in March

1913, just as suffrage supporters were lobbying the state legislature to amend Delaware's constitution to enfranchise women, and clubwomen were planning the groundbreaking ceremony for the women's college. Pointing out that "two million women will have the right to vote" in the 1916 presidential election, the ad got to its sponsor's point: "twenty million women have already voted for the emancipation of American womanhood by serving Shredded Wheat for Breakfast." "Votes for Women" may have been an attention-getting heading, but a shrewd copywriter had undoubtedly also noticed the hoopla that surrounded the February arrival in Delaware of "General" Rosalie Gardiner Jones and her band of suffrage "pilgrims" marching from New York to Washington, D.C. to attend a planned national suffrage parade on March 3, 1913, the day before President Woodrow Wilson's inauguration. Welcomed on February 18 to Arden, Delaware's newly founded economic and artistic experiment in community-building, the group made their way through the state before arriving at the home of Delaware College and the future Women's College two days later. "All Newark," turned out for the spectacle, which included an escort for the marchers (and their Wilmington supporters) by a cadet corps of young men from Delaware College. After lunch at the Deer Park Tavern, a "weary" Rosalie Jones addressed a crowd assembled on the college grounds with a plea for "justice and the right to co-operate with mankind." At four in the afternoon, to the sound of a bugler's call, the women headed for Elkton, Maryland, then on to D.C.[42]

Stunts, advertisements, and parades were new means to a longstanding end. Not only did they usefully spark public discussion of suffrage, but they also worked to shake up older styles of protest and organizing, and when added to established tactics—such as legislative lobbying and petition campaigns—became ways to achieve the goal of statewide suffrage. To get to that goal, suffragists would need the constitutional amendment passed in two legislative sessions by two-thirds votes in both houses. Given that Delaware's legislature met biennially, in odd-numbered years, the effort required substantial organizational and human resources. Delaware suffragists possessed both, along with extraordinary reserves of sheer doggedness. Marrying new methods to old, they basted together a loose coalition of individuals and groups who often had nothing in common except a commitment to winning "Votes for Women," an accessible, plural term that was rapidly replacing "Woman Suffrage," with its singular "woman" and its sepia-toned nineteenth-century aura.[43]

Figure 3. In advance of the massive suffrage procession planned for Washington, D.C., on March 3, 1913, "General" Rosalie Gardiner Jones (1883–1978) and a group of suffragists drew attention to the cause by trekking from New York to Washington. In Newark, Delaware, they stopped for speeches and then lunch at the Deer Park Inn. A photograph shows the bundled-up suffrage pilgrims surrounded by supporters and curious onlookers, including children. In the background, the group's wagon, sporting a flag, is loaded with baggage, leaflets, and buttons. Credit: Newark Historical Society, Newark, Delaware

The very existence of anything resembling a coalition of suffrage sup-porters in Delaware testified to the changes that were roiling suffrage advocacy on both the state and national levels. Unlike in 1897, when a few individuals from the state's lone suffrage organization had pleaded their case before the state constitutional convention, in 1914, individuals calling themselves suffragists joined not only the Delaware Equal Suf-frage Association and its local affiliates, but also the African American Equal Suffrage Study Club, the Arden Suffrage League, the Grange, and the Franchise Department of the WCTU, both of which supported suffrage. Pro-suffrage politicians within the Republican Party, many of them energized by the new national Progressive Party and its pro-suffrage leader, former President Theodore Roosevelt, added votes for women to the other planks in their platform.[44] As with most coalitions, the suffrage bloc encompassed members of widely varying positions and politics whose adherents agreed on only one goal: women's right to vote.

Figure 4. Emily Perkins Bissell, c. 1895. Credit: Delaware
Historical Society.

By 1914, their deeds and words, as well as those of national and international leaders visiting the state, were all receiving prominent coverage in the state's daily and weekly newspapers. So, too, were the words
and deeds of an increasingly visible and vocal opposition. Emily Bissell, president of the Delaware Anti-Tuberculosis Society, founder of
the Christmas Seals campaign to raise money to eradicate tuberculosis,
and sponsor of Hope Farm, a sanatorium outside Wilmington for white
tuberculosis sufferers, was the best-known of Delaware's anti-suffragists.
A busy single woman and published author, Bissell was active in a variety

of social welfare causes, including efforts to regulate child labor. By 1914, she increasingly shared the stage—and newsprint space—with Mary Wilson Thompson, an elite socialite married to a wealthy textile manufacturer, who led the newly formed Delaware Association Opposed to Woman Suffrage. Suffrage in Delaware had really arrived: the existence of a vocal and well-connected opposition offered proof positive that the issue was both visible and controversial.[45]

The Delaware legislature killed the 1913 suffrage amendment. Both suffragists and anti-suffragists anticipated rallying their forces in 1915 for yet another effort to enfranchise women by revising Delaware's 1897 state constitution. In nearby New Jersey and Pennsylvania, too, suffrage referenda on fall 1915 ballots looked promising. State-level campaigns were succeeding in other states. Why not in Delaware? In 1914, Delaware remained a divided state, with only scattered support in Kent and Sussex Counties for altering state constitutional restrictions on voting. The potential for yet another defeat at the state level prompted some white suffragists to increasingly embrace a strategy that their African American counterparts had consistently favored: supporting a federal amendment enfranchising women across the United States. In 1909–1910, the Delaware Equal Suffrage Association, in conjunction with the state WCTU (Martha Cranston led both organizations), had participated in NAWSA's National American Suffrage Petition for a constitutional amendment, contributing 3,012 signatures to the 400,000 names delivered to Congress.[46] Whatever the prospects for a national approach, however, most Delaware suffrage leaders were still keeping their eyes focused on Dover. In 1913, a local journalist, summing up the political terrain that the state's suffragists sought to tame, made a particularly dire prediction: "Many persons think that Delaware will be the last State in the Union of States to extend liberty to her women, and [that suffrage] will only be won by a National Constitutional Amendment."[47]

CHAPTER 2

Energy and Fracture, 1914–1917

On May 2, 1914, Wilmington witnessed Delaware's first big suffrage parade. On a pleasant Saturday afternoon, more than six hundred marchers proceeded from the corner of Front and French Streets up Market Street to the steps of the old county courthouse at Tenth Street, where they listened to suffrage speeches. Heading the line of the march, behind the First Regiment Band, were the members of the Delaware Equal Suffrage Association (DESA), led by Florence Bayard Hilles and two other white suffragists. Each woman carried a yellow banner; each represented one of the state's three counties. Further back, behind the Homemakers division, the Newport suffragists' float, the mortarboard-wearing College Women's group, the Men's Equal Suffrage Club, the doctors' and nurses' section, the children's division, and the Wilmington Fife and Drum Corps, came the Wilmington Equal Suffrage Study Club, the "colored" contingent led by Blanche Williams Stubbs. Behind the Study Club were the representatives of the Arden, Delaware, single tax colony, the YWCA, some socialists, and a "boys section." Local newspapers pronounced the parade a "striking success" and commented particularly on the supportive and decorous behavior of the onlookers who lined Market Street.[1]

A week later, a small contingent of Delaware women and men took the train from Wilmington to Washington, D.C., in order to participate in the capital city's suffrage parade on May 9. The Washington parade's orderly nature, noted Wilmington's Sunday newspaper, contrasted sharply with suffragists' experience fourteen months earlier on March 3, 1913, when suffrage marchers in the national parade—some eight thousand strong, including a Delaware contingent—had been "spat upon, slapped in the face, tripped up, pelted with burning cigar stubs, and insulted by jeers and obscene language." Shaken and fearful, the marchers had stood their ground against the threatening mob and an indifferent police presence, and asserted their rights to claim public space and engage in political speech.[2]

Whether or not the organizers had explicitly designed the March 1913 D.C. procession to evoke hisses, the crowd's behavior—contrasted with the marchers' decorum—drew enormous publicity for the suffrage cause. By planning the event to coincide with Woodrow Wilson's first inauguration, organizers had hoped to steal the spotlight from the new president. Indeed, one report had Wilson asking plaintively, "Where are the people?" as he arrived at Union Station, only to be told that they were watching the suffrage parade.[3] Subsequent Senate hearings into the police handling of the pre-inaugural procession cast suffragists' assertion of their citizenship rights—particularly their right to assemble—in a new and more positive light. The organizers soon began to plan bigger nationwide events for May 1914.

Chief among the planners in both 1913 and 1914, New Jersey's Alice Paul was fresh from participating in the in-your-face tactics of the British suffragettes, including parades, demonstrations, and confrontations leading to arrest, imprisonment, and hunger striking. As a hunger striker in Britain, she had experienced the brutality of forcible feeding some fifty times. Already a celebrity with a charismatic reputation when she returned to the United States in 1910, Paul was eager to try out militant, but peaceful tactics at home. (As a Quaker, Paul renounced the violent methods in which some British suffragettes indulged.) More immediately, as chair of the Congressional Committee of the National American Woman Suffrage Association (NAWSA), soon to begin operating semi-autonomously as the Congressional Union for Woman Suffrage (CU), Paul was determined to redirect the energy behind the suffrage movement from tedious state-by-state campaigns into a push for a constitutional amendment enfranchising women, similar to the Fifteenth Amendment (1870). Indeed, a month after the pre-inaugural 1913 procession, suffrage leaders, including Martha Churchman Cranston of Delaware, lobbied each state's congressional delegation on behalf of the national approach. "Nation-wide Suffrage by a Constitutional Amendment," read a banner the suffragists waved as they marched toward the Capitol. Changes in both suffrage strategy and suffrage tactics were in the air.[4]

A national approach appealed to many, especially African American suffragists, who saw it as a way to counteract the virulent opposition coming from Wilson's supporters, many of them from Southern states that had disfranchised almost every potential African American male voter. (Wilson was a Virginian with deep ties to white supremacist movements in the ex-Confederate states. As president, he facilitated the systematic segregation of the civil service and of federal offices.) As they marched on the eve of his inauguration in 1913, they were fully aware that a constitutional amendment would double the voting population at a time when Southern Black male disfranchisement was virtually complete. They had a faith in such federal amendments born from their belief in the transformative significance of the Fourteenth and Fifteenth Amendments, a faith that their organizations echoed in repeated calls for the enforcement of both amendments. Their experiences at the pre-inaugural event itself surely tested that faith. A contingent of Black women graduates and students of Howard University, led by Mary Church Terrell, marched as planned. But Chicagoan Ida B. Wells-Barnett, president of her city's Alpha Suffrage Club, encountered and rejected an organizer's "suggestion" that her members avoid offending segregationists' sensibilities by marching at the rear of the procession. In concert with two white allies, she marched with the Illinois group instead, but African American suffragists were unlikely to forget the insult.[5]

In May 1914, then, as Delaware's suffragists participated in their first home state parade, in conjunction with parades being held across the country, the ground on which they trod was shifting. Within NAWSA, debates flared on both strategy and tactics: strategically, should the group continue primarily to pursue statewide suffrage, or put most of its resources into the quest for a federal constitutional amendment? Tactically, was patient grassroots organizing and lobbying the way to go, or were the unabashedly aggressive British suffragettes who inspired Alice Paul offering more effective techniques? To complicate the geography of suffrage, the national suffrage coalition was itself undergoing redefinition and expansion, as new individuals and groups made places for themselves in an ever-expanding domain, and state and national organizations struggled to manage the reorientation that resulted. Southern white women, through their clubs and organizations, for instance, expressed increasing enthusiasm and support for woman suffrage. Their growing presence raised key questions that had surfaced at the 1913 D.C. event: how might their dedication to maintaining white supremacy affect the interests of African American suffragists? Could Black suffragists pursue their efforts to re-enfranchise Black men and promote their own voting rights when other suffragists adamantly opposed both goals? Both NAWSA and its state affiliates continued grappling with those questions.[6]

By 1914, too, the suffrage coalition included substantial contingents of young, college-educated women like Alice Paul, referred to in the media as "New Women," some of whom termed themselves "feminists." It also included white working-class and immigrant women, dubbed "labor feminists" by historians, who connected their own demands for workplace rights to their need to have a voice in choosing their rulers. Indeed, working-class women in cities like New York regularly used street protests and parades as a way to draw attention to their demands. "Why," asked the New York Wage-Earners' Suffrage League in a flyer distributed in March 1911, "are you paid less than a man? Why do you work in a firetrap?" The answer: "because you are a woman and have no vote. Votes make the law." Circulated in the aftermath of the cruel deaths of 146 individuals, most of them young Jewish and Italian immigrant women, in the Triangle Shirtwaist Factory Fire, the leaflet made a direct connection between women's economic and political rights.[7]

As Delaware suffrage supporters marched in May of 1914, each of these issues was on someone's mind. Some, such as Hilles, were finding the Congressional Union (CU) an appealing option within NAWSA. Others, such as Stubbs, brought to woman suffrage a perspective that saw voting rights for women as part of a larger civil rights project that might improve educational, civic, recreational, and cultural resources and opportunities for the children who participated in the Garrett Settlement House's activities. Suffrage would also bring equity with African American male voters in Delaware, adding heft to African American men's and women's common work in the local NAACP. Still others, such as Annie Melvin Arniel, with white working-class roots and concerns, envisioned suffrage as an emancipatory project that would improve working and living conditions, wages, and opportunities for women like themselves. The CU's sharp focus on one cause and its nimbleness on the ground no doubt resonated, in Arniel's mind, with the need for labor unions to champion women's rights in the workplace.

In the years that followed the 1914 parade, Delaware's suffragists energetically pursued both state and national amendments. As they did, they experienced moments of united purpose, but often found their efforts fractured by ideological, racial, class, generational, strategic, and tactical divides. A promising 1915 effort to amend the Delaware state constitution came to nothing. The parting of ways between NAWSA and the CU, and the creation of the National Woman's Party (NWP) in 1916, exposed major divisions within suffragist ranks. Yet another effort to amend the state constitution in 1917 brought a halt to collaborations between the Delaware Equal Suffrage Association and the Delaware Congressional Union, as CU members joined the NWP in new, more confrontational tactics, particularly silent picketing of the White House. Looming over all of the discussions and disagreements was the European war, commenced in 1914. By 1916, it was pushing suffrage news off the front pages and by early summer 1917, the cheerful unity that reigned over the 1914 Wilmington suffrage parade had dissipated like a morning's fog.

New Energy, New Tactics, New Fissures

Florence Bayard Hilles went to the Delaware State Fair in September 1913 to exhibit her prize show dogs. Until that day, a suffrage colleague recalled, the forty-seven-year-old Hilles "had simply lived the life of a woman of her rank, was more or less athletic, a lover of dogs, etc." But at the fair, a Damascus Road moment left her transformed; she became a suffragist and subsequently a lifelong devotee of women's equal rights. Chalk it up to her encounter with Mabel Vernon, a Wilmington native, Swarthmore College graduate, and CU suffrage organizer who was at the fair site in Wilmington to staff the DESA tent and give a speech. No sooner had Hilles signed a card declaring "I believe in women suffrage" than she became passionately committed to the cause. Possessed of wealth, social position, a talent for leadership, a sense of the injustice of women's second-class status, as well as close ties to Delaware's Democratic Party, Hilles was a dream recruit. She could count among her male relatives and ancestors a large group of prominent politicians, five of whom served as U.S. senators, including her grandfather

James Ashton Bayard, her father Thomas Francis Bayard, and later, in the 1920s, her brother Thomas F. Bayard, Jr. As a girl, she lived part of the year in Washington, D.C., where her father served as Secretary of State under Grover Cleveland. There, she made her social debut under the patronage of Phoebe Apperson Hearst, whose husband George was a senator from California. As a young woman, Florence Bayard traveled to Great Britain after her father's appointment as U.S. Ambassador to the Court of St. James.[8]

Thirty-year-old Mabel Vernon had only recently returned to her native state to open a local field office for the Congressional Union. Youthful, optimistic, energetic, and fiercely dedicated to that one goal, members of the CU, like their founder and lodestar, Alice Paul, embraced attention-getting methods. From her small perch in the Equal Suffrage Association/Congressional Union office at Seventh and Shipley Streets, Vernon broadcast CU ideas and undertook CU tactics, such as giving impromptu street-corner speeches from an open air automobile along with Arden suffragist Frank Stephens. As she remembered them, her Equal Suffrage Association coworkers were "nice women, older women, not very gifted women but good women," who needed the push she provided because "I had some position in Delaware" and "could do a great deal more for suffrage than most" members of the Association. In November 1913, Vernon incited controversy by defying the leadership of the Delaware Equal Suffrage Association and inviting the radical British suffragette Emmeline Pankhurst to give a talk in Wilmington. "We are learning politics by disagreeing amicably," Vernon told a reporter from the Wilmington *Every Evening*. Pankhurst turned out to be "a perfectly delightful little woman" with a "soft and gentle voice," hardly the militant bomb-throwing banshee of popular press depictions. Nevertheless, Vernon's coworkers' ire at her insubordination foreshadowed ruptures within both the state and national organizations over tactics.[9]

As a CU organizer, Vernon spent much of her time out of state. Hilles, by contrast, was a Wilmington resident, married since 1898 to lawyer William S. Hilles, with a teenage daughter. She had social position, political visibility, economic resources, household help, and a commanding personal presence, assets she quickly put at Vernon's disposal, providing the use of her motorcar (and chauffeur) for transporting Pankhurst during her brief Wilmington visit. Hilles and other recruits would carry the flag for the CU within the Delaware Equal Suffrage Association. By late winter of 1914, Hilles was chairing a newly formed Delaware CU committee and planning the May parade.[10] Retaining a lively interest in DESA's work, Hilles planned the parade as the association's representative, even as CU's single-minded determination to win a federal amendment slowly brought it and its parent organization, NAWSA, to a strategic and widening fork in the road. The May 1914 Wilmington parade was a particularly visible result of Hilles's newfound commitment to woman suffrage, as was her participation in the Washington, D.C., gathering a week later.[11]

A photo of the Delaware delegation to Washington would have revealed to sharp-eyed observers the ways in which the makeup of Delaware's suffrage leadership was changing, as a broad and potentially more fractious coalition of supporters was now forming. Represented among the delegates were members of DESA, the state's leader in the cause since 1895, and newer CU adherents, as well as individuals from the Arden single-tax colony. To take one example, Mary de Vou, Corresponding Secretary of the Equal Suffrage Association, had a résumé testifying to her long and dedicated service to the group as its liaison with NAWSA; she had dutifully signed on to contribute to the Congressional Union as well.[12] From Arden, Delaware, came Elenor Getty Stephens and her husband Frank, along with Frank's son Donald. Founded around 1900 by Frank Stephens and others, Arden was a distinct community dedicated to both Henry George's single tax ideas and the artistic endeavors championed by the Arts and Crafts movement. Like the Stephenses, many Arden residents identified with socialist politics, and most were full-throated suffragists.[13]

As the group posed for their photograph, de Vou might have noted the presence not only of the Arden residents, but also of Annie Melvin Arniel, a widowed working mother accompanied by her fifteen-year-old daughter Rebecca, and Annie Stirlith McGee, the daughter of immigrants from Ireland and France, and also a working mother, both of whom brought to the suffrage cause very different life experiences from those of either Hilles or de Vou. Sixteen-year-old Mamye (or Mamie) Statnekoo, the American-born daughter of a Russian-born Wilmington merchant, was probably a schoolmate of Rebecca Arniel, seen partially hidden behind her mother Annie. Hilles stood in the center. At the time, her central position was undeniable. Not only had she led the Wilmington parade a week earlier, but she also had the status and tenacity needed

Figure 5. A group of suffragists heading to a Washington, D. C. suffrage parade, May 9, 1914, was photographed at the Wilmington train station. Wilmington [Delmarvia] *Sunday Morning Star,* May 10, 1914, 1. Front row, L-R: Mabel Fowler, Josephine W. Thomas, Annie Melvin Arniel, Mayme Statnekoo, Mary deVou, Agnes Keehan Yerger, Annie Stirlith McGee [aka Magee]. Second row, L-R: John F. Thomas, Rebecca Arniel [partially hidden], Donald Stephens, Marguerite C. Wallace, Florence Bayard Hilles, Frank Stephens, Elise Stokes Satterthwaite, May Keehan Stroman [partially hidden]. Credit: Delaware Historical Society

to hold together—for the moment, at least—a group with such divergent interests and backgrounds.[14]

Absent from the photo were any individuals from the Equal Suffrage Study Club. Although Hilles was acquainted with at least two club members, Alice Dunbar and Blanche Williams Stubbs, and although the club's participation in the Wilmington parade had received due notice in local newspapers, Delaware's racially segregated practices rendered an integrated contingent unlikely. (Delaware's schools remained segregated until 1954; as late as 1958, a member of the Wilmington City Council was refused service at a local coffee shop because he was Black.) Besides, both Dunbar, the club's president, and Stubbs, its parade leader, were juggling a number of commitments. For Dunbar, they encompassed her teaching duties as well as her own writing and publishing projects, including her 1914 book, *Masterpieces of Negro Eloquence.* For Stubbs, they included launching the Garrett Settlement at its new, enlarged location, and attending the National Association of Colored Women's annual convention as state president of the Federation of Christian Workers. Along with other members of the club, the two women were also in the process of starting an NAACP chapter in Wilmington.[15]

As suffragists added parades, processions, tableaux, and pageants to their list of tactics, they had good reason to be optimistic that a long-sought goal was in sight, whether achieved by a state or a national strategy. Across the globe, women had full national voting rights in New Zealand, Australia, Finland, and Norway. In the United States, by the end of 1914, women had full voting rights in eleven states plus territorial Alaska, presidential suffrage in Illinois, and other types of limited suffrage in several more states. The success of state-level suffrage campaigns in Washington state in 1910, California in 1911, Arizona, Oregon, and Kansas in 1912, and Montana and Nevada in 1914 likely confirmed the faith of those who adhered to the state-by-state strategy (although in 1914 five other state campaigns went down to defeat). On the national front, a constitutional amendment's prospects received a boost when the Seventeenth Amendment went into effect in 1913. Now, the voters of the states (rather than the legislatures) would elect U.S. senators, just as they had always elected members of the U.S. House. Women voters in full-franchise states could help shape Congress's composition by electing pro-suffrage members who would then support a federal constitutional amendment. And, indeed, in the summer of 1913, the Senate committee on woman suffrage had, for the first time in two decades, voted favorably on just such an amendment, the first step in sending it to the full Senate for consideration. Whether individual marchers favored putting their energies into state-focused efforts, or preferred to push for a national constitutional amendment, or both, the stars looked to be aligning and full suffrage for all seemed to be coming into view.[16]

For Delaware suffragists, 1915 presented yet another opportunity to bring their vision to fruition through statewide suffrage. Working together, DESA and the CU, having patted themselves on their collective backs for the "perfectly harmonious" "fraternal relation" the two groups enjoyed, had a bill amending the state constitution's voting requirements ready to present when the legislative session began in January.[17] At the same time, neighboring New Jersey and Pennsylvania would be holding statewide suffrage referenda in the autumn. Both referenda and state constitutional provisions had worked as tools to enfranchise women, California by referendum in 1911, and Arizona via state constitution in 1912, when it became the forty-eighth state. Members of the Delaware branch of the CU were no doubt aware that their national leadership was encouraging members to pursue statewide organizing primarily as a way of drumming up "a nationwide demand" for a federal amendment. In addition, the CU's Alice Paul was giving form to the wisp of an idea: to use the power of current women voters both to sway national politics and to make suffrage a political issue in state races. Between 1914 and 1916, she shaped the thought into a platform with two planks: hold "the party in power responsible" for women's lack of the franchise, and assemble women voters into a "woman's party." The CU's pressure for a change in strategy provoked NAWSA to respond with a "Winning Plan," announced in September 1916 by the group's president, Carrie Chapman Catt. Although continuing to see state-level campaigns as the surest road to success, particularly in the South, Catt endorsed a parallel strategy of petitioning Congress for a federal amendment. The latter, she predicted, would become part of the Constitution by 1922.[18]

The 1915 effort to amend the Delaware state constitution fizzled, just as it had in 1913. This time, however, the bill made it onto the floor of both legislative chambers before failing to secure the required two-thirds majority for passage. This time, too, suffragists introduced a variety of new and colorful CU-inspired tactics to Dover and to the legislature. The Equal Suffrage Association inaugurated the campaign by opening a headquarters in Dover, trumpeting their cause with speeches from a "gaily decorated" automobile (likely Florence Bayard Hilles's) and a musically accompanied procession from the Dover train station to the new headquarters, "greeted with apparent interest" by Dover residents who lined the parade route. Mabel Vernon and other CU members followed up by driving a "suffrage flier" on a couple of "whirlwind tours" around the state to rally support. Despite the lighthearted approach that suffrage supporters took, Wilmington newspapers used the language of war to evoke the scene: "Suffragists Invade Dover," read one headline; "Equal Suffragists Storm the Capitol," read another. A parade was, a reporter concluded, both an "unusual spectacle" and "an innovation" for the state's capital city. In March, as the final legislative votes were being taken, suffragists from across the state, once again accompanied by music, walked in procession from their temporary headquarters to the Dover Green, rallied in front of the State House, then marched into the galleries to watch the vote. After witnessing the amendment's defeat, they pronounced themselves undaunted, held a street meeting in Wilmington from another "gaily decorated automobile," followed by an "informal luncheon" at the Hotel Du Pont, and began planning for a renewed effort when the legislature reconvened in 1917.[19]

By the time of the 1915 campaign in Dover and the "farewell luncheon" in Wilmington, however, noticeable cracks had appeared in the surface unity of pro-suffrage Delawareans. The luncheon's sponsor, for instance, was not the Delaware Equal Suffrage Association but the "Delaware Campaign Committee on Equal Suffrage," chaired by the CU's Florence Bayard Hilles. Among the seventy guests were the presidents of both the Delaware and the Wilmington Equal Suffrage Associations, each of whom made brief remarks, but the event clearly belonged to Hilles and the CU. The fault line separating the two organizations had begun to develop in the aftermath of the May 1914 parades in Wilmington and Washington, D.C., when, having "outgrown" the existing headquarters at Seventh and Shipley in Wilmington, they moved to new headquarters on Delaware Avenue, near Tenth and Market Streets, in June. Heralding the move, the CU organized a parade from the old to the new headquarters, with Hilles and Annie Stirlith McGee carrying banners with CU-devised "suffrage colors" of white, yellow (or gold), and purple. They then decorated the new space with evocations of the newly designated yellow "suffrage rose" in curtains and wallpaper. Although the new space was shared by two organizations, if one skimmed newspaper descriptions, it would appear that the Congressional Union was its sole occupant.[20]

In these and other activities, adapted from successful state-level campaigns in states such as California, CU members exhibited a talent for tailoring their activities to reach varied audiences. Through publicity-seeking stunts and choreographed events, they cultivated a high profile, using newspaper notices to keep their organization regularly before the public eye. At the same time, afternoon "parlor meetings" held in suffragists' homes brought information about their cause into domestic spaces and enabled women to attend who might be concerned about propriety or be unwilling or unable to attend meetings that took them away from family responsibilities. These meetings proved especially effective in building enthusiasm for the May 1914 parade. Another tactic, posting "voiceless speeches" on placards in downtown shop windows, called attention to women's lack of a "voice" in public affairs while also evoking the traditional belief that women should exert their moral influence silently. Decorating their headquarters with suffrage-yellow window curtains and wallpaper, CU members softened public spaces with domestic imagery. Women's needlework in suffrage colors appeared on tri-colored flags and "Votes for Women" banners, and "The Little Yellow Rose of Equal Suffrage," a song with lyrics by Wilmingtonian Mary H. Askew Mather, rebranded the yellow rose as a suffrage symbol. Simultaneously, CU women laid claim to spaces that were clearly not domestic, via open air meetings on street corners, rallies, and processions, and mass meetings on city streets or in downtown halls. By 1914 and 1915, of course, women were familiar sights on downtown streets, as workers and shoppers. Traversing those same streets and buildings (such as department stores), suffrage advocates reached a variety of audiences with the message that women were political actors who had the same rights as men to occupy political spaces. To be sure, their stunts relied upon their white racial identification; African American suffragists who wished to take part would need to "pass," to become invisible.[21]

The CU's leadership was particularly adept at creating an image that suffrage advocacy was fun and a bit daring, and that they themselves were youthful and energetic. When a CU organizer, Elsie Hill, arrived in Wilmington in June 1914, the morning paper dutifully printed the group's description of her as a "live wire," and the group itself as working with "renewed . . . zeal" at their new headquarters. Suffragists led by Hilles apparently participated in so many public events in 1914 that a Wilmington reporter concluded they "made a record of having marched in more parades here this year than any other organization." In August, Hilles and Elsie Hill, touring the entire state in Hilles's suffrage-decorated car, gave open air talks, distributed literature, and cultivated affiliations. From the press's breathless description of the tour and the number of places visited (Newark, Dover, Frederica, Camden, Kitts Hummock, Harrington, Milford, Wyoming, and Felton), it might have appeared that the women were on the road for an extended time rather than the two days the trip had taken. Automobiles themselves and women drivers were new and unusual enough in 1914 that the description of Hilles on a "flying trip through the little State" created an image of modernity and carefree autonomy. The motorcar, an "emblem of . . . women's emancipation," as Virginia Scharff has noted, served as a useful speaking platform and could be a means to attract men curious about a newfangled piece of machinery, regardless of their interest in suffrage.

By contrast with the CU's vivid and multifarious public presence, the larger and more established Delaware Equal Suffrage Association could appear wan and faded. To underscore the contrast, ahead of the 1914 Wilmington parade, the CU supplied dueling photographs of Hilles and Martha Cranston, the longtime leader of DESA, to the Wilmington *Evening Journal*, along with text on suffrage history that foregrounded the CU's work. Cranston, aged sixty-seven, looking grandmotherly with white hair and a demure shirtwaist blouse, appeared more than a generation older than the almost fifty-year-old Hilles, whose direct gaze, jaunty hat and scarf, and self-possessed demeanor conveyed both seriousness of purpose and the modernity of the "new woman." A July photo in the CU journal *The Suffragist* conveyed a similar message.[22]

There is little doubt that the CU, both locally and nationally, appealed to both college-educated and "self-supporting" women.[23] In Delaware, the most significant way in which the CU differentiated itself from DESA was in its outreach to working-class white women. Although members of both groups cultivated working women's support, visiting local factories and shops and speaking to women workers, the CU leadership had more success in addressing their concerns and placing them in noticeable leadership positions. Elsie Hill's summer work in 1914 provides an example of the CU's outreach, employing street meetings conducted in "an entertaining manner" as people headed home from work and arguments that echoed the language and approach of New York's Wage Earners' Suffrage League. That "working women need the ballot to regulate conditions under which they work," and businesswomen need it "to secure for themselves a fair opportunity in their business," were CU talking points that she highlighted, along with more conventional appeals to motherhood and child protection.

Although some CU stunts derived from British examples, they also bore a significant resemblance to the tactics of the U.S. labor movement. Working women in the Women's Trade Union League, founded in 1903, for instance, employed "militant" tactics, particularly street-corner protests and mass marches that were a new experience for their middle-class allies. The 1909 "Uprising of the 20,000" garment workers strike in New York and the massive 1911 protests that followed the horrific Triangle Shirtwaist Company fire would have been fresh in the minds of Delaware's

Figure 6. In this July 1914 photo taken at the joint Delaware Equal Suffrage Association (DESA)—Congressional Union (CU) headquarters on Delaware Avenue in Wilmington, the contrast of images between the CU's Florence Bayard Hilles and DESA's Martha Churchman Cranston is evident. Hilles, in suffrage white with a tri-color sash, holds one side of a banner demanding a federal constitutional amendment; Cranston stands behind Hilles and to her right. The others are Cranston's daughter Helen A. Cranston (to her mother's right); Mary R. de Vou (standing between the two Cranstons); Ella Weldin Johnson from Newport (seated l); Alice L. Steinlein from Arden (seated r); and Mary Conkle, a national CU organizer, holding the other side of the banner. Credit: Photo #1914.001.047, National Woman's Party Photograph Collection. Courtesy of the Belmont-Paul National Historical Monument, Washington, D.C.

labor suffragists when CU speakers addressed them. And when the CU's leadership made plans to march in Wilmington's Labor Day parade, secured an endorsement from the skilled male workers belonging to the Wilmington Central Labor Union, and then assured the men that all CU printing would not only be done in union print shops but would also bear a union label, working-class women undoubtedly got the message.[24]

The experiences of three working-class CU partisans reveal the concerns that led them to suffrage and to the CU in particular. Of the three—all seen in the May 1914 Wilmington train station photograph—Annie Melvin Arniel had already been to Washington, D.C., in February 1914 as part of a CU delegation of five hundred working women seeking to meet with Woodrow Wilson to press him into supporting a federal amendment. They were "women workers who toil daily in the mines and in the sweatshops and the factories of the nation" for "inadequate wages under conditions that undermined health." Arniel, a widow in her mid-forties with a teenage daughter, came from a family where men worked in the building trades or on the railroads, women took "women's work," and family members helped each other out when they could. In 1913, she had tried unsuccessfully for a job as police matron in Wilmington, a position made particularly attractive because it had a pension attached.

Agnes Keehan Schopferer Yerger knew something about the harsh realities of working-class life. Oppressive job conditions had killed her first husband, Charles Schopferer, a foundry worker who collapsed and died in ninety-five-degree June heat at the age of thirty-nine. Now remarried to the owner of a frame shop on Shipley Street, Agnes, along with her fifteen-year-old daughter Naomi, lived at and worked in the family enterprise. Annie Stirlith McGee, aged forty-one in 1914 with four surviving children, came from a family of immigrant workers. Her French-born father was a rag dealer, several brothers of hers went into the scrap iron business, her husband Thomas worked at a gas plant, and her brother Frank spent his days at the DuPont powder mills, manufacturing explosives. Described by a suffrage colleague as a woman of "strong physique," Annie McGee stood out as the tallest woman in the train station photograph. The CU likely appealed to these and other women because putting their energy into a federal amendment would enfranchise all working women, not those of one state alone. Moreover, CU leaders did not merely address working women's concerns directly; they also made a point of inviting women like McGee and Arniel to take the foreground in parades and at the local office. By 1915, for instance, Arniel was managing the CU's Wilmington headquarters as the group's executive secretary.[25]

During the 1915 legislative campaign, some of the differences between DESA and its CU members hardly mattered. But once the possibility of state suffrage had again gone down to defeat, cracks in the surface of suffrage unity gradually became fissures and fissures produced rupture. In May, the DESA "withdrew from headquarters" that it had by then shared with the CU for almost a year. Soon, members were no doubt startled to read the headline in their evening paper, "Mrs. Hilles Heads State Suffragists." Wasn't Martha Churchman Cranston still DESA's president? She was, but the state's CU branch, at its two-day "first convention," had elected Hilles president, placing the organization on a separate, seemingly equal, platform as its parent. Less-informed readers might be forgiven for confusing the two groups. And indeed, there were some prominent members of the Equal Suffrage Association present at the CU convention, notably Dr. Josephine White De Lacour, a pioneering physician who was serving as president of the Wilmington Equal Suffrage Association. Her comment about the need for the two groups to "work harmoniously together," however, was buried deep in the newspaper article. At the convention itself, the activities and resolutions were curated to call attention to the CU's chosen tactics and goals. A convention-opening parade up Market Street, led by Hilles carrying an American flag and McGee wielding the CU's "new official" banner of purple, white, and gold, featured the flags of the eleven states where women enjoyed full suffrage. Speakers such as Mabel Vernon made clear the group's commitment to a federal amendment (now christened the "Susan B. Anthony Amendment" to differentiate it from alternate proposals), and their rejection of any version that fell short of guaranteeing votes for all women. Hilles might still have considered herself a member of the Delaware Equal Suffrage Association and would have supported another run at amending the state constitution, but her message to other DESA members was clear: Delaware's Congressional Union branch would walk its own path, the one heading in the direction of a federal constitutional amendment.[26]

During the months between May and November in 1915, Cranston continued to insist publicly that her organization enjoyed "friendly feeling" with its CU members. Privately, she seethed, convinced that Hilles was engaging in deliberately misleading practices and working to undermine the older organization. Delaware, she told Alice Paul, "is too small a state to support two entirely independent suffrage organizations." Now that it had two, the groups delineated the lines between them ever more distinctly. Throughout those months, led by a seemingly indefatigable Hilles, CU members traversed the state, enlisting support and organizing CU affiliates in towns where the Equal Suffrage Association had experienced almost no success. In upbeat reports to the local press as well as to the CU's national periodical, *The Suffragist*, Hilles and her coworkers described "an active campaign for members" in Sussex County. An equally indefatigable Mabel Vernon represented Delaware at a CU-sponsored suffrage event at the Panama Pacific Exposition in San Francisco. Hyperbolically described as the "first political convention ever held by women in the history of the world," the gathering proposed to use the clout of women voters in full-franchise states "for the enfranchisement of the non-voting women of the nation." By contrast, at its annual meeting in November, the Equal Suffrage Association, while touting the "parades, public meetings, all kinds of affairs for raising money, open air plays, parlor meetings, &c." as useful tactics employed throughout the year, was still looking for a suffrage organizer "to go down through the state to form clubs." As if to confirm the inevitable, at its November 1915 convention, the association's leaders announced a decision they had made in April: they had "severed ties" entirely with the Congressional Union. Cranston then announced her retirement; as the "Susan B. Anthony of Delaware" and DESA's "first and only President" since 1895, she would thereafter serve in an honorary capacity.[27]

The rift in Delaware mirrored that which was occurring at the national level, as NAWSA and Alice Paul's Congressional Union increasingly followed different signposts toward national suffrage. While officially nonpartisan, the CU offered the promise of electing pro-suffrage members of Congress who would then endorse a constitutional amendment. CU's leaders took the promise one step further by insisting on "holding the party in power"—namely the Democrats—responsible for a failure to bring a federal suffrage amendment up for consideration. In effect, this meant that, in the 1914 (off-year) elections in the full-suffrage states, the CU would campaign against all Democrats, regardless of an individual candidate's suffrage position. In 1916, the group would do the same, this time during a presidential election year when Woodrow Wilson sought a second term. The results were distinctly mixed, but 1914 saw two more states—Nevada and Montana—enfranchise women.[28]

With its "party in power" approach, the CU appeared to follow a road map laid out along British parliamentary lines, where a defeat for the ruling party would bring down a government. Paul's grasp of American electoral politics seemed questionable. Not only did the strategy require that voters in the small number of full-suffrage states oppose pro-suf-frage Democrats, but it also ignored the imbalanced sex ratios in some of those states, where women voters' electoral strength could be dimin-ished by a surfeit of male voters. It further assumed that women voters all shared the same priorities. Although the strategy appeared quixotic, Paul was not merely tilting at windmills. She was single-minded in her passionate belief that a federal amendment was the most direct means by which to achieve nationwide suffrage, and like other suffragists, she had high hopes for the four state campaigns (in Massachusetts, New Jersey, New York, and Pennsylvania) being decided in October and November 1915. Not one of the four succeeded, however. When NAWSA met in its annual convention in December, the state-by-state strategy was looking depressingly unworkable.

By then, too, changes to NAWSA's leadership threatened any attempts to keep Paul's faction within the NAWSA fold. (Many in that faction, including Paul herself, were members of both the CU and NAWSA). The election of Carrie Chapman Catt as NAWSA president in late 1915, replacing Anna Howard Shaw, had a perceptible impact. While Shaw was widely admired for her oratorical abilities, and indeed had spoken in Delaware on numerous occasions, Catt was an organizer. Her return to the presidency after over a decade away from the position almost guaranteed a clash with Paul. At the NAWSA convention, the CU's tac-tics came up for discussion under the rubric of "another problem." A December 17 meeting aimed at reconciling NAWSA and the CU did not go well. "Mrs. Catt explained to Miss Paul," wrote a NAWSA reporter, "that the association could not accept as an affiliated society one which was likely to defy" its policy of non-partisanship. As Paul was unwilling to "guarantee that the Congressional Union would observe this policy," the two groups parted company, although not without recrimination and finger-pointing that would only become more bitter as CU leaders established their group's complete and separate identity, culminating in the formation of the National Woman's Party in 1916.[29]

Race, Class, and the Anti-Suffrage Argument

The 1915 state amendment campaign exposed other, older fault lines within the ranks of the Delaware leadership, particularly those of race and class. The divergences played out somewhat differently, however, from their unfolding earlier in Delaware's history, largely due to the increased prominence of an organized anti-suffrage cohort with its own signal (red) flower and song, "The Anti-Suffrage Rose." This cohort's objections were familiar: they claimed that the majority of women did not want to vote; that expanding the electorate would unnecessarily increase the cost of running elections; that women's voting in the full-suffrage states had been a failure; that "any further political activities" by women would "menace" "the interests of family and home"; that most women were "unprepared" to vote; that "no one can point to a single substantial grievance . . . suffered by women" merely because they lacked voting rights; and that, in fact, "woman" exercised substantial "influence" on the "progress . . . [of] civilization" despite (or perhaps because of) being voteless. Emily Bissell remained a familiar figure espousing such arguments, on occasion engaging in public debate with Hilles. But in 1914–15, Mary Wilson Thompson, an upper-class white socialite with deep roots in the state, gained increased prominence. Through the newly formed Women's Committee of Delaware Opposed to Woman Suffrage, which Thompson chaired, Bissell and Thompson drew upon their own political influence, social connections, and organizational experience to channel and promulgate the views of the "antis." And as was true of anti-suffragist arguments in general, their claims often rested upon a particularly narrow view of "woman" and a set of notable blind spots on the question of how "she" might be able to exercise "influence."[30]

In disseminating their views, Thompson and Bissell had help from local political leaders who raised alarms about the prospect of "illiterate" or "ignorant" women crowding the polls on Election Day. In January 1914, for instance, when Delaware's Republican senator Henry A. du Pont met in Washington with a small "deputation" requesting his support for federal suffrage, he largely repeated a response he had given in 1910. It would not be wise, he told the group, to "increase the national electorate by two million illiterate women." Making it clear that he was referring to "illiterate foreigners" who, he believed, should be excluded from immigrating to the United States, he endorsed educational and literacy qualifications for woman suffrage. But there was a racial aspect to his argument as well: suffrage was a state matter and should be "properly limited." Not every woman in Delaware "colored as well as white" should vote; there should be educational or property qualifications to do so.[31]

Newspaper editors actively introduced the anti-suffrage position into public conversation. To be sure, journalists generally represented both groups' leaders in a respectful fashion, but editors of the three Wilmington dailies especially esteemed "Miss Emily P. Bissell." Bissell had achieved local hero status for her endeavors, including lobbying successfully for the passage of Delaware's first child labor law as well as the state's first maximum hour law for women workers in 1914. With her long history of involvement in Wilmington's Associated Charities, Red Cross (from the start in 1904), Consumers' League (she was its first president), and New Century Club, as well as the West End Neighborhood House (she was a founder), and other undertakings carried out in both women-only and gender-integrated contexts, Bissell embodied the type of female self-sacrifice that antis accused suffragists of lacking. By 1915, too, she had seemingly single-handedly spun fundraising straw into gold by pioneering the use of Christmas Seals in the campaign against tuberculosis. For white Delawareans afflicted with the deadly disease Bissell's crusade was lifesaving, leading to the opening of a "tent sanitarium" in 1906 and then a permanent hospital (Hope Farm) in 1909. As permanent president of the Delaware Anti-Tuberculosis Society from 1908 until her death, Bissell collaborated with a wide-ranging roster of male politicians, businessmen, physicians, clergymen, and philanthropists. When she sought funds for any of her undertakings or lobbied for legal changes, these men took her phone calls. Their female kin were her colleagues in the New Century Club. Key to understanding Bissell's anti-suffrage position was her belief that suffrage would cause "women" to lose the "influence" they already enjoyed. As a non-voter, she had all the "influence" she wanted for her concerns. Moreover, if all Delaware women, including immigrant and African American women, could vote, then the influence that any one woman possessed would dissipate—even if that woman was "Miss Emily Bissell." She would be merely one voter among the mass of female voters.[32]

Local editors embroidered anti-suffrage scenarios about who had influence, and who should have it. Enfranchising women, contended Merris Taylor, the editorialist for Wilmington's Democratic paper *Every Evening*, meant enfranchising African American women, diluting the influence of white women, and bolstering the power of the Republican Party. Given the "well-known capacity of Delaware negroes for registering and voting," because Black men have "solidly and unthinkingly" supported Republicans, and because "nearly one-half" of white women "would not vote at all," woman suffrage "would double the numerical advantage of this Republican party asset," namely, the "negro vote." Any "fair consideration" of "the equal suffrage question" on its own "merits" was impossible; no Democrat would vote for it. In the states of the former Confederacy, where the systematic disfranchisement of African American men was carried out between 1890 and 1905, the specter of Black men voting was a useful device to whip up white fears. Now, in Delaware, as in most of the white south, fear of any expanded access to suffrage had another target: African American women.[33]

White suffragists were compelled to address the racial hobgoblin circling around their campaign in 1915, just as they regularly countered other anti-suffrage claims. Some stuck to the general principle that suffrage was a matter of simple justice for all women. In testifying before the legislature, Martha Churchman Cranston framed her formal remarks in that way: "we want to say under what laws we shall live." Similarly, Bogotá, Colombia-born Mary Ospina, who made headlines in July when she became, according to the *Evening Journal*, "the only [single] woman who has ever obtained final naturalization papers in this city," took the opportunity to underline the unequal citizenship that naturalization conferred upon her. "I have not come into the same rights and justice," she wrote in a published letter, that her male counterparts "instantly acquired." She looked forward, she said, "to the day when I shall enjoy inalienable rights" as well as the freedom to express "my opinion by the ballot."[34]

But in both informal and formal comments, Hilles, with a surfeit of Democratic politicians and known anti-suffragists in her family, chose to respond directly to the anti-suffrage argument that, as a reporter explained it, "there is danger from the female negro vote." At first, Hilles dismissed such talk as rubbish. Delaware's white female population was "three times as many" as that of the entire Black population, and besides, the "immoral vote is more dangerous" than the "illiterate vote." Testifying before a legislative committee, however, she sharpened the racial edge of her argument by invoking white supremacy. In an echo of Mary Ann Sorden Stuart's complaints in an earlier era, she cited the example of an illiterate "colored man" living at the gatehouse of her rural estate at Ommelanden who, "simply because he is a man, can vote" and even affect the valuation of the property on which she paid tax. The injustice of denying voting rights to educated, tax-paying women like herself seemed clear. At no point, however, did she contend that Black men should be disfranchised, or that only white Delawareans should vote. Rather, she presented white dominance as a permanent condition, and race-based arguments against Black women voting as irrelevant. The state's demographics ensured that "this is a white man's and a white woman's State and always will be."[35]

Faced with anti-suffrage arguments that demeaned them, and perhaps unsurprised that their suffrage allies willingly stereotyped African Americans, two members of the Equal Suffrage Study Club confronted the racial specter directly. Each took her stand on the grounds of justice and the common interests of Black and white women, interests that assumed a shared middle-class identity. Club member and Wilmington NAACP chapter vice-president Mary J. Woodlen forthrightly presented herself in a letter to the editor of *Every Evening*, "as a colored woman and one who believes in Equal Suffrage." Black suffragists, like white women, were "anxious . . . that justice be done . . . [and] especially anxious to improve conditions among our own people." Informing her readers that Black and white women were "travelling side by side" in "works of charity and social uplift," she evoked the delicate diplomacy middle-class women like herself employed to bring improved educational and housing opportunities to their communities. She then skewered the subtext of the argument of "those who fear us so," that African American women were not "fit" to vote. "The only menace that threatens this State" was "ignorance, dense ignorance" of the sort the editor represented. No "thoughtful" Black woman would vote "blindly" for Republicans. "This is our house," she pointedly reminded him, "and we expect to remain here and help in making it a 'fit' place in which to live."[36]

Her colleague, Blanche Williams Stubbs, who had led the Equal Suffrage Study Club contingent at the 1914 Wilmington parade, astutely sent her own rebuttal to the city's other afternoon daily, the Republican *Evening Journal*, which had a larger circulation. Like Woodlen, Stubbs emphasized the common interests of all woman suffragists, and tartly accused the editor of being "a slave" to his prejudices against African American women. She offered him a history lesson. What did he think African American women had been doing since the days when "the spirit of Abraham Lincoln dominated the Republican party"? She answered, "We have neither been sitting down dreaming [n]or standing still, but have been advancing like other women in thought, in culture and in character." Invoking the name of "dear old Sojourner Truth," she reminded him that, since 1848, "colored women have been joining hands with the noble white women of this country in every reform movement." In her view, they continued to do so. Moreover, if any group of potential voters posed a "menace," it was "the poor, illiterate immigrant women who have not been reared under our flag and constitution, and with our language and customs their birthright." Once women acquire suffrage, she concluded, indulging in a bit of strategic dissemblance, "the vote of the colored women cannot be counted on as an asset to any one party." In actuality, Stubbs and her sister suffragists fully understood which party supported African Americans' voting rights.[37]

Stubbs's and Woodlen's evocations of an interracial suffrage sisterhood might appear strange, given the sorts of comments from white suffragists that they were encountering daily, particularly Hilles's cartoon version of her employee at Ommelanden and her blithely dismissive suggestion that African American women shouldn't expect their votes to matter very much. Framed for a largely white audience, their statements suggest the delicate choreography that African American suffragists had to perfect if they were to win their voting rights without sparking a white racist backlash. By presenting themselves as the educated, cultured women that they were, they might help displace the imagery that racist anti-suffrage editorials used to represent "colored women voters." Moreover, Hilles and other white suffragists, unlike some of their cohort in Deep South states, were not endorsing white-only suffrage.

The CU, in particular, was increasingly mobilizing the power of women voters in the full-suffrage states, such as California, where African Americans faced no voting restrictions, and championing working women's concerns. In addition, the CU's opposition to Democratic office-seekers and its focus on a federal amendment (in tandem with the Delaware group's involvement in the 1915 state constitutional amendment effort) dovetailed with African American suffragists' own Republican leanings and their faith in constitutional amendments and federal enforcement as the surest way of guaranteeing suffrage to both African American women and men. The Congressional Union had already roundly rejected a version of the suffrage amendment that would have had the effect of making woman suffrage entirely a states' rights issue. Given that context, Stubbs's presence at the March

Figure 7. Blanche W. Stubbs, c. 1920. In a formal portrait photo, Blanche Williams Stubbs presented a contemplative image. Credit: Photo courtesy of H. Gordon Fleming

11 "farewell luncheon" for those who had labored in Delaware during the legislative session and who would now begin planning "the 1917 campaign" might not be entirely surprising. To be sure, she was the only known African American to attend the luncheon, but it seems unlikely that she simply passed into the otherwise all-white gathering, for several women in the group knew her personally. As her letter to the editor revealed, she had in common with some of them a sense of privilege based on her class and educational status, and a willingness to entertain the idea of "educational qualifications" for voters, as long as they were "justly administered." At least part of her grievance was with powerful white individuals who lumped all Black women with "the lowest" group.[38]

Perhaps no one so well understood—and negotiated—the complex steps that African American women had to master in their relationships with white suffragists as Alice Dunbar. After the failure of the 1915 Delaware amendment, Dunbar took a position as a field organizer for the campaigns for two Mid-Atlantic suffrage referenda (New Jersey and Pennsylvania), with "financial support from [white] philanthropists with whom she is personally acquainted" and "voluntary contributions" from audience members. Traveling around Pennsylvania between July and November, with occasional forays into New Jersey, she spoke to varied audiences, pressing men in particular to vote to enfranchise their mothers, sisters, and daughters. She gave talks in churches, at women's club meetings, to men's groups, and to mixed audiences. In press reports, she appeared as "Mrs. Paul Laurence Dunbar," or the "Negro Poet's Widow," titles that conferred upon her an unusual visibility while also erasing the reality of the Dunbars' deeply troubled marriage. She enjoyed and cultivated her celebrity, as her scrapbook of press clippings from the campaigns makes clear. Handbills announcing her appearances often included her glamorous youthful studio photo; her beauty, poise, and eloquence were recurring themes in both white and Black newspaper reports. She was "a woman of unusual beauty," one "in whom the race can take great pride," with "a voice beautifully modulated and an easy flow of forceful, logical arguments." Having just recently published *Masterpieces of Negro Eloquence*, which she dedicated to "the boys and girls of the Negro race," Dunbar was aware of the conventions of oral argumentation, including the importance of tailoring one's arguments to one's audiences.[39]

To be sure, Dunbar's first purpose was to persuade male voters to approve the suffrage referenda, and so she rehearsed a few common suffragist pleas ("taxation without representation is tyranny"; that women as "natural homemakers" needed the vote in order to become better homemakers). More often, she emphasized larger themes, particularly the needs of working women and families, and the benefits of "favorable housing conditions" to Black residents—and by extension their white neighbors. As she had in a 1914 speech to the NAACP, she regularly reminded listeners about the needs of Black working women, especially "the woman who is forced to earn her living by her hands." Any argument about women "belonging" in "the home" erased their experiences. In Chester, Pennsylvania, joined by Blanche Stubbs, she lauded clubwomen for their successful "betterment of the [N]egro woman industrially, socially, and intellectually." In Pittsburgh, she testified against permitting the racist film *The Birth of a Nation* to be screened on the ground that it threatened the "amity" that "now exists" between the races. In her self-presentation and her public advocacy, Dunbar embodied the beautiful and cultured African American colleague with whom white suffragists could work. As she did, she did not shy away from enlisting African American men in the suffrage struggle. Whereas Woodlen and Stubbs carefully framed their published letters for white audiences, dismissing any suggestion of bloc voting by African Americans, when Dunbar had the opportunity to address African American men directly, she told them simply that enfranchising women would "double" the "political power" of "our race." If they voted favorably on the referendum, she predicted, when African American rights were at stake, "the women will stand with the men on the matter." Perhaps this was a risky strategy that could bolster the racist anti-suffrage arguments being bandied about in Wilmington, but then Dunbar was shrewd enough to know that her hometown newspapers would not cover her speeches.[40]

While African American suffragists such as Dunbar (after her April 1916 marriage to Robert Nelson, Dunbar-Nelson), Stubbs, and Woodlen put forth pro-suffrage sentiments in speeches and in print, simple self-protection made them guarded in their dealings with white women. They did not recognize themselves in the fun house mirror image of the "colored woman voter" that cropped up each time a statewide suffrage amendment came up for discussion, and they no doubt were fully aware of NAWSA's and the NWP's skittishness about championing Black suffragists' concerns. Their experiences working with white philanthropists in the Garrett Settlement, temperance supporters in the WCTU, and allies in the local NAACP chapter shaped their understanding of the extent and limits of cross-racial collaboration. (Only one white church in Wilmington, the First Unitarian Society, included African American members as equals.) Suffrage advocacy was one arena within which they generally preferred to keep their own counsel. For that reason, it was notable when, on a few occasions, African American and white suffragists met in each other's spaces. In July 1916, Dunbar-Nelson accepted Florence Bayard Hilles's invitation to attend the CU conference as a "fraternal delegate" from the Garrett Settlement House. She and Stubbs then made the settlement house available for a CU meeting at which Stubbs presided. At the meeting, the CU announced plans to organize Wilmington's voters by ward in order to mount an "aggressive fight" for a national suffrage amendment. Endorsing that approach, Dunbar-Nelson became the CU's Sixth Ward chairman. As a Republican, Dunbar-Nelson had concerns that dovetailed with those of the CU and the National Woman's Party, namely, defeating Woodrow Wilson's bid for a second term. There is no record of any comparable contacts between the members of the Equal Suffrage Study Club and the Delaware Equal Suffrage Association.[41]

Another State Campaign, 1916–1917

Pennsylvania's voters defeated the 1915 referendum for which Alice Dunbar lobbied so strenuously. (New Jersey's fall referendum failed, too.) With state-level suffrage thwarted next door as well as at home in 1915, Delaware's suffragists turned once again to planning for the next legislative session. Once again, too, the 1917 state-level effort would be part of a wider national push. For instance, New York suffragists were organizing to put another referendum on the ballot and were prepared to wage a fierce campaign for women's enfranchisement. A victory in Delaware would be important, but to take effect it would require a second triumph at the 1919 legislative session. Success in New York would be earth-shattering. An East Coast state with a substantial female population and the largest delegation in Congress (forty-five members), and thus the largest number of electoral votes, New York could change the entire suffrage calculus. Even before any 1917 state-level effort took place, in the 1916 national elections, women could vote for president in states with a combined ninety-one electoral votes, a total that had been boosted in 1913 when Illinois, with twenty-nine electoral votes, adopted "presidential suffrage," permitting women to vote for U.S. president and some local offices.[42]

Throughout 1916, as Delaware suffragists gathered the personnel, resources, energy, and funds to mobilize for yet another attempt to scale the state legislature's fortifications, it remained an open question as to how suffrage groups would work together toward common goals. After the bruising disagreements over strategy and tactics that had led DESA and the CU to a seemingly permanent parting of ways at the end of 1915, the prospects of achieving comity appeared remote. Those disagreements marred any attempt to stitch together a common suffrage strategy. In particular, the question of how much energy and resources to put into working for a federal as opposed to a state constitutional amendment roiled white suffragist ranks. So, too, did the matter of acceptable tactics, as the Congressional Union brought additional tools to the work, resulting in shifting alliances when some individuals defected both from its ranks and from the ranks of the Delaware Equal Suffrage Association. Looming over all discussions and decisions that suffragists made were the European War and the upcoming 1916 elections.

For much of the year, DESA experienced a "struggling time," drift-
ing along on scanty funds and scarce personnel, under the direction of
a new leader, while the CU seemed always to find the wind to propel its
organizational ship forward. In January, for instance, the Equal Suffrage Association doubled annual member dues from fifty cents to a
dollar. Even so, by August, the group, with sixty-five paying members,
was unable to send more than thirty dollars of the one-hundred-dollar
contribution to NAWSA that it had requested, and five dollars of that
had to be borrowed from the Wilmington Equal Suffrage Association,
by far the largest of DESA's affiliated groups. A major two-day conference announced in February was soon postponed until April, and
then put off until the autumn, and finally canceled, ostensibly because
NAWSA's Carrie Chapman Catt could not fit the event into her schedule. In March, a majority of members of the New Castle Equal Suffrage
Association (Hilles among them) voted to secede from the Delaware
group and instead to affiliate with the CU. Wilmingtonian Sallie Topkis Ginns, married to a local theater owner and active in Jewish war
relief work, defected too.

At DESA's annual convention in Wilmington in November, the
executive committee hyperbolically reported having done "much
active work" before conceding that most of that activity took place
in Wilmington. When the group's new president, Mary Clare Laurence Brassington, accompanied by a NAWSA organizer, went "down
the State" to Lewes, Georgetown, and Dover, they met with local suffragists, but concluded that "lack of local support" doomed any effort
to organize affiliates in either Kent or Sussex County, each of which
had once hosted the group's annual convention. Still, they took some
solace in knowing that they "had an opportunity to enlighten the
people concerning the difference between the Congressional Union
and the National Association." Prodded to participate in NAWSA's
"National Amendment Day" in October, the group responded with a
band, speeches, an "Emancipation" pageant featuring "several young
women," and distribution of suffrage leaflets.[43]

Surely it galled DESA members that, after two decades of dogged
labor, their organization's leadership star appeared dim by contrast
with the work of the CU, and especially the celebrity that accompanied Florence Bayard Hilles's every move. By their own reports, Hilles
and the CU cruised from triumph to triumph in 1916, buoyed by cash

from wealthy donors, including Hilles's dear friend California philan-
thropist Phoebe Apperson Hearst. In January, just as the Equal Suffrage Association was announcing its need to raise dues, Hilles and
Josephine Anderson du Pont (Mrs. Victor du Pont, Sr.) were giving
"glowing accounts" of a trip to Sussex County with a CU staff member,
and planning an all-day conference in Milford that would "complete
the [CU's] organization" of that county. Already in the CU camp were
Lewes's Leah Burton and Mabel Lloyd Ridgely of Dover, now chair
of the CU organization in Kent County. The latter's name resonated
of Delaware history: the Lloyds and Ridgelys owned land and at least
one historic house in Dover's town center, a short walk from the state
capitol building.[44]

At a well-publicized CU conference in March, to which Hilles
invited the Equal Suffrage Association's leadership, and in sharp contrast to the older organization's troubles, Hilles and others trumpeted
the CU's success in organizing the entire state, claiming eighteen
branches (seven in Sussex County alone). In July, a CU-sponsored
convention in Kent County attracted sixty attendees. Hilles might
have described the CU's relationship with DESA as "most friendly,"
but the winds of historical change seemed always to be in the newer
group's favor. Even if not all of the shiny objects that the CU presented
to local and national newspapers were quite as lustrous as appeared
at first glance, the group enjoyed a reputation for energy and momen-
tum. The appearance of brilliant grassroots organizing may have been
the point. They had no reason to scuff the shine by acknowledging
their inability to replace the group's Sussex County chairman, Phyllis
Mason, a Laurel schoolteacher, when she moved to New Castle County
after less than a year of service.[45]

In a contest of imagery, the CU believed that it had a distinct
advantage over DESA. Hilles made that case when she compared "the
old and the new woman" suffragist in her speech at the March CU
conference. In her telling, "the chief distinction between" the two had
to do with temperament and style. The "old" suffragist "is patient and
persuasive," but the "new" is "aggressive, self-assertive, and determined." "To her," she predicted, "will come the victory!" Throughout
the year, as the state affiliates of both NAWSA and the CU increasingly
focused on securing congressional passage of a federal amendment,
the divergence sharpened between those who engaged in "patient and

persuasive" methods and those who demanded action. Arguing, as Hilles put it, that "woman suffrage is now practical politics," the CU's leadership took the striking step of mobilizing women who already had the right to vote. With the 1916 presidential election firmly in her sights, Alice Paul convened 1,500 suffrage-state delegates in Chicago in June and gained their consent to form a political party, the National Woman's Party (NWP). Not coincidentally, the Republican Party was meeting—at the same time, in the same city—to nominate its candidate for president. The prospect of women forming "a third party" was sensational indeed. Introducing the new party to readers of Wilmington's morning paper, Hilles went further, stating baldly that party members "hold the balance of power to determine the next presidential election."[46]

In advance of the Chicago meeting, Hilles signed on for another event that exhibited CU devotees' flair for the dramatic. On April 9, she was one of twenty-three CU notables who boarded a "Suffrage Special" train from Washington, D.C., to California and back. It was an ingenious, attention-getting device to promote suffrage and recruit new members. Living and working in railway cars for a month, the group recruited delegates for the June conference and garnered substantial contributions. (They also grew heartily sick and tired of each other and of the sooty and uncomfortable conditions aboard their rolling campaign carriages. Only those with the resources to do so could trade the train car for a hotel bed at nighttime.) Still, they batted out reams of publicity on their typewriters, providing copy to every local newspaper along the way. "This is biggest act for suffrage that has ever been 'pulled off,'" Hilles wrote from Oregon.[47]

Even as the CU and the NWP made headlines, the leaders of DESA followed the course laid out by the Catt-energized NAWSA leadership, appointing a chairman to its Congressional Committee, tasked with lobbying members of Congress for a federal amendment, while also deciding how much to press for a state amendment when the legislature reconvened in 1917. The group's executive committee followed the new path faithfully, deputizing Mary Ospina to write regularly to the state's congressional delegation members regarding the suffrage amendment. "We ask only for justice," her standard letter read, "will you give it to us?" Their responses were tepid, to say the least. Whereas Democrat Willard Saulsbury, Jr., whose wife, May du Pont

Saulsbury, was a firm anti-suffragist, agreed to give the matter "careful consideration," his about-to-be elected fellow Democrat Josiah Wolcott told Ospina bluntly that a federal amendment required "forcing suffrage upon the states whether they favor it or not." He did not favor it. Ospina also pressed delegates to both of the national political party conventions to work to include a federal suffrage amendment in the party platforms. In June, Mary Clare Brassington, the new state Equal Suffrage Association president, received a public send-off as she headed for the two national political conventions. She took along the "new state suffrage banner," explicitly designed to trumpet the group's 1895 founding date and to counter the upstart CU's branding efforts. Bearing the banner and a bouquet of yellow roses, she boarded a train for Chicago. Once there, she participated in a joint NAWSA/ NWP march down Michigan Avenue to the site of the Republican convention, whose delegates approved their first-ever platform plank endorsing the Anthony amendment. The Democratic convention defeated a comparable proposal.

Toward the end of the year, the association welcomed Lola Trax, another NAWSA national organizer, sent to Delaware on an "aggressive" five-week organizing campaign, with special attention to the state's "lower end." No doubt, NAWSA president Catt intended Trax to light a fire under the Delaware group, to move them out of their comfort zone in Wilmington. It would take more than Trax's kindling to set the group ablaze, however. At its November annual conference, the membership, now up to 270, dithered indecisively over whether to introduce a suffrage amendment at the 1917 legislative session, and listened nostalgically to an address by an aging Anna Howard Shaw.[48]

However one evaluates either the Delaware Equal Suffrage Association's or the Congressional Union's suffrage advocacy during 1916, the results of that year's statewide elections were deeply disappointing. It was the first time that Delaware voters could choose a U.S. senator, as there had been no open seat when the Seventeenth Amendment went into effect. Democrat Josiah O. Wolcott defeated the incumbent Republican Henry A. du Pont. When Congress convened in 1917, the state's two Senate seats would be occupied by Democrats, both of whom were hostile to a federal suffrage amendment. In the vote for the U.S. House, Democrat Albert F. Polk of Sussex County defeated pro-suffrage Republican Thomas W. Miller, a former governor who was just completing his first, and only, term in Washington, D.C. In the presidential race, Woodrow Wilson's unsuccessful Republican challenger Charles Evans Hughes took Delaware's three electoral votes. The one bright spot at the statewide level was the election of Sussex County Republican John G. Townsend, Jr. to the governor's position. At his inauguration in January 1917, Townsend declared his support for woman suffrage.[49]

The 1916 elections also constituted a daunting test for the National Woman's Party's—and Alice Paul's—policy of "holding the party in power responsible." In October, NWP organizers fanned out across the full-suffrage states, with New York's Inez Milholland, renowned as "the beautiful flying envoy of the Woman's Party," attracting large crowds during her thirty-two-city Western swing. At the presidential level, the approach failed. Not only did Wilson win reelection over the Republican Hughes with 52 percent of the electoral vote, but with the exception of Oregon, the full-suffrage states went for Wilson. In Illinois, where women were voting for presidential electors for the first time, Hughes was the victor. In Congress, Wilson's party, in coalition with a few third-party representatives, narrowly retained control of the House, while the Senate, when it convened in 1917, would be Democratic with a margin of fifty-four seats (56 percent) to the Republicans' forty-two. Although such results offered suffragists very little to celebrate, they took some comfort in the election of Montana's Jeannette Rankin to the House, only two years after the state's women had won the right to vote. Rankin, a Republican and former president of the Montana Woman Suffrage Association, a NAWSA affiliate, had spent time in Delaware lobbying the legislature during the 1913 suffrage campaign. The members of the Delaware Equal Suffrage Association took the occasion of their November annual conference to "rejoice" that "for the first time a woman . . . can take her place among our national legislators."[50]

While Wilson had campaigned in 1916 on the slogan "he kept us out of war," New York suffragist Harriot Stanton Blatch had pleaded for anti-Wilson votes with the cry "Wilson kept us out of suffrage." As Blatch and her allies recovered from the stinging loss of the New York State suffrage referendum in 1915, she and other CU/NWP leaders remained committed to keeping the pressure on Wilson on the question of a federal suffrage amendment. In pursuit of their goals, they found creative ways to press their cause. On December 4, 1916, for example, during the president's address to a joint session of Congress, Mabel Vernon and Florence Bayard Hilles concocted a way to confront him. As Vernon recalled it, Hilles's large winter coat served as camouflage for a banner the two women smuggled into the visitors' gallery. Unfurled from on high while Wilson spoke, the banner read: "Mr. President, What Will You Do for Woman Suffrage?"[51]

But it was Inez Milholland's tragic late November death that provided an unexpected opportunity to command Wilson's attention. Milholland had collapsed during her grueling suffrage swing around the West, endured a month's agonizing treatment in a Los Angeles hospital, then died of aplastic anemia. She was only thirty. Major newspapers covered her illness, printing regular updates; when her death came, it evoked an outpouring of stunned grief. Encouraged by her sister Vida, NWP leaders began canonizing Inez as a suffrage martyr. Securing the right to use the Capitol Building's Statuary Hall on Christmas Day, Alice Paul orchestrated a "great national memorial," attended by a thousand people, including Milholland's grieving widower, Eugen Boissevain, and Delaware's Vernon and Annie Arniel. Paul then followed up with an invitation to Wilson to meet with a three-hundred person "Milholland Memorial Deputation" in January. The President welcomed the group to the White House and sat stiffly, with increasing discomfort, through eulogies to the lovely suffragist and appeals for him to take action "in the name of this gallant girl." Wilson could be forgiven for feeling that he had been ambushed. Concurrently, Delaware's CU/NWP contingent held a mass meeting at Wilmington's Majestic Theatre, featuring a striking poster of a white-robed Milholland on horseback at the 1913 Washington procession in a Joan of Arc pose, wielding a banner reading "Forward out of Darkness!" One day after the Wilson meeting, the NWP inaugurated a silent vigil outside the White House.[52]

Such confrontational tactics generated publicity, strong reactions, and new recruits for the NWP, but also defections. In Delaware, those tactics ripped apart the fraying seams that still linked the Delaware Equal Suffrage Association with the Congressional Union. Truth be told, there was little comity left between the organizations except for a planned joint effort to amend the state constitution through a bill striking the word "male" from the list of voter qualifications. In

January 1917, Florence Bayard Hilles moved quickly to take charge of the process—and, not incidentally, to elbow the older organization out of the way. The Majestic Theatre gathering, with the Milholland poster and speeches by NWP organizers Maud Younger and Lucy Branham, supplied copy to local papers placing the CU in sole charge of the legislative suffrage campaign. It did not hurt, either, that the event raised one thousand dollars to pay for two CU organizers to staff a temporary headquarters in Dover while the legislature was in session.[53]

Caught flat-footed, and pressed by NAWSA chairman Catt, the Equal Suffrage Association signed on to cosponsor the state amendment bill. But the leadership wanted it clearly understood that "our money" and "our own speakers" were to be employed separately from any CU work for the amendment, and that "we are not to be connected" in any way with "any public demonstrations as are being done in Washington." With the suffrage bill about to be introduced, Hilles was "out of town" when DESA's executive committee sought a strategy meeting. Soon, it became "too late for a Conference," and when Hilles, in a fairly obvious power play, asked the association's president to confer at the CU headquarters, the only serious option left was for the association to "publicly endorse" the bill that the CU had at the ready. The leadership agreed to do so. At a February hearing in Dover, no representative from the Equal Suffrage Association spoke. Only Hilles, "who is recognized as the leader of the suffragists in Delaware," and Anna McCue, a working-class Philadelphia CU organizer referred to as "the Factory-Girl Orator," represented the pro-suffrage side. Emily Bissell and Mary Wilson Thompson, both of them already caught up in war "preparedness" fever, lobbied for the anti-suffrage position. The Delaware Senate took no action; the House defeated the amendment on February 23.[54]

By then, the "public demonstrations . . . being done in Washington" were receiving national attention. Initiated on January 10, with Vernon leading the first phalanx, the NWP's "silent sentinels" were standing picket duty outside the White House gates, promising to keep at it until Wilson's second inauguration in March. Bearing banners with questions directly addressed to Wilson, they employed the time-tested suffrage tactic of accentuating feminine silence to make their point. Invoking Milholland's memory, one popular banner used an edited version of the dead woman's alleged final words to ask, "Mr.

President, How Long Must Women Wait for Liberty?" The purpose of this "new policy of mild militancy," noted one Wilmington newspaper, was to make it "impossible for the President to enter or leave the White House without encountering a sentinel . . . pleading the suffrage cause." Among the NWP/CU affiliated Delawareans who took stints during the cold and wet weeks leading up to Inauguration Day were Hilles, Agnes Yerger, her daughter Naomi Schopfer, Arniel, and another working-class Wilmingtonian, dressmaker Mary E. Brown. Now, the NWP strategy of "holding the party in power responsible" had a sole focus: Wilson himself. Arguing that the president had the power to force Congress to bring the Anthony amendment up for consideration, the sentinels accused him of not having the will to do so. Over time, the picketers' banners grew more pointed and more personally insulting. It became a contest of wills between silent, determined suffragists and a president ignoring them while hearing growing calls for the United States to enter the European War.[55]

Throughout the early months of 1917, as the picketing continued, leaders of both NAWSA and the NWP made decisions that reverberated in Delaware, and moved their local affiliates farther apart. Most pressing was the question of whether to encourage members to participate in the "preparedness" campaigns being undertaken in case the United States entered the Great War. A NAWSA resolution and local war talk led DESA to discuss "whether . . . in case of a crisis in the affairs of our nation," its members should "offer ourselves as an organization to the Government." In other words, if war came, would the cause of suffrage take a back seat to the cause of national defense? The NWP made its position clear in March: woman suffrage was an essential prerequisite to any decision to go to war. "We must do our part," the leadership agreed, "to see that war . . . shall not be entered upon without the consent of women." Following the national group, the Delaware CU merged with the NWP and held its first convention under the NWP banner—and with the Milholland poster—in April. Held a little over a week after Congress agreed to Wilson's request for a declaration of war, the convention welcomed a scant thirty-four attendees of the five hundred statewide party members. In a "spirited defense of the Party's methods," Hilles reiterated the NWP stance: despite the war, the party would not stand down from its assertive tactics. By early summer, onlookers critical of that posture began to scuffle with picketers, crowding the sidewalks and ripping their banners. As the confrontations escalated, local police responded by arresting the suffragists, among them Vernon and Arniel and, on July 14, Hilles herself.[56]

Patching up the relationship between the two Delaware organizations was now largely impossible, as exasperation over the NWP's tactics boiled over. Responding to a letter from NAWSA President Catt, DESA assured her that the group would "stand by the National [Association] . . . during the present crisis." More to the point, the Delaware association concurred with NAWSA that "the work of the picketing was doing . . . harm" to "normal suffrage work" such as lobbying. Invited to a meeting at Josephine Anderson du Pont's home, Equal Suffrage Association secretary Mary de Vou, a former CU member, found that she was being asked to sign a letter "praising the [picketing] work" and "extending sympathy" to Hilles over her experience of arrest and brief imprisonment. De Vou "took a very decided stand against the picketing and declined to sign the letter." Only when the authorities' treatment of incarcerated picketers became appallingly harsh did the association's members, while deploring the "recent tactics of the Woman's Party," condemn "the injustice of the unusual and extreme punishment" being inflicted upon "the women who are using these methods." Still, the success of New York's suffrage referendum in November, they believed, "vindicated the methods of the National American Woman Suffrage Association" over those of the NWP.[57]

Conclusion

Between 1914 and 1917, Delaware's suffragists had backed two efforts to amend the state constitution, while also coming to the conclusion that a federal constitutional amendment was likely to be the only way they would reach their goal. On the question of how to get there, DESA and the CU/NWP reached fundamentally different conclusions. Throughout, despite the insults they endured from anti-suffrage quarters and the marginalization they suffered at the hands of white suffragists, members of the Equal Suffrage Study Club continued to assert their right to be heard on matters of such grave importance as voting, citizenship rights, and racial justice. Throughout, too, anti-suffrage arguments received regular airing in the press and in legislative halls.

When rumors of war turned into war itself, both suffragists and anti-suffragists confronted decisions about how to prioritize their time, resources, and energy. Moreover, they needed to determine the tactics that promised the most success in bringing about a federal amendment. War has a way of both creating opportunities to challenge existing gender arrangements and reinscribing traditional gender roles. British suffragettes had suspended their militant agitation during wartime. What the Great War might bring to the suffrage cause in the United States remained as yet unknown.

CHAPTER 3

Suffrage in Wartime

"Delaware AWAKE!" exhorted the enormous painting. At five-and-a-half feet tall and almost three feet wide, it commanded attention. Below the heading, which unrolled on a scroll, was the figure of a white woman seated on clouds, resting on an outline of the state, and looking as though she was responding to the arresting call. Clad in a loose royal blue, short-sleeved shift, and wearing flat sandals, hair in flowing curls, she was adorned only with a diamond-shaped blue brooch and a spray of small blossoms. An image of sunrise illuminated her auburn hair and youthful face. Delaware viewers would readily identify the painting's references: the state's "diamond" shape; the peach blossoms, the state's flower; the Blue Hen at the lower right; the state seal on the left. But the overall message would be clear to even the most literal-minded observer. "Buy MORE Bonds. The Liberty of the World is at Stake," read the caption.[1]

Created in 1918 by Wilmingtonian Ethel Pennewill Brown for a World War I campaign, reproduced as a poster, and then donated to the Delaware Women's College in Newark, the painting called upon women to do their part in the war effort, particularly by participating in the fundraising drives of the Liberty Loan campaigns. They might not be soldiers, subject to wartime conscription, but they could awaken to their responsibility as citizens. And they did. Middle-class suffragists and clubwomen such as Wilmington's Alice Dunbar-Nelson and Sea-ford's Mary Phillips Eskridge, and elite women such as Dover's Mabel Lloyd Ridgely, threw themselves into a variety of war related patriotic activities, particularly through Red Cross and Liberty Loan work, but also through direct government service. White working-class suffragists such as Annie Melvin Arniel, Catherine Thornton Boyle, and Annie Stirlith McGee, along with the occasional middle-class ally, took war jobs, often in dangerous circumstances, such as filling ammunition shells at a munitions factory. In taking these actions, they actively endorsed the view expressed by the Women's College dean, Winifred Robinson, that "it is, too, a woman's war . . . all working together for one thing—Victory." They also actively rejected the perennial anti-suffrage position that, in order to be a full citizen (read: voter), one needed to be able to rise to one's country's defense and take up arms against its enemies. At the same time, they drove home the argument that, because they were indeed rising to their country's defense, they deserved full citizenship.[2]

Throughout, Delaware's suffragists grappled with the challenges of promoting a federal suffrage amendment while the country was at war. By April 6, 1917, when Woodrow Wilson signed the congressional declaration of war, the Delaware legislature had already rejected yet another state constitutional revision bill. Members of both the Delaware Equal Suffrage Association (DESA) and the state's National Woman's Party (NWP) affiliate had little appetite to try again at the state level; both groups now gave full attention to a federal amendment. How to pursue that goal in wartime created numerous dilemmas, not the least of which was whether to suspend political agitation "for the duration" or use the wartime context to press even more insistently the cause of "votes for women." Already at odds with each other, the two organizations experienced ever more turbulent tidal cross-currents in the wake of the declaration of war. Cleavages on tactical matters proved especially wrenching for members of the Equal Suffrage Study Club. However accustomed they might have been to racial animus within the suffrage ranks, they understood what a declaration of war might mean for their pursuit of racial justice for their communities and for gender equity within those communities. On the one hand, there was the age-old argument that, if African American men simply proved their patriotic devotion through wartime heroism, then rewards would arrive in the form of expanded civil rights. On the other hand, there was the concern that war-borne rights would be temporary or would extend to men only.

Anti-suffragists experienced no comparable dilemmas. A call for women's wartime service fit neatly within their understanding of women's civic roles. Women served their families and communities; when called upon, they served the state. This was a sacrifice of self, freely given in order to support the men who made decisions and carried on wars. This war, however, changed them. Moved to do their duty through community agencies such as the Red Cross and armed services women's auxiliaries, they participated in Liberty Loan drives, marched in a preparedness parade, and ramped up their lobbying of Delaware politicians. As the Great War did for the state's suffragists, it reshaped the attitudes and tactics anti-suffragists would use in pursuit of their political objectives. The import of that alteration took a bit of time to come into focus, but by war's end, anti-suffragists had become as skilled at swimming in the deep pool of politics as their suffragist counterparts were. As historian Lynn Dumenil has argued, because the war "focused attention on questions of citizenship, patriotic service, and democratic rights" for suffragists of all persuasions, it could be a moment during which to "make a claim for an enlarged sense of citizenship," including full voting rights. The wartime moment remade anti-suffragists, too, though with a distinctly different understanding of women's citizenship.[3]

Preparedness

The outbreak of war in Europe in 1914 prompted, first, a determination that the United States would stay out, and then, widespread planning in case it got in. By the time Woodrow Wilson ran for a second term in 1916 with the slogan "he kept us out of war," "preparedness" had become a watchword that shaped domestic policies and decisions in widely varying ways. Delaware's suffrage leaders, as such, had little to say on the topic; they considered it "a matter for individual opinion." In other words, when suffragists engaged in preparedness activities, they did so through their other commitments, particularly women's voluntary organizations and clubs, as well as civic associations, churches, and synagogues. Dover's Mabel Lloyd Ridgely and Winifred Morris were fairly typical. Like many other white suffragists, they volunteered for the Red Cross, which in 1914 began collecting funds for "the stricken nations" of Europe and the "starving Belgians," and sponsoring events fashioning and collecting hospital supplies for overseas use. Concern about children caught up in war zones and interest in facilitating a negotiated peace settlement animated a number of club and church undertakings. Some projects engaged women's domestic skills, such as sewing, knitting, and bandage making, while others tapped into their fundraising talents. Wilmington's Sallie Topkis Ginns, for example, an early Congressional Union (CU) recruit, participated actively in Jewish relief efforts throughout the war.[4]

"Preparedness" itself soon evolved. From a program that envisioned preparation as a way to guarantee peace, it became a call for mobilization in the event that the U.S. became involved in war. By the summer of 1916, the word itself had acquired modifying adjectives: military, civilian, industrial, home. Each modifier conveyed a different idea about what preparedness entailed, and each also laid out different roles for women and men. By then, both women's associations and the gender-integrated organizations in which women worked in tandem with men were involved in a wide range of traditionally feminine activities, whether providing relief for victims of the widening conflict in Europe and the Middle East, supporting the various U.S. armed services, sponsoring training for nurses who would go overseas, schooling members in first aid, donating supplies, or knitting and sewing for the cause. A few individual women signed up for the Women's Land Army or attended preparedness camps, learning everything from signaling to first aid, or, in a volley aimed at the anti-suffrage view, took up arms through membership in gun and shooting clubs. Indeed, "preparedness" became such a widely used—overused—term, that local shops routinely used it in ads for underwear, millinery, candy, movie tickets, and other items far removed from armed conflict.[5]

Up and down the state, Delaware's suffragists participated in all such "preparedness" enthusiasms and more. So did its well-known anti-suffragists. The two most visible, Mary Wilson Thompson and Emily Bissell, were on the front lines of preparedness campaigns. For Bissell, Red Cross work had been a particular commitment since 1905, and had led her into the anti-tuberculosis planning and fundraising (via Christmas Seals) that now consumed most of her working hours. Bissell had long collaborated with suffragist colleagues in both the Red Cross and the Wilmington New Century Club. She and they were used to putting aside political differences to achieve common goals, though that became harder once she and Thompson were officers in the Women's Committee of Delaware Opposed to Woman Suffrage. In July 1914, for instance, a kerfuffle over whether suffragists had attempted to claim an unambiguously pro-suffrage position for the state's white clubwomen produced front-page headlines about a supposed "war" within the Delaware Federation of Women's Clubs. Nevertheless, preparedness provided the balm that soothed any rancor, as clubwomen and Red Cross volunteers gave time and energy to labors that all endorsed. Even pacifist colleagues signed on as long as preparedness included work to mitigate the worst of wartime suffering, end the war, and prevent future conflicts.[6]

When military readiness began eclipsing other sorts of preparedness, the goals of preparedness campaigns became increasingly oriented toward readiness for war. In January 1916, as Woodrow Wilson embarked on a national speaking tour, a local Episcopal minister linked preparedness to a masculine definition of patriotism, urging Delaware men to enlist in order to bolster the armed services with "men for national defense." In March, a group of Boy Scouts heard that their organization stood for "manly preparedness." The shift in language and tone subtly redefined preparedness. Initially, it had encompassed activities in which women shared equally with men, but the prevailing stance now was that preparedness required, first and foremost, manliness and masculinity. African American commentators, among others, remained ambivalent as to how the preparedness mania might affect the men of their communities, but the lure of soldiering as a route to full citizenship was indisputable. It was a hope that had accompanied Black men into volunteering for the armed services since the American Revolution, and as recently as the war with Spain in 1898; it held out the promise that valor on the battlefield would be rewarded with improved rights at home. As one advocate of school-based training and drilling commented in the *Baltimore Afro-American*, echoing an existing slogan, "the best soldiers make the best citizens."[7]

As military mobilization spread its reach, it relegated other kinds of preparedness to the margins of public life and raised concerns, particularly among peace advocates, that "preparedness . . . had dangerous possibilities" toward "militarism." When "Preparedness Day" events became popular in 1916, organizers took varying approaches to the participation of military-style groups. A New York parade in May featured over 136,000 marchers, bookended by uniformed groups: the city's mounted police, and the state militia, along with 728 veterans of the war with Spain. Representatives of the U.S. Army and U.S. Navy joined the mayor on the reviewing stand, and various regimental bands and fife and drum corps headed parade sections. The "women's section," comprising 2.4 percent of the marchers, did not arrive at the reviewing stand until 7 pm, more than eight hours after the initial group. Wilmington's June 10 event, sponsored by the city's Chamber of Commerce, banned mounted riders but included several uniformed marshals and war veterans, the state militia, a contingent of Boy Scouts, and "several hundred women." In both New York and Wilmington, women marchers fulfilled second-ary, supportive roles. Men were to be the warriors. Only at San Fran-cisco's July parade, where women marched both in their own section and with male colleagues, did a protest against such demonstrations as sym-bols of a "militaristic government" become deadly. A suitcase bomb left on a sidewalk killed six and injured several others.[8] At the Wilmington event, peaceful protests occurred at the periphery, where members of the Delaware Woman's Peace Party distributed literature to both marchers and spectators. Both literally and symbolically, the leafletters were on the sidelines, a place to which they were increasingly relegated as war talk shut out discussions of negotiation or reconciliation.[9]

Indeed, one can map the arc that the "preparedness" concept traced in Wilmington, from peace advocacy to military mobilization, in the history of the Peace Party. Founded early in 1916 as an affiliate of the national Woman's Peace Party, whose president, Jane Addams, was one of the most admired women in the United States, the Delaware group had a core of Quaker women whose network of ties ran through the Federation of Women's Clubs, the Society of Friends, the Equal Suffrage Association, and the local chapter of the Fellowship of Reconciliation, and who were members of the Delaware Peace Society, a male-led orga-nization founded in 1895. Suffragists such as Mary H. Askew Mather and Emma Worrell were part of "an ardent group of peace advocates." To their minds, preparedness meant efforts to prevent war or resolve con-flict peacefully. The Delaware Woman's Peace Party activities encom-passed engaging in efforts to keep military training out of local schools, awarding prizes for student essays on the topic of peace, sponsoring a Fellowship Room with reading materials, and hosting lectures setting forth the proposition that true preparedness required finding an alter-native to war. Initially treated respectfully, the national party eventu-ally became the object of critics who scorned its members as part of the "Peace-at-any-price-crowd" and then ratcheted up their language to claim that members were simply unpatriotic dupes of a vicious German government. By July 1916, in the aftermath of the San Francisco horror and the Senate's vote to allocate $700 million for preparedness, party members were finding it prudent to retreat from the public eye.[10]

The shifting fortunes of preparedness altered the positions that both suffragists and anti-suffragists maintained toward questions of peace and war, and of women's roles and responsibilities in wartime. As individuals, white women on both sides of the suffrage cause participated in preparedness activities, particularly through the Red Cross. But when military preparedness surged to the forefront of the undertaking, it was the anti-suffragists who most enthusiastically adopted it as a cause. In the process, their participation changed them. Mary Wilson Thompson's involvement in Wilmington's June 1916 parade planning offers a key example. Early on, she signed up as chairman of the parade's women's committee, promising 1,800 female participants (in actuality, substantially fewer marched). Soon, she was elevated to the rank of women's section "grand marshal." Thompson drew upon her work in the women's auxiliary of the Navy League, the Daughters of the American Revolution (DAR), and in the Red Cross to join with other "citizens who are supporters of . . . military preparedness" in participating in the parade. She did not, in other words, directly represent the anti-suffrage cause, though one newspaper captioned her portrait by mentioning both her roles on the Women's Committee of Delaware Opposed to Woman Suffrage and as women's grand marshal of the parade. Still, Thompson's willingness to take to city streets as an advocate for a cause indicates that she no longer considered such public participation and display as unwomanly. In evaluating women's public processions, it was the cause that mattered, not the fact of parading. As long as marching women represented feminine self-sacrifice in the interests of a specific version of patriotism, not women's rights, they could expect to be applauded for the "splendid support" they exhibited. Women's roles in the preparedness parades were secondary, supportive, and voluntary, fitting the general anti-suffrage understanding of womanhood, while also inserting feminine figures into the tableau of a country heading for war.[11]

Yet the visual style that Thompson adopted for herself and her marchers looked as though it had been borrowed from suffrage parades, where women actually were at the center. Her marchers dressed in white, with tricolor sashes across the front. Unlike suffrage sashes, however, these were red, white, and blue, complementing the American flags that parade participants waved. Like suffrage parades, the Wilmington prepared-ness parade had contingents of professional women, such as nurses, as well as factory workers, dressed in white and carrying tricolor pennants. Clearly, Thompson had learned something from observing pro-suffrage events. There were significant differences, however. The women workers participating in the preparedness parade were employees of the Electric Hose and Rubber Company, marshaled by their plant's male general manager to demonstrate their "enthusiasm for preparedness." They were not the unionized or militant women workers whose traditions of protest had helped shape suffrage parades. In fact, the male leadership of Wilm-ington's Central Labor Union explained that its members would not be participating in the parade because they did not want "patriotism to be degraded by militarism." Nor were any of the women participants in the June 1916 parade African American. Although Wilmington's lone Black city council representative, pharmacist John O. Hopkins, accepted an appointment as chairman of the parade's "Negro division," and agreed to make "every effort" to get local civic groups to participate, only an "especially strong . . . body from the Howard School" turned out, march-ing in the public schools' section.

Still, the Wilmington event represented a change in the way that anti-suffragists such as Thompson believed it was permissible to be a woman advocating policy in public. They might continue to condemn suffrage parades as examples of women "flaunting themselves in the streets," as historian Susan Goodier has described their attitude, but they evaluated marching for preparedness quite differently. Doing so placed women marchers in the position of supporting men, not advocating for their own sex. As the Wilmington Sunday paper summed up the city's event, "it was a day when men stood as men—and had their women folks with them."[12]

Marching and other preparedness-related activities both altered the work of Delaware's anti-suffragists and remade the arguments they employed against woman suffrage. Because most peace activists in the state were also known to be pro-suffrage, anti-suffragists found it easy to make them targets when complaining that suffragists were unpatri-otic or worse. The "Woman's Peace Party (suffragist)" was fomenting an "Anti-Preparedness Program" that represented their "unpatriotic spirit," argued the writer of "Anti-Suffrage Notes" for the women's page of one of Wilmington's evening newspapers in 1916. It was also easy to extend the charge of lack of patriotism to all suffragists, not just the pacifists among them. The anti-suffragists contended that they alone brought to the current crisis "constructive and practical ideas of democracy, citizenship, patriotism and preparedness with special regard to the aspirations and achievements of woman." They would put "America First," supporting the Red Cross and serving as a clearinghouse for local women looking for ways to help by volunteering their time and (unpaid) labor. As the United States entered the war, the anti-suffragists' future agenda was already over-determined. Wartime volunteerism would take precedence over anti-suffrage activism. In Delaware, where the by-now biennial effort to amend the state constitution in 1917 was feeble and marked by divisions among the major suffrage groups, the anti-suffragists' distraction from their oppositional stance may not have mattered much. But in New York State, inattention had consequences. There, suffragists won a November referendum amending the state constitution to allow for full suffrage, breaking through the solid phalanx of no-suffrage Eastern states and setting up the possibility that the 1918 elections would bring to Washington a Congress in a more pro-suffrage mold.[13]

Suffrage Organizations in Wartime

On April 2, 1917, as Congress was about to convene for a joint session at which Woodrow Wilson would ask for a declaration of war against Germany, the two rival national suffrage organizations hosted the nation's first congresswoman, Montana's Jeannette Rankin, at a celebratory breakfast. At the table of honor, Rankin sat between the National American Woman Suffrage Association's president, Carrie Chapman Catt, and the National Woman's Party's leader, Alice Paul. Anyone with even the dimmest awareness of the rancor that now characterized relationships between the two organizations and their two leaders would have understood that Rankin's position was an uncomfortable one. Few would know, however, that Rankin's discomfort was likely amplified by the effort of each leader to influence her vote on the war resolution. For Paul, a Quaker, Rankin's entrance into an institution that had been a masculine bastion for almost 130 years offered the opportunity to validate her view that "women were the peace-loving half of the world" and that putting women into positions of political power "would diminish the possibilities of war." Rankin should vote "no." For Catt, a longtime

Figure 8. Delaware Red Cross Chapter Motor Messenger Corps, 1919. Young women's commitment to wartime volunteerism included participating in Red Cross activities such as the Motor Corps, ferrying people and materials around the state. As they lined up for a photograph, the women adopted a stance that, together with their "regulation uniform and insignia," projected the "precise and military manner" that the corps sought to instill. Suffragist Ethel Ball Staniar (#10) was the group's "Captain." Standing at the rear was Evangelyn Barsky (#20), who in 1923 became one of the first two women admitted to the Delaware Bar. Source: Wilmington *Evening Journal*, February 26, 1919, 14. Credit: Delaware Historical Society

pacifist and honorary vice-chairman of the New York branch of the Woman's Peace Party, the possibility of war offered the potential for a period of shared "sacrifice and service" that would lead to a national suffrage amendment. Rankin, who had been president of NAWSA's Montana affiliate, should vote "aye."[14]

In the end, Rankin cast her vote against the war resolution. To her mind, war "destroyed" women's work in "raising human beings, and war destroyed human beings to protect profits and property." Her decision won approval from pacifists and others who had witnessed the militarization of preparedness and felt a sense of dread as preparations assumed an aura of inevitability. Others whose gender assumptions marked women as more peace-loving than men applauded because they adopted the argument that, if women voted and ran political institutions, wars would end. Along with Paul herself, the NWP expressed its "approbation" for Rankin's vote, then added its determination to press forward with demands for a federal suffrage amendment, even during wartime. If "women together with men share the burdens of taxation, responsibility, and horrors of war," as the Delaware branch averred, then they should have equal citizenship rights.[15]

True to her single-minded pursuit of suffrage, however, Paul took no public stance on the war. In a letter to NWP colleagues describing the conflicting pressures buffeting the group, she insisted that "no action on war" should ever be taken "without the consent of women." Pacifism now carried the taint of an assumed disloyalty to the nation, a taint pungent enough to put off most suffrage supporters. Recognizing that reality, and understanding the effect that preparedness activities had wrought among the legions of white clubwomen suffrage supporters, Carrie Chapman Catt decided that NAWSA would do "double duty," lobbying for suffrage through its Congressional Committee while promising its members' full engagement with the war effort. Through demonstrations of their patriotic service, she clearly expected, NAWSA members would make their case for women's full citizenship—for suffrage. She accepted an appointment to the Woman's Committee of the Council of National Defense, chaired by her predecessor as NAWSA president, Anna Howard Shaw. The New York branch of the Woman's Peace Party then expelled Catt. The leaders of the NWP and NAWSA would follow different roadmaps, but each hoped, by war's end, to arrive at the same place.[16]

The Delaware affiliates of the two national organizations followed the routes that their leaderships marked out. During the nineteen months of war, the membership of the Delaware Equal Suffrage Association continued their suffrage advocacy alongside their war work, while the state's National Woman's Party branch pressed ahead with direct action in support of demands for a federal amendment. African American suffragists such as Alice Dunbar-Nelson, recognizing that wartime military service made particular demands on the men of their communities and believing that demonstrations of patriotic service would heighten the visibility of their contributions, generally set aside their qualms about militarism. Indeed, in a short play entitled *Mine Eyes Have Seen*, Dunbar-Nelson anticipated the position of W.E.B. Du Bois that African Americans must "forget our special grievances and close our ranks . . . with our own fellow white citizens" because a German victory would spell "death to the aspirations of Negroes and all darker races for equality, freedom, and democracy." Like some other African American suffragists, Dunbar-Nelson later joined the pacifist Women's International League for Peace and Freedom. Yet, throughout the war, she remained fully alert to the conflicting possibilities that wartime service presented to Black women and men.[17]

Having already agreed with NAWSA in March 1917, that they would "offer [them]selves as an organization to the Government in case of a crisis in the affairs of our nation," upon the declaration of war, the Delaware Equal Suffrage Association's members immersed themselves in the sort of volunteer service that had begun with preparedness activities. On March 30, many of them were in the audience at Wilmington's white high school to help form the Wilmington Women's National Defense League and to pledge "unconditional loyalty" to the federal government in the event of war. Among the eight hundred attendees were clubwomen and neighbors on rival sides of the suffrage question, including anti-suffragists and members of the Delaware branch of the NWP. The three leaders chosen that night were Abby Woodnut Miller, wife of recently retired Republican governor Charles R. Miller, Jeannette Eckman, an energetic teacher and child welfare advocate, and Eliza Corbit Lea, whose late husband Preston Lea had been a prominent local banker and onetime governor. Lea was an anti-suffragist, Eckman a suffragist, and Miller took no public position on the issue. Soon, when Woodrow Wilson authorized the creation of the Council of National Defense, with a Woman's Committee as part of its composition, Miller became Delaware's committee chairman.[18]

Thereafter, suffragists affiliated with the Equal Suffrage Association would be filling their daily and weekly calendars with suffrage meetings, but also with events at which they interacted with colleagues who were both the "militants" of the NWP, from whom their organization was rapidly distancing itself, and committed anti-suffragists, who had recently helped defeat a state constitutional suffrage revision. The extent to which such interactions proved discomfiting is difficult to gauge. Delaware was, after all, a small state, and the white middle-class population of Wilmington and nearby towns was small enough so that many mainstream suffragists, militants, and anti-suffragists already belonged to the same women's clubs and churches. In the New Century Club, for instance, the groups had developed a *modus vivendi* that permitted common labors while excluding discussion of divisive matters. Yet they also read the same daily newspapers, in which suffrage and anti-suffrage "notes" might appear next to each other on the same "women's page," and in which women from both groups published editorial commentary.[19]

For those reasons, one could imagine the scene at the New Century Club in June 1917, where members, including teachers and "all other patriotic women" rallied in support of "report day" (June 5), when men would begin registering with their local draft boards for conscription into war service and clubwomen would sell Liberty Bonds. If the group included anti-suffragists Thompson and Bissell, along with the Delaware Equal Suffrage Association's first vice-president, Rose Hizar Duggin, there might have been whispering and some foot-shuffling. The preceding month had seen all three women taking to the columns of local newspapers to press their respective cases on whether woman suffrage might become a reward for wartime service. Adapting some by-now familiar anti-suffrage arguments to the war context, Thompson and Bissell's joint letter to *Every Evening* raised the specter that suffrage might be "Forced Upon Woman" as just such a reward. They would have no part of a bargain like that. Their ideal "woman" provided a "service to the State, as [she did] to the family," but it was a commitment that was "unbought, unselfish, unconditional, and unremitting." Voting would seduce women away from a traditionally feminine self-sacrificing "nonpartisan" form of service, making them partisans and, worse, requiring them to choose between "their duties as women [and] their duties as voters." They could not do both. The ballot, the anti-suffragist leaders argued, was nothing but a "burden" to already overburdened women.[20]

Clearly annoyed by the content and tenor of that argument, Rose Duggin penned a riposte, sending it to the rival evening paper, the *Evening Journal*, which published it a few days later. Born in Wilmington in 1884, Rose Hizar had grown up in California, attended the University of California, Berkeley, and graduated in 1907. While a student, she had been editor-in-chief of the *Women's Daily Pelican*, a satirical student newspaper, and served as vice-president and then president of the university's English Club. California women won the right to vote in a 1911 referendum, an effort for which her sister Margaret was an earnest organizer. Rose, now married to Californian William Duggin, and the mother of a baby boy, promptly registered as a Republican to vote in the 1912 elections. But in 1913, when the couple left California and relocated to a farm outside Wilmington, Rose was disfranchised. As a woman who had once been a voter and now was not, Duggin could "speak with . . . authority" to her readers, assuring them that Thompson and Bissell's position was simply "not good sense." With sarcasm and crisp argument, Rose refuted the two women point by point. Suffrage, she wrote, "is a right" and a "comfortable function" for women, just as it is for men. She signed the letter with her full name: Rose Lippincott Hizar Duggin. Thereafter, she contributed regular suffrage columns to the *Evening Journal* and, at the Equal Suffrage Association's annual convention in November, shared her experience with other attendees with a talk entitled "How it Feels to Be a Voter." Her untimely death in February 1918 of puerperal fever, one of the cruel but common dangers of childbirth in her era, deprived the association of a "valued member."[21]

Like Duggin, members of the Delaware Equal Suffrage Association followed the NAWSA slogans of "sacrifice and service" and "suffrage and service" during the war years, balancing suffrage-specific events and meetings with added war-specific events. Their contributions to the Red Cross and especially the four wartime Liberty Loan campaigns drew upon their organizing talents, fundraising skills, and club and church networks. Those campaigns also brought into their orbit women whose involvement in local women's clubs had made them savvy organizers and lobbyists, even if not yet committed suffragists. Mary Phillips Eskridge, who headed up the Victory Loan Committee for six Sussex County towns, raising $85,000 in the process, was one of many such individuals. The daughter and wife of Democratic Party politicians, before the war she had been president of Seaford's women's club, the Acorn Club, spearheading its effort to establish a town library and representing the club at annual meetings of the Delaware Federation of Women's Clubs. There, Emalea Pusey Warner and other leading clubwomen and suffragists from around the state became her coworkers. The shared work of supporting the war effort in everything from selling bonds to holding canning demonstrations and food conservation drives established new connections that might, in turn, build a sturdy scaffolding for future, postwar projects. At war's end, Warner, who understood the value of having a talented and well-connected Sussex County woman like Eskridge as a member of the suffrage fold, nominated Eskridge for service on the Equal Suffrage Association's Executive Committee. Eskridge accepted.[22]

The same shared war work engaged the members of the Equal Suffrage Study Club—in segregated settings. Through the Garrett Settlement House and its director, Blanche Stubbs, African American suffragists participated in a range of projects, including sponsoring or teaching classes in food conservation, first aid, and home nursing; appointing a public nurse, whose services were particularly crucial during the 1918 influenza epidemic; and establishing a baby-weighing station, a wartime undertaking aimed at promoting what contemporaries termed "human conservation."[23] Wartime also provided an opportunity to press for health improvements at Wilmington's "colored" schools, at least one of which was appallingly substandard due to the high incidence of tuberculosis among the pupils, and to highlight the needs of "destitute" or "delinquent" African American youth. As director of the Garrett Settlement and president of the Delaware Association of Colored Women's Clubs, Stubbs expanded the ambassadorial role that she had filled for some time. She now found herself in constant demand to stand in for, represent, or speak for members of her race in all-white settings. Through meetings of the "women in industry" and food conservation subcommittees of the Council of National Defense Woman's Committee, and the Red Cross's "educational department for colored citizens," she became a key point of contact between official wartime agencies and local African American women. On a couple of occasions, her diplomacy brought white women into Black public spaces, such as churches or the Garrett Settlement, to discuss areas of common interest, including suffrage.[24]

As the demands of war work cast suffrage-oriented activities in semi-shadow, the Equal Suffrage Association's leaders took their cues from NAWSA's leadership and its "double duty" approach. They would, they agreed, "stand by the National in the work they are endeavoring to carry out at the present crisis"—for who knew how long the war might last—while also accepting a NAWSA directive that they appoint a "politically . . . influencial [sic]" member to head up a state Congressional Committee, and organize affiliates in each of the state's three counties. At their November 1917 convention, group members reported on both "patriotic work" and suffrage-related events in all three counties: there was the usual tent at the state fair at Wawaset Park in New Castle County; in Sussex County, a suffrage-decorated automobile took part in Lewes's Fourth of July parade; and in Kent County, members of the Dover group held a parade in Wyoming and lobbied the governor to appoint educator and suffragist Mabel Lodge as county superintendent of schools. Pressed by the national leadership, in late November 1917, DESA's leaders scheduled a dispiriting "interview" with two of the three Democratic members of Delaware's congressional delegation. House member Albert F. Polk was downright insulting; he "paid no attention to the discussion [but rather] smoked and said that he was irrevocably opposed to suffrage." True to his word, he voted against the House bill for a constitutional amendment in January 1918, which nevertheless passed with the required two-thirds majority. Senator Willard Saulsbury, whose wife May du Pont Saulsbury was an anti-suffrage stalwart, took a familiar tack in opposition to the amendment: "then colored women would vote, too." Senator Josiah Wolcott begged off the meeting with DESA representatives, pleading illness. Outside of Delaware, though, congressional passage of the federal amendment had begun to appear possible in the aftermath of the New York suffrage victory and in the context of war.[25]

When the suffrage bill passed the House in January 1918, American participation in the war was entering its second year. All future action on the suffrage front focused on getting the Senate to its own two-thirds vote. But the Delaware Equal Suffrage Association leadership believed that neither Saulsbury nor Wolcott could be moved to vote "aye." Even as NAWSA's general activity around the amendment hummed ever more loudly, the Delaware branch seemed unable to catch the general rhythm. The group's coffers ran low. In February, the Executive Committee could envision no way in which to raise the sum of five hundred dollars it had earlier promised to NAWSA. By borrowing forty dollars from the Wilmington Equal Suffrage Association, the officers were able to make a partial payment, but in October, they were still in arrears. In March and April, the group spent no money at all. Also in March, they decided that they had no use for the services of a national suffrage organizer and declined NAWSA's offer of a "travelling library . . . as at present there is no demand for it." DESA held no meetings at all during the summer of 1918, and when the time rolled around to make the routine request for a suffrage booth at the 1918 state fair, its stalwart supporters were too busy with other obligations. "The usual working members were not in a position to give the requisite time," noted the secretary's minutes.[26]

Militancy

The National Woman's Party's militant tactics—making Woodrow Wilson and the Democratic Party targets of suffragist ire—presented a clear contrast with NAWSA's grassroots lobbying approach and its leaders' participation in the National Defense Council. The NWP's members opposed Wilson's reelection and did what they could to defeat other Democrats running for Congress. NWP activists like Delaware's Mabel Vernon embraced their role as the annoying pebble in Wilson's shoe, heckling him and then picketing the White House, so that he had to pass them if he wanted to get to his golf game. Once the United States entered the Great War, the NWP raised the discomfort level considerably by not only continuing the picketing but also crafting picket signs that threw back at Wilson his own words about "democracy" and "the right . . . to have a voice in [one's] own government," even demonizing him as "Kaiser Wilson." The NWP's single-minded pursuit of suffrage while the country was at war, even as its members also contributed to the war effort through paid work and unpaid volunteer labor, fit Alice Paul's understanding of the organization's stance. "Those who wish to work for preparedness, those who wish to work for peace," she advised, "can do so through organizations for such purpose." But, she continued, "our organization is dedicated only to the enfranchisement of women." War or no war, the NWP would remain steadfast in its drive toward its "sole purpose": "securing political liberty for women." And the group would relentlessly blame Wilson for any roadblocks in the way.[27]

When it came to suffrage, members of the NWP's Delaware branch followed the national leadership. When it came to the war effort, many individuals actively supported organizations such as the Red Cross and defense agencies, as well as the Liberty Loan campaigns. Both Sallie Topkis Ginns and Florence Bayard Hilles served on the executive committee of Delaware's Woman's National Defense Committee, which recruited women for war service in arenas such as public health, community welfare, nursing, Americanization, community gardens, motor service, and recreational activities. In April 1917, in her capacity as head of the subcommittee on "enrollment for service," Hilles recruited over two hundred women who expressed their willingness "to serve the community" in various ways, but particularly through taking up war work in occupations ranging from accounting and bookkeeping, and nursing and police work, to signal and wireless operation. "Let us have no idle women during this war," she exhorted those who signed up.[28]

Unpaid voluntarism might fit common images of self-sacrificing womanhood, but by including paid war work as a form of national service, Hilles revealed the extent to which her acquaintance with working-class suffragists in the Delaware NWP had shaped her understanding of their lives. Only some women, such as herself, had the time and resources to commit themselves to full-time volunteer labor. Paid war work offered different opportunities, and members of the group's working-class contingent seized them. Among them were Annie Arniel, who had participated in the "silent sentinel" protests outside the White House; eighteen-year-old Naomi Schopfer Barrett, who became a munitions worker; and forty-four-year-old Annie Stirlith McGee, a coal-grinding operator at the General Chemical Company works in Claymont. At the Bethlehem Steel Loading plant just outside of New Castle, which began expanding operations in 1915 and eventually employed some fifteen hundred women and men, several working-class NWP suffragists spent their days loading explosive powder into shells, something that, as a coworker understated it, "should be done with dexterity and quickness." They included Arniel, Catherine Thornton Boyle, a woman in her thirties with a toddler at home who also took in boarders at her New Castle home, and Adelina Piunti, a teenaged Italian immigrant who had arrived in the United States only three years before her new country entered the war. Eventually, the employee roster also listed Hilles's name. Hers was an exploit that connected the demand for suffrage with her call for war service; it also satisfied the adventurous spirit that had inspired Hilles (with Mabel Vernon) to unfurl a banner in the congressional gallery while Woodrow Wilson spoke, and, at some point, to acquire a purple and gold "CU" tattoo on her right arm. Her stint as a munitions worker provided a quick introduction to some of the realities of working-class life, as well as enabled her to find additional recruits for NWP activities. Hilles thus added paid labor to her suffrage militancy and unpaid voluntary service.[29]

With their country at war, Delaware's NWP members, like their counterparts from other states, found that continuing to participate in the highly visible White House picketing made them objects of controversy. The wartime context brought accusations of disloyalty and behavior unbecoming to women. An activity that earlier had been interpreted, variously, as brave, unusual, patient, endearing, or even childish or undignified, now could be interpreted more harshly as selfish, pig-headed, disloyal, and unwomanly. Whereas earlier in 1917, pickets had drawn "curious or dismissive looks" from bystanders and "a muted, sometimes condescending response from the press," now, in wartime, they attracted hostility from White House staff and passers-by alike, along with openly hostile commentary in the press. Not surprisingly, Wilmington's anti-suffrage editor of *Every Evening* lumped all suffragists into the NWP camp (an approach that the Delaware NWP had encouraged by framing themselves as the state's premier suffrage organization) and pilloried them as women who "put country below cause" and suffrage before patriotism at a time of "national peril." In a rhetorical move that became an increasingly common element in anti-suffrage language during the war, the paper's editor stirred suffragists into the poisoned mélange of "feminism, socialism, and Mormonism." It served anti-suffragists' interests to do so, even as NAWSA's "double duty" was designed to achieve suffrage as a "war measure." The group, Catt assured Woodrow Wilson, would exercise womanly patience, while the pickets offered daily reminders of other suffragists' impatience. Catt took a different tone with Paul, rebuking the picketing for the "serious antagonism" it evoked, and claiming that the pickets' presence "is hurting our cause in Congress."[30]

Despite deepening criticism, Delaware's NWP members remained committed to the strategy they had chosen: war service, yes, but also putting continued pressure on the president, in turn, to press Congress to pass a federal suffrage amendment. By June 1917, their commitment was being tested by more than the Washington, D.C., weather. The District police began arresting pickets for disturbing the peace. On June 26,

Arniel and Vernon became the first of Delaware's NWP members to be arrested; they received sentences of three days in the Washington, D.C., jail. Ever quick to seize an opportunity for publicity, the NWP circulated a photo of Arniel and Minnesotan Florence Youmans being placed under arrest outside the White House gates. Arniel, Youmans, and others became, as two NWP historians have put it, "the first women imprisoned in the United States for demanding the right to vote." Upon their release, they attended a celebratory breakfast at which Vernon explicitly rejected the call for patience: "women have been too patient for the past fifty years." Now was the time to make "a demand for political freedom so insistent that the government can no longer deny" it.

Other Delawareans continued on picket duty, which was now weekly instead of daily. Then, on Bastille Day, July 14, 1917, Arniel and Hilles were among a group of sixteen women arrested and charged with blocking traffic. Given the option of paying a fine or accepting stiff sentences in the Occoquan Workhouse in Virginia, the women took the sixty-day sentences. Entering the dingy courtroom, the fifty-one-year-old Hilles was jolly, remarking with reference to her English sojourn during her father's stint as U.S. Ambassador, "Well, girls, I've never seen but one other court in my life and that was the Court of St. James. But I must say they are not very much alike." She soon turned serious and, with the aplomb of a seasoned suffrage speaker, reminded her listeners that she, like her distinguished male relatives and the president himself, was a Democrat. Pointedly contrasting the arrest of women seeking voting rights with Woodrow Wilson's claim that the U.S. had gone to war "'for the right of those who submit to authority to have a voice in their own government,'" she wondered "what a spectacle it must be to the thinking people of this country to see us urged to go to war for democracy in a foreign land, and to see women thrown into prison who plead for that same cause at home." Three days later, Wilson pardoned all sixteen women.[31]

Soon, however, the pardons came to an end. As the NWP ratcheted up its insults to Wilson (the "Kaiser Wilson" banner made its debut in mid-August), his personal ire at the pickets and larger public reaction, which ranged from mere irritation to serious outrage, made it increasingly likely that the arrested women would be made to serve out their workhouse sentences. That likelihood came to pass in September when Arniel, the fieriest of the Delaware group, received a sixty-day sentence to the Occoquan Workhouse, a term from which there would be no

For
EVERY
FIGHTER
a
WOMAN
WORKER

UNITED
WAR
WORK
CAMPAIGN

CARE
for
HER
through The YWCA

Figure 9. "For Every Fighter a Woman War Worker." A wartime poster from the Young Women's Christian Association drew a direct correlation between women war workers' production of munitions and men's war service. The additional text, "Care for her through the YWCA," underlined the YWCA's commitment to protecting single young white women workers by offering them safe, respectable, and affordable housing. In Delaware, African American working women were excluded from segregated YWCA residential facilities. Credit: Delaware Historical Society.

respite or pardon. In October, Alice Paul received a seven-month sentence, to be served in the District of Columbia jail. The following month, she began a hunger strike in order to underscore the NWP's stance that the imprisoned suffragists were political prisoners (not criminals) and should be treated as such. A close coworker, Rose Winslow, joined her in refusing nourishment. Transferred to the jail's psychopathic ward on orders of District Commissioner Gwynne Gardiner, Paul was then subjected to forcible feeding twice a day, a grueling, intensely painful, health-endangering reminder of her experience in England in 1909. A letter smuggled out to the *New York Times* describing the atrocious conditions under which Paul and others were being held drew attention to their protest and catalyzed a variety of reactions across the country.[32]

Although no Delaware NWP member had yet participated in the hunger strikes, the responses to all NWP activities throughout the summer and fall of 1917 reflected the range of conflicting emotions that party tactics evoked. When it became clear that the Woman's Party would continue to picket the White House during wartime and even magnify the messages emblazoned on pickets' banners, some Delaware suffragists defected from the ranks. Most notably, Mabel Ridgely, who had signed on as the CU/NWP chairman in Kent County, dropped her membership, spending the rest of the war years as Delaware state chairman of the Women's Liberty Loans project and dedicating time to the Red Cross. There were defections in other states as well, most noteworthy among them New Yorker Harriot Stanton Blatch, Elizabeth Cady Stanton's daughter. One historian puts the number of membership losses after the "Kaiser Wilson" banner appeared at "dozens." Even supportive pickets thought twice when they learned that sixty-day workhouse sojourns might be their fate. Working women, for instance, could afford neither the loss of wages nor the ignominy that would follow them if they were arrested. African Americans could hardly risk being thrown into notoriously awful segregated local jails. Still other NWP enthusiasts expressed doubts about leaders' decision-making, especially when some of their individual decisions appeared downright puzzling. In particular, Alice Paul seemed to court incarceration despite her frail health, on one occasion refusing even to speak after an arrest for obstructing traffic and then appearing to dare the authorities to respond with a heavier hand.[33]

At the same time, the grim reality of the jailed suffragists' situations evoked sympathy even from critics such as those in the Delaware Equal

Suffrage Association. Arniel's two jail terms, totaling sixty-three days in 1917, and her eventual return to Wilmington "much broken in health as a result of her sacrifice for democracy," undoubtedly reminded Delawareans that some of the suffragists being pilloried or praised in the local press had suffered heroically for their actions. Signaling her willingness to endure more, Arniel told a local newspaper, "my experiences may have to be repeated before the great cause for which we women have endured so much is finally won." Some hard hearts in the Equal Suffrage Association may have melted at the thought, even though the group had scorned Arniel's NWP during the early months of the war, exasperated by what they viewed as the wrong-headedness of White House picketing. Now, after refusing to sign a July 27, 1917, letter "praising the work" of the pickets or "extending sympathy" to Hilles for her own three-day incarceration, DESA's membership approved a November resolution "condemn[ing] the injustice of the unusual and extreme punishment, which is being inflicted upon the women who are using . . . the recent tactics of the Woman's Party."[34]

Such expressions of sympathy relied, of course, on enduring stereotypes of femininity, crosshatched by racial and class assumptions. Earlier representations of women pickets—whether as peculiar, childish, unfeminine, pigheaded, or disloyal—gave way to grudging admiration for the sacrifices they were making for their cause. The NWP leaders framed their suffering sisters' stories in ways that facilitated the shift. Despite the incarceration of working-class white women such as Arniel, NWP publicity highlighted the situations of respectable middle- or upper-class white women, contrasting the assumed privacy and cleanliness of their daily existences with the filthy, claustrophobic, vermin-infested, and embarrassingly public lives they were forced to live in jail or the workhouse. An editorial cartoon appearing on the cover of a September 1917 issue of *The Suffragist* played upon those contrasts. Originally drawn by North Dakota's U.S. House member John M. Baer, the sketch called out the treatment of "refined, intelligent, society women" who were being "thrown into" the Occoquan Workhouse "with negroes and criminals." The implications were clear. Not only were the pickets committing no crime by exercising their "constitutional right to petition," but also their daily contact with women who might have sold their bodies for money or were, simply "negroes," exponentially increased the horrors of their suffering. In actuality, jailed suffragists often found Black women inmates to be helpful or sympathetic. But the publicity value of contrasting white "society women" with "negroes and criminals" as a way to promote the suffrage cause was too useful to admit much nuance.[35]

Alice Paul brought NWP picketing to a halt when she and the remaining group of twenty-one suffragists jailed with her after her fall 1917 arrest, "some too weak to walk," were suddenly released from custody just before Thanksgiving. The decision apparently reflected political leaders' fears, as one of Wilson's Democratic supporters argued, that Paul intended to "'permit herself to be starved to death for the suffrage cause.'" Whether done at the behest of Woodrow Wilson or of his private secretary, Joseph Tumulty, who had warned Wilson that the suffrage prisoners were "'being treated very harshly,'" the women's discharge came shortly after the success of the New York suffrage referendum and not long before Wilson at last declared his support for a federal suffrage amendment.[36]

Patriotism and Loyalty

In pressing the case for a federal amendment, both the NWP's picketing, protesting, and hunger-striking (along with lobbying) approach and NAWSA's more measured vote-counting, interviewing, and reinterviewing strategy played out against the wartime backdrop. Expressions of dissent became suspect in a home front setting characterized by the policing of people's loyalties, the growing censorship of official information, the expansion of a federal bureaucracy that intruded in new ways into the lives of Americans, and a concomitant push for ordinary individuals to conform to the patriotic sentiments presented to them by their government. Suspicion of peace or reconciliation advocates, many of whom were known to be suffragists, which had grown during the "preparedness" era, became more overt and threatening in 1916 and 1917. Individuals learned to silence their public statements, or, as did Jane Addams, agreed to support relief for war victims in the hope of preventing future wars. (Her work with the federal Department of Food Administration in 1918 did not exempt her from Department of Justice surveillance, however.)[37] The Delaware suffragist whose adherence to pacifist ideals proved particularly costly was twenty-seven-year-old Donald Stephens, a member of the Arden single-tax community who refused to register for the draft. Immediately labeled a "slacker" by the local morning newspaper, he was arrested. While being publicly castigated for "moral cowardice," Stephens sought but was denied conscientious objector status, resulting in a nine-month sentence to the New Castle County workhouse, followed by induction into the armed services "whether he likes it or not." Stephens's appeal to the U.S. Supreme Court, claiming the draft violated his constitutional right to freedom of conscience, was unsuccessful; the Court simply reaffirmed his sentence. But by the time of his release, the war—and the draft—had ended.[38]

Stephens's persistence in the face of powerful opposition was aided in large part by his family's resources and by the support of the Arden colony. Other Delawareans no doubt found it difficult to stand up against the wave of hypervigilance that washed across the country, challenging the patriotism of anyone who questioned the war or its aims. Remaining afloat could be challenging as anti-suffragists or civilian vigilance groups such as the National Security League lashed pacifists as "allies" of "German agents," and sought pledges of loyalty even from the three-man Delaware congressional delegation. In its zeal to attach labels of disloyalty to members of Congress, the Security League ran into trouble, but other vigilance committees, such as the American Protective League, "operating under the direction of the Department of Justice, Bureau of Investigation," created a statewide organization working to track down "German propaganda" and "enemy alien activities." More troubling was the leadership's pressure on "loyal citizens" to report "disloyalty, enemy propaganda or activity" to its inspectors. Delawareans reported "slackers" whom they encountered on Atlantic City beaches during the summer, and sought the removal of German-language books from libraries as well as of German language classes from school curricula. In September 1918, Delaware joined thirteen other states in banning the teaching of German. The women's national committee of the American Defense Society urged patriotic local women to "start a garden" in order to avert possible food shortages, and evoked the specter of German "outrages" (that is, rapes) committed against Belgian and French women in a plea for local Christmas boycotts against German-made toys.[39]

To be sure, no one in Delaware suffered the lethal terrors inflicted elsewhere upon individuals labeled unpatriotic, such as German-American Robert Prager, lynched by a mob in St. Louis in 1918, or the "ugly fires of vigilantism" that scorched left-wing labor groups such as the Industrial Workers of the World (IWW), and facilitated the brutal murder of IWW official Frank Little in Butte, Montana. But the use of postal censorship to silence nonconforming writers, press collaboration with the Wilson administration to erase any war stories not deemed sufficiently upbeat, and the circulation of wartime propaganda by the exceedingly effective Committee of Public Information squelched potential dissent. Headed by George Creel, a Wilson supporter, Progressive reformer and muckraking journalist, and self-identified feminist, the committee produced, among other undertakings, a daily "official bulletin" of curated war information. More than a few Americans, including some in NAWSA's leadership, became giddy at the prospect of censoring their own opponents' press coverage. For a time, women in NAWSA's press office sought to apply "the remedy of silence" to NWP activities by enlisting Creel to convince the national press associations to limit their coverage of the rival group. Creel's committee adopted the practice of presenting only NAWSA as a representative of the suffrage movement. By far his committee's most wide-reaching projects, though, were those that employed new forms of communication, particularly arresting posters, movies, photographs, and short, pithy speeches delivered by "Four Minute Men," who could present a patriotic message within the established time limit. By July 1917, Delaware had a state "Four Minute Men" chairman recruiting local speakers for talks; and by the summer of 1918, all three Wilmington dailies were routinely—and uncritically—reprinting photographs, articles, and advertisements from Creel's committee. Delawareans learned one specific version of patriotism, which championed service to the nation at war and chastised opposition to the war, or dissent from current policy, as unpatriotic.[40]

Patriotism became entangled with ideas about masculinity and femininity, ideas that suffrage supporters questioned at their peril. Just as Donald Stephens was accused of lacking manly virtues, White House pickets encountered slurs against their characters and their femininity, as well as their wartime loyalty. And while the mainstream suffragists of NAWSA managed a more calculated use of ideas about femininity through their embrace of "sacrifice and service," as well as "suffrage and service," they still found anti-suffragists excoriating them for supposedly serving the nation only for the political benefits they would collectively gain. In their May 1917 statement, Thompson and Bissell adopted that position, claiming that in the suffragists' world, "women wish the vote

as a form of payment or reward for services rendered." In their own uni-
verse, "patriotic women want no reward." Theirs was a cosmos made up
of women who expressed their patriotism by volunteering for a long list
of service agencies, as well as their churches and schools, all the while
spending nine hours a day, as did the "average adult woman married and
the mother of three children . . . doing her own housework for a family of
five." It hardly mattered that neither Bissell nor Thompson actually lived
in the world of their imagining—Bissell was a single professional woman
and Thompson relied upon a bevy of servants for household labor—as
they were articulating a constellation of ideas that tied patriotic womanhood and women's experience of citizenship to unpaid service to the
nation.[41]

In the antis' realm, to put a "political price on women's patriotism"
would be to demean their service. Yet, for African American suffragists,
the dilemmas presented by the dual issues of patriotism and wartime
service required a great deal of negotiation. These suffragists understood
the war's economic benefits to their poorer neighbors, including those
newly arriving in Delaware, in the form of better and better-paying job
opportunities. They were loath to question a war that was enabling Black
women to leave demeaning domestic service jobs for "men's work" on
railroad tracks and in yards, in munitions and other factories, and in
jobs that required "skill rather than brawn" as elevator attendants and
machine-shop operatives. Indeed, in July 1918, the Women's Branch of
the U.S. Employment Service complained that it was "utterly impossible" to fill all domestic service openings in Wilmington because "now
a considerable number of colored women are employed in various positions . . . in factories." Wartime patriotism could take the form of a better
job with better pay. Teacher-suffragists were likely to see their students
entering the best job market in their memories; they hoped that war's
economic effects would linger in the aftermath. Even if the postwar era
brought a return to domestic service jobs, noted Dunbar-Nelson, young
workers would—and should—now expect better working conditions.
Moreover, as clubwomen and churchwomen, middle-class Black women
were used to using their skills in voluntary service to their communities.
Perhaps wartime service to the nation would bring bonuses, including
suffrage.[42]

For the men of their families, schools, and community institutions,
the war held out the prospect of advancing their civic status through

military service. In registering for the draft or volunteering for the armed services, African American men looked to show their patriotism and expected the promise of "manhood rights denied to them as civilians" to be fulfilled. By the summer of 1918, some four hundred Howard School alumni had been inducted into the armed services, and individual suffragists' families had relatives in the segregated army. Blanche Stubbs's brother, Lieutenant A. Hugo Williams, served in France, for instance, and Helen Wormley Anderson's nephew Spahr H. Dickey attended officer training school in Des Moines, Iowa. To be sure, Wilmington's middle-class teachers worried about what an influx of African American draftees into nearby Fort Dix, New Jersey, might mean for the rules of personal conduct they sought to inculcate in the young women they taught. "The lure of the khaki," as Dunbar-Nelson put it, that is, the "relationship of the young girl and the soldier," required some managing. YWCA "Hostess Houses," the closest of which was at Fort Dix, offered men "a bit of home" and opportunities for "social activities," but required measures that "safeguarded the moral life of women and girls." Concern for girls' morals added a layer of urgency to promoting a project that African American clubwomen had planned for almost two decades: opening an "industrial school" for girls deemed troublesome or "incorrigible," in the language of the day. "The khaki" lured men, too, not only in the appeal of wearing a uniform but also in the prospect of providing well-paid work and perhaps even job training.[43]

There was a careful line that African American suffragists had to tread in order to avoid raising questions about their loyalties. After the war, Dunbar-Nelson became a strong advocate for peace and an enthusiastic member of the Women's International League for Peace and Freedom.[44] But during the war and for a brief time afterward, she found it prudent to orchestrate displays of African American loyalty and service to the nation. For Flag Day, June 14, 1918, she arranged a patriotic parade for and by Delaware's "colored citizens." Like the 1916 preparedness parade, it had didactic purposes, in this case displaying for spectators the strength of Black Wilmingtonians' commitment to the nation's central symbol and providing some pointed history lessons. Unlike the 1916 parade, in which a "Negro division" was clearly an afterthought, the Flag Day parade placed the African American organizers' interests at the center. On the reviewing stand, along with the mayor, a former governor, and members of the City Council (including the lone African

American councilman, John O. Hopkins), stood Emmett J. Scott, Assistant Secretary of War in the Wilson administration. Led by Dr. Conwell Banton, who served on the city's Board of Education, several thousand women, men, and children carrying flags marched in groups representing social, religious, fraternal, and workers' organizations, including the Red Cross, the Garrett Settlement, and the State Federation of Colored Women's Clubs.

Although woman suffrage received no mention, members of the Equal Suffrage Study Club participated both as organizers and as marchers, in their roles as teachers or civic leaders. As the participants walked "through the principal streets" of the city, accompanied by lively bands, they "formed as pretty and uniform a line as was ever seen in parade," one city newspaper commented. The presence of three Civil War veterans furnished a living history lesson, while banners and signs mentioning African Americans' long history in the United States and the service of Black men in every war since the Revolutionary War offered a clear alternative narrative to what white spectators might have learned in school. Simultaneously, women and girls with sons or brothers in the armed services marched as a unit, carrying service flags, and Howard High School's principal Edwina Kruse rode in an automobile with a banner reading "She Trains Our Youth for Uncle Sam." This was, as one newspaper editorialized, "a striking display of patriotism," precisely echoing the organizers' purpose.[45]

Soon thereafter, Dunbar-Nelson took a leave from teaching in order to serve as a field representative to Southern Black women from the Woman's Committee of the Council of National Defense. The position, created at the behest of Emmett Scott, came as reports of unrest among African Americans in the South were worrying the War Department. Widespread racial discrimination against Black soldiers and the cold shoulders given to Black women who sought to participate in war volunteerism was undermining patriotic sentiment, Scott heard, and perhaps even producing openness to German propaganda. In a wartime atmosphere characterized by suspicion and concerns about disloyalty, Dunbar-Nelson's role was to promote cooperation between the (separate) Black and white women's organizations affiliated with the Woman's Committee and report back.

As she undertook a grueling travel schedule, Dunbar-Nelson had to deal not only with the often depressing conditions she encountered, but also with a white supervisor, Hannah Patterson, who felt authorized to scold her field representative on various matters—minor as well as major. Both women were suffragists, and had met before Dunbar-Nelson's appointment, but their relationship during her stint with the Woman's Committee apparently snagged on the prickly fence of a unionizing drive by Black Louisiana domestic workers. The women hoped that collective action during wartime, when their talents were in heavy demand, would lead to "fair wages and reasonable hours" and perhaps even better-paid war jobs. But their employers accused them of being German spies. Dunbar-Nelson's sympathies were not entirely with working-class women, for as historian Nikki Brown has argued, middle-class clubwomen like herself often "placed patriotic activity ahead of civil rights." Nevertheless, on her Southern tour, including to her native Louisiana, Dunbar-Nelson came to her own views on how patriotism might be leveraged to achieve greater rights. By the time she completed an essay on "Negro Women in War Work" in 1919 for Emmett Scott's edited collection, she adopted an unambiguous celebratory tone lauding the enthusiasm and contributions of women who, despite the racism of white women in agencies like the Red Cross, "put great-heartedness and pure patriotism above the ancient creed of racial antagonism."[46]

Patriotism, Suffrage, and Democracy

When Alice Paul, newly released from jail, ended all suffrage picketing in late November 1917, the NWP's protest tactics seemed to have brought the desired result. Woodrow Wilson signaled his endorsement of a federal amendment "as a necessary war measure," then made his pledge a reality in advance of the House vote on January 10, 1918. A positive vote, coming a short month after the full Congress had sent the Prohibition Amendment (the Eighteenth) to the states for ratification, thrilled suffrage leaders. Surely a Nineteenth Amendment could not be far behind. "Wasn't [it], splendid?" Florence Bayard Hilles wrote to her friend and patron Phoebe Apperson Hearst, on January 29. She explained, "It meant an awful lot of hard work [but] we have a good chance for the Senate now." Her optimism was premature. During the Sixty-fifth Congress, the Senate voted twice on the amendment, first on October 1, 1918, then again on February 10, 1919; both times it failed by tiny margins. Among those pushing it over into the abyss were Delaware's two senators, both Democrats, Willard Saulsbury and Josiah Wolcott.[47]

For as long as Hilles's initial optimism about the Senate prevailed, the NWP's Delaware branch seemed to follow NAWSA's script. With picketing stopped, on January 18, Hilles and several of her coworkers—including Wilmington's Arniel, Mabel Vernon, and Sallie Topkis Ginns, along with Middletown's Marie Lockwood—joined a group of labor leaders in visiting Saulsbury and Wolcott to ask for their support of woman suffrage. Wolcott, who had not bothered to meet with the Equal Suffrage Association delegation a few months earlier, promised "to give full consideration to the views expressed." Whatever "consideration" he gave the issue, not even an "ardent appeal for [his] support" from Woodrow Wilson, tying the amendment to "the fate of the war—and by implication the fate of the world" could move him. The Delaware NWP's courtesy visit in January aligned with the approach now taken by Paul, who, throughout the spring and summer of 1918, "refrained from new demonstrations," instead "counting on lobbying and the pressure of the fall elections" to shift senators' votes. When a federal appeals court ruled in early March that the arrest and imprisonment of pickets during the preceding year was an unconstitutional violation of their right to assemble peaceably, the ruling validated one of the NWP's tactics. For now, however, that tactic sat on the shelf.[48]

A new pressure tactic, inaugurated during the interlude in spring 1918 while Senate consideration of the amendment dragged on, proclaimed members' willingness to demonstrate their patriotism by taking war jobs. Along with volunteering for the Red Cross or Liberty Loan campaigns, a few high-profile NWP members punched time clocks in war-related industries. The Delaware branch received national publicity when Hilles, the state chairman, took a paying job at the Bethlehem Steel munitions plant outside New Castle in late April 1918. Local NWP press releases framed her decision as fulfilling her "patriotic duty" to "replace men" in the industries. For a "considerable length of time" by her reckoning, perhaps three months on and off, Hilles traveled three miles daily to the factory from her River Road farm, "Ommelanden," at least once in a milk delivery truck. She donated her pay to the Red Cross. In describing the work that she and her coworkers performed, Hilles provided details about what it was like to be doing dangerous factory labor, details that readers of *The Suffragist*, the NWP's periodical, might not previously have noticed. By printing contrasting photographs showing Hilles in her munitions worker's uniform and in her usual fashionable attire, the NWP furnished a visual cue that evoked earlier scenes of respectable suffragists in jail sackcloth. Hilles particularly stressed the "lesson in democracy" being learned by her new coworkers, the "many groups of women who have never before seemed to have anything in common" and who now understood that Woodrow Wilson's "own words" about "'the right of those who submit to authority to have a voice in their own government'" should translate into woman suffrage. By highlighting the activities of former pickets such as Hilles, the NWP connected war work, democracy, and suffrage. Whereas at the war's outset, the NWP had vowed to pursue its "sole purpose," a federal amendment, now that the amendment was before the Senate, party leadership found it useful to emphasize that members were "working alike for war and for suffrage," both of which, they reminded Wilson, were struggles for democracy.[49]

Hilles's visibility as a socially prominent suffragist enabled her and the NWP to cast her war work into a mold that fit their new tactic. During a lull at the factory in late May, she accompanied a group of five coworkers to Washington, D.C., where they awaited an "audience" with Wilson in order to discuss democracy and suffrage. Their work, the women argued, was as important as that of soldiers, yet as women they were "discriminated against in many ways." To draw attention to their purpose, the women waited daily for several hours in a White House waiting room, then extended their stay by a second week. They waited in vain. As their story spread, a group of eight women from Baltimore's Bartlett Haywood munitions operation made plans to join them. In a statement read into the *Congressional Record* by Maryland's sympathetic Senator Joseph I. France, the Baltimore group noted that "we face the risk of injury as soldiers face it" when taking men's places "handling the highest explosives," yet "in our rights we are not made equal with men." Wrapping war work, women's economic rights, democracy, and suffrage into one package for delivery to Wilson and recalcitrant senators represented a new approach to rendering suffragism as a supremely patriotic undertaking.[50]

Such "stunts," a sympathetic government overseer of factory work argued, "are necessary in putting over propaganda where the public mind must be aroused." And, indeed, throughout the struggle to get the amendment through the Senate, NWP publicists posted regular reminders that the party's ranks included war workers, women who needed the weekly pay envelope and hoped that achieving suffrage would improve

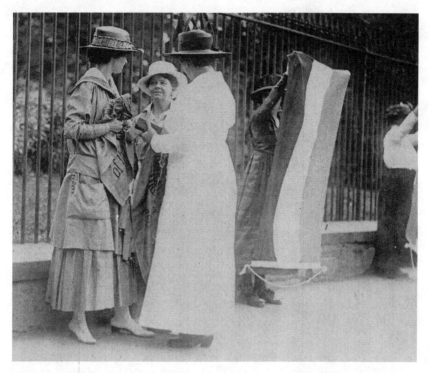

Figure 10. "Policewoman [in white] arrests Florence Youmans of Minnesota [left] and Annie Arniel of Delaware [center] for refusing to give up their banners," June 1917. Annie Melvin Arniel eventually served eight jail sentences for a total of 103 days. Credit: Library of Congress, www.loc.gov/item/mnwp000073/

their working conditions and their earnings. By early summer, as the amendment languished in the Senate, getting tangled up in more procedural skeins than many knew existed, the group's leadership watched nervously as the days ticked by while interminable filibusters and other delaying tactics kept the Anthony Amendment swaddled to the point of near-smothering. On this point, the NWP and NAWSA agreed: if the Sixty-fifth Congress adjourned without Senate ratification, advocates would have to start all over again when the Sixty-sixth Congress convened. It was not scheduled to do so until December 1, 1919.[51]

Determined to loosen the knots tying up the amendment before the current congressional session ended, Alice Paul and her coworkers at

NWP headquarters devised an approach that blended old and new tactics. On August 6, 1918, invoking the sainted memory of Inez Milholland, for it would have been her thirty-second birthday, the party inaugurated almost daily protests in Lafayette Park, across from the White House. "How Long Must Women Wait for Liberty?" read their banners, evoking the legend of Milholland's final words. The targets of their ire were both the Senate, which had gone into recess in mid-July, and the President, whom they accused of not doing enough to pressure Democratic senators into voting for the amendment. Over the next few days, arrests commenced again. Among those arraigned and jailed were Annie Arniel (again) and Catherine Boyle; Arniel joined some of the prisoners in a hunger strike before all were released without charge. In mid-September, the protesters' pageantry introduced a new use for an old symbol—a flaming liberty torch—by publicly burning Wilson's "empty words" and promises. Along with the addition of this attention-getting tactic, "watch fires of freedom," as the participants called them, the NWP instituted daily picketing of both the White House and the Capitol.[52]

As the Senate moved toward taking a vote on the amendment, Wilson made a dramatic appearance in the chamber in the early afternoon of September 30. With his wife observing from the gallery, the president gave a short speech that included virtually every talking point that both the NWP and NAWSA had honed throughout the war. Woman suffrage was "vitally essential" to winning the war. Both political parties favored the amendment. "Workaday folk" wanted democracy, and they believed that "democracy means that women shall play their part alongside men and on an equal footing with men." Dismissing the "voices of foolish and intemperate agitators" as irrelevant background noise, he characterized his decision to support the amendment as a noble recognition of the importance of democracy. When the senators finally cast their ballots on the following day, however, the amendment failed by two votes.[53] With the fall elections a scant few weeks away, both Wilson and the NWP leadership apparently had counted on his authority and political arm-twisting to secure the necessary votes. Both, it seemed, were wrong. Yet to Alice Paul, there was no reason to question the NWP's relentless emphasis on Wilson's culpability; his endorsement, while welcome, was "too reluctantly and too tardily given." Besides, the Sixty-fifth Congress would sit until March

1919; the necessary two votes might still be turned before then. Others within the NWP had some doubts, however, wondering whether Paul's emphasis on Wilson's power to move senators' votes had been "wrong-headed."[54]

In Delaware, Florence Bayard Hilles had no such misgivings. Although she was not part of the nightly scenes in Lafayette Park, she used the arrests there to issue a "protest" against the violation of the demonstrators' rights and then to decry the approach of those suffragists who, as she quoted Elizabeth Cady Stanton, "'continue the activities of past generations,'" simply "'rehearsing the old arguments which have done duty for fifty years.'" Wilson was blameworthy, she reiterated, as was "the inaction of the Democrats in the Senate." Once again, and likely with an eye toward the 1918 elections, Hilles targeted the "party in power." She also aimed her quiver at NAWSA and its affiliate, the Delaware Equal Suffrage Association.[55]

To an extent, she was correct about the Delaware branch, which had largely relied upon "the activities of past generations" while its members were dedicating much of their time to war work. She slighted, however, NAWSA's operatives, who had been doing the patient, grinding, exhausting labor of lobbying, cultivating, and counting votes in Congress while its leader, Carrie Chapman Catt, worked at maintaining a cordial relationship with Wilson.[56] Catt and her organizational team were often annoyed, at times to the point of exasperation, with their Delaware coworkers. In May 1918, visits from Catt and national NAWSA organizer Maud Wood Park were clearly designed to rouse the group and get it primed for the ratification struggle that would follow if the Senate approved the amendment. (The Delaware legislature's biennial meeting would commence early in 1919.) But DESA was suffering from a leadership vacuum that worsened with the May resignation of its president, former YWCA Secretary Agnes Y. Downey.

Only when first vice-president Eva Halpern Robin took charge and then agreed to assume the presidency did the group experience a palpable quickening in the pace of its activities. Born in Russia in 1878, Eva Halpern had immigrated to the United States as a young child. By 1903, she and her physician-husband Albert Robin were living in Wilmington, where Dr. Robin became widely admired as a bacteriologist, state pathologist, and medical director of the sanitarium for (white) tuberculosis patients outside the city. While raising four children, the last of whom was born in 1917, Eva Robin joined the New Century Club and, through it, honed her passionate advocacy for children's welfare and for establishing a juvenile court in Delaware. As a Jewish woman, she was fully aware of the city's restrictive real estate practices and likely endured some casual anti-Semitism within the overwhelmingly Protestant New Century Club. Yet her organizational and public speaking talents, well known within suffrage circles, as well as her social position, made her the members' choice to lead them at a crucial juncture.[57]

By autumn, after hearing from the NAWSA luminaries, Robin led the DESA membership in agreeing both to conduct a petition drive designed to demonstrate to Senators Saulsbury and Wolcott the strong statewide support for the amendment and to accept the assistance (paid for by NAWSA) of a national organizer, Mabel Willard, in collecting petition signatures and energizing downstate affiliates. Eventually, some eleven thousand Delawareans (perhaps 12 to 15 percent of the state's adult population) signed the petition. But in October 1918, both senators voted in the negative. Now, a strongly worded resolution approving Wilson's framing of suffrage as "a necessary war measure" but expressing "profound regret . . . [at] the attitude of our two Senators" struck a different tone from that of earlier DESA statements. There is little doubt that Eva Robin drafted it. Sex, the statement argued, should no longer be "the determining factor in the making of citizens." "We assert," the women wrote, "that we desire no longer to be represented by proxy at the ballot box, but we wish to express, unfettered by any assumptions of masculine superiority, our own political convictions at the polls." For the women of the Delaware Equal Suffrage Association, the work they had done in wartime, as "war workers" and "homemakers," as well as suffragists, had become both a record and a cudgel to wield in their claims to full citizenship.[58]

Using that weapon, the group began a thinly veiled campaign against the 1918 reelection bids of both House member Albert Polk and Senator Willard Saulsbury. (Democrat Josiah Wolcott, who hadn't bothered to meet with the women, had four years left in his term.) Such a direct intrusion into the electoral process marked a major tactical departure by DESA and by NAWSA. Whereas the NWP had targeted the "party in power"—the Democrats—NAWSA and its affiliates had insisted on a strictly "non-partisan" stance. Now, NAWSA willingly urged voters to oust any anti-suffrage member of Congress, regardless of party. Building coalitions with labor and other groups that would attack incumbents' voting records, NAWSA sought to shape a new, pro-suffrage Congress. Mabel Willard and the Scottish journeyman machinist who accompanied her, Hannah Black, cultivated suffrage endorsements from Wilmington's male craft unions. Ads targeting Saulsbury attacked his votes on matters of concern to "wage earners," such as protective tariffs. "Mr. Labor Man, Vote against Saulsbury," ran one ad line. Despite what one historian has termed "the timidity of Delaware suffragists," Willard convinced DESA members to recruit volunteers who would visit over one hundred precincts on Election Day in order to hand out "suffrage literature at the polls," and provided a couple of volunteers from NAWSA headquarters as well. To be sure, some longtime members "held up their hands in horror," as Catt later recalled, at the prospect of abandoning a "non-partisan" stance, but Robin framed the Election Day literature distribution as an "educational campaign," simply providing literature in a non-partisan fashion. It "should not be construed as a militant act."[59]

Nevertheless, with some prodding from NAWSA headquarters and a new leader, the Delaware affiliate had taken a key step toward accepting tactics that had theretofore been associated with the NWP. Older members of DESA, particularly its honorary president, Martha Churchman Cranston, complained that some aspects of the "educational campaign" had crossed a line by doing more than simply informing voters. Cranston asked Eva Robin to lodge her grievance with the national organization, a request that Robin apparently did not fulfill. She calmed the waters by blaming the NAWSA volunteers for crossing the line by "disregarding and misrepresenting" the "non-partisan attitude" of the Delaware affiliate.[60]

The outcome of the 1918 midterm elections substantially altered the composition of the state's congressional delegation. Not only did anti-suffrage Democrat Albert Polk lose his House seat to Georgetown's pro-suffrage physician Caleb R. Layton, but also Democratic Senator Willard Saulsbury, who remained a defiant anti, was defeated by Republican L. Heisler Ball. In October, Ball had assured the Delaware Equal Suffrage Association's executive committee that "the women of America who have so faithfully and untiringly shouldered war work for our country have proved their fitness to be trusted with the ballot."

If elected to Congress, he would vote "yea." The extent to which either DESA or its NWP branch contributed to Polk's and Saulsbury's defeats is almost impossible to gauge. Saulsbury's support among voters is particularly difficult to determine, as he had been elevated to the Senate not by popular election but by the state legislature, the last Delaware U.S. senator to be so chosen, before the Seventeenth Amendment went into effect. Regardless of whether woman suffrage figured in the defeat of both men, the 1918 campaign marked a tactical departure by DESA. Like NAWSA, it was learning to use electoral muscle as a "single-issue pressure group," cultivating allies and moving away from appeals to women's wartime service as an essential rationale for suffrage.[61]

Across the country, the 1918 elections brought several suffrage referenda that would alter the calculus for the 1920 presidential election. In South Dakota, Michigan, and Oklahoma, women won full voting rights, bringing to fifteen the number of full-suffrage states. Combined with several states that provided "presidential" suffrage, the total number of presidential electors in states where women would be voting was 339 (out of 435), or almost 78 percent of the total. If they wanted their nominee to win the presidency in 1920, politicians in both parties would have to pay attention to women voters, and to the demand for woman suffrage.[62]

Six days after Election Day, on November 11, 1918, the Armistice ended World War I. Like their counterparts elsewhere, Delaware's suffragists began winding down their war work, wrapping up their Liberty Loan fundraising, retiring their "Delaware Awake!" posters, and turning their attention to winning a federal amendment. Woodrow Wilson, who had endorsed the Nineteenth Amendment and trekked to the Capitol in September to provide his personal endorsement of "the extension of suffrage to women as vitally essential to the successful prosecution of the great war," was headed to Paris to negotiate a peace treaty. Before he left, he included in his December 2 annual message a plea urging the new, Sixty-sixth Congress to pass the amendment when it met the following December. In the meantime, suffragists pinned some remaining hope that the lame-duck Senate might decide to reconsider its October vote.

Looking ahead to that session, the NWP and DESA adopted different stances, which demonstrated a key shift in each organization's understanding of how to win the constitutional amendment. Gone were the appeals to women's wartime sacrifices as a rationale for suffrage. Instead, the two groups evidenced a forthright view that suffrage was a political matter, a right that women would claim with political methods. On the NWP side, on November 6, 1918, the day after Saulsbury had been defeated at the polls, Florence Bayard Hilles took out an ad in a Wilmington newspaper. In it, she asserted that the NWP deserved credit for his loss (and Heisler Ball's victory) and then warned both Saulsbury and Josiah Wolcott that "the women of Delaware are organized. They are in earnest." Both should recognize that "Delaware believes in political liberty for women." More to the point, she was sure that Saulsbury "has now the political vision to see that" and would "take advantage of this lesson in democracy." Wolcott, too, because of Saulsbury's "decisive defeat," should understand that he had "a mandate from the people of Delaware as a guide for his official action on the suffrage question." In short, she believed the men to have been chastened by the election results, and hence should now be willing to support the amendment when the current Congress returned to Washington. The state's NWP branch, which she claimed now enrolled seven hundred members, would hold them accountable if they did not.[63]

The Equal Suffrage Association's approach was similarly grounded in practical politics. Once again prodded by NAWSA president Carrie Chapman Catt and led by an energetic Eva Robin, the members began looking ahead to the ratification process. At their November convention, after passing resolutions rejoicing in the "growth of freedom everywhere, and . . . the promise of woman's complete liberation into the great arena of the world," they heard from Catt on "The Coming Democracy." A week later, the group approved Robin's plan for an "intensive" effort to recruit new dues-paying members and cultivate supportive individual and organizational allies across the state in order to whip up "enough public sentiment . . . to influence our legislature to take favorable action" when the amendment passed. In the meantime, Robin would begin contacting every member of the General Assembly to determine "how they stand on the question of the Federal Amendment." No longer using language about "sacrifice and service," the group forthrightly laid a claim to the "great need" for "the participation of women in our government."[64]

Securing Congressional Approval

As the amendment continued its tortuous slog through Congress, the postwar political strategies of the two national organizations came into clear focus. In order to get the lame-duck Senate to follow the House and ratify the amendment, the National Woman's Party undertook another of its attention-grabbing campaigns. As before, the party focused its fury on Woodrow Wilson, insisting that he had not done enough to get Democratic senators to vote in favor of ratification. They felt that he should use all of his political clout on recalcitrant members, such as Delaware's Saulsbury, to get them to change their votes. In their long struggle with Wilson, the NWP's leadership was not mollified when, on December 2, 1918, the president explicitly exhorted the incoming (Sixty-sixth) Congress to pass the Nineteenth Amendment and send it to the states for ratification. Waiting another year was unacceptable; the NWP refused to relent.[65]

No sooner had Wilson left for Paris and Alice Paul had recovered from a bout with influenza (the dangerous "Spanish Flu" that wracked the country during the autumn of 1918) than the NWP instituted a new round of "watch fire" demonstrations. By burning Wilson's speeches (including, by some accounts, those in support of the federal amendment), the party asserted that, until the Senate acted affirmatively, Wilson's "every word on democracy will be fit only for flames of public scorn," as Paul declared in Lafayette Park on December 16. The following day, a contingent of sixteen Delaware Woman's Party members participated in a Boston Tea Party commemoration, with Catherine Thornton Boyle putting the flame to a Wilson text following a speech by Florence Bayard Hilles. As in the past, the group included elite members of the du Pont family (Alice du Pont Ortiz, Josephine Anderson du Pont), middle-class supporters such as Sallie Topkis Ginns and Marie Lockwood, and working women such as Annie Arniel, Mary E. Brown, Annie Stirlith McGee, and her sister-in-law Elizabeth Bussier Stirlith. Whatever the prospects for a positive response from the incoming Congress were, the NWP—including its Delaware branch—was determined to employ its accustomed tactics in the here and now.[66]

The National American Woman Suffrage Association's leadership was moving on, however. Convinced that further attempts to wring

Figure 11. Studio portrait, "Mrs. Catherine Boyle, 908 Young Street, New Castle, Del.," c. 1916. Catherine Thornton Boyle's commitment to the National Woman's Party is evident in her decision to have a formal photograph taken with the party's flag. When she died in 1955, her obituary prominently featured her role as "a member since its beginning of the National Woman's Party." Credit: Library of Congress, https://www.loc.gov/item/mnwp000091/

a positive vote out of the stony Senate would be largely futile, Carrie Chapman Catt and her "Front Door Lobby," led by Maud Wood Park and Helen Hamilton Gardener, began looking ahead to the new Congress and instituting renewed organizing in the states, while also continuing their lobbying efforts in the current Senate. If the Senate surprised everyone by ratifying, then NAWSA's leadership would be ready with ratification campaigns in the states. If the amendment failed the Senate once again, then the new Congress would offer reasonably good chances for passage when it convened. NAWSA would still be ready to secure the necessary three-quarters of state legislatures needed to vote for the amendment to secure ratification. To be sure, the leadership was realistic about the low chances of ratification in some Deep South states, where states' rights platforms and white supremacist legislators held sway. They also knew they needed to mount organized grassroots campaigns in enough likely supportive states to get to the thirty-six required for final ratification.

Delaware was one state that looked promising, largely because it had a Republican governor and legislature. DESA, already energized by the infusion of NAWSA guidance and by the spark of Eva Robin's leadership, welcomed the arrival in mid-January 1919 of one of NAWSA's organizers, Maria S. (Mrs. Albert) McMahon. She quickly got the group focused on four tasks: lobbying the state's legislators to press Senators Willard Saulsbury and Josiah Wolcott to vote "aye" when the amendment came up for another vote; beginning a fundraising effort in order to create a ratification account; undertaking a robust organizing drive in Kent and Sussex Counties; and establishing a satellite office in Dover. If, by chance, the current Senate's vote was positive, then the group would be ready to press for ratification when the state's legislature convened for its biennial session later in January. If it was negative, then grassroots organizing for ratification would be well under way by the time the new Congress met.[67]

As NAWSA's Delaware branch was stitching together the pieces laid out in accordance with the national organization's pattern, the women of the Delaware NWP were enthusiastically following Alice Paul's design. Beginning on New Year's Day 1919, to the tolling of a bell at NWP headquarters, successive phalanxes of protestors gathered in Lafayette Square in Washington, D.C., to tend the urn that had been employed in the first watch fire protests. To keep a "watch fire of freedom" going continually, NWP stalwarts arrived in regular stints, the changing of the guard marked by the tolling of a bell. Each contingent had some relic of Wilson's spoken or written words ready for incineration. It was classic political theater, as dramatic and attention-getting as earlier NWP activities, such as 1917's "silent sentinels" and the "monster picket" leading up to Wilson's second inauguration, had been. The protest also invoked symbols deeply embedded in American history, especially bell-tolling and, in echoes of the Boston Tea Party, invocations of patriotic destruction in the cause of freedom. Pushing at the boundaries of protest, as the NWP generally did, the watch fire participants ignored the terms of their city-issued permit, which confined their activities to Lafayette Park, by moving a smaller urn onto the White House sidewalk. There, as a crowd gathered, the behavior of hostile spectators and the arrests of the suffragists provided some striking photographs for use in NWP publicity: servicemen charging the urn and stamping out the fire; women being knocked over; and city police officers rounding up the suffragists for "violating park regulations and lighting fires on government property." Once jailed, some of the women began hunger strikes.[68]

Among those arrested at these watch fire protests were several Delaware NWP members. Annie Arniel in particular garnered attention as perhaps the feistiest and most committed of the arrestees. By then, she was already the Delawarean with most jail stints to her name, as well as the most days served. Arrested with Paul and three others on January 4, 1919, Arniel posted bond, returned to participate in the protest, and was promptly rearrested. Along with the others, this time she refused to post bond and was sentenced to five days in the District of Columbia house of detention, where she joined a hunger strike. On successive days, other Wilmington and New Castle working women arrived in police wagons, some of them munitions workers from the Bethlehem Steel plant, which was being mothballed. Naomi Schopfer Barrett and Adelina Piunti—at ages nineteen and seventeen, respectively, the youngest of the Delaware arrestees—were factory workers, as were Catherine Boyle and Annie McGee. Mary E. Brown, at age fifty-one, the eldest of the Delaware arrestees, a skilled dressmaker and longtime NWP member, took the whole thing in stride. Notifying her husband, John L. Brown, of her arrest in a January 13 telegram signed "Mother," she indicated that she expected to receive a five-day sentence and let him know that Arniel would be "home tomorrow." She soon received a message from her Philadelphia-based son reading, "Congratulations on Your Fight for Democracy." Upon her return home to Wilmington, Brown told the *Evening Journal* that her jail experience "was of no severe nature. . . . We all went on a hunger strike. . . . Outside of being told not to make so much noise when we talked the prison matron was fairly kind to us, [though when] we asked to have fresh air in our cells . . . the prison authorities decided to turn the heat off entirely and freeze us out." As with earlier protests, the watch fire experience proved important as a bonding process, reinforcing the Delaware NWP members' commitment to the cause through their commitment to each other.[69]

Alice Paul followed up with souvenirs of the women's experiences. Each member who had served a jail, workhouse, or prison term received a "prison pin" of Paul's devising: a brooch in the shape of a prison cell's locked door. Some, such as Arniel, Mabel Vernon, and Hilles, already wore them. But Brown, Barrett, and Boyle received theirs at a "festive . . . luncheon" in Wilmington on January 22 where they were guests of honor. (McGee received hers a few days later; Piunti was arrested but not sentenced to jail. She would be eligible for a "picket pin.") "Proud that they had been imprisoned for the cause of political freedom for women," in the words of a local reporter, the former inmates shared the spotlight with Hilles, for whom the event had originally been planned as a "farewell luncheon."[70]

Farewell? What could take Hilles away from the suffrage struggle? She was leaving for France to join the American Committee for Devastated France, a philanthropic women's group interested in helping with postwar reconstruction. The startling decision would take her far away from any action on the suffrage front—away, in other words, from the cause to which she had been converted in 1913, and that had consumed so many of her waking hours ever since. Her suffrage work had long been a source of friction with her husband, William S. ("Billy") Hilles, who expected her to provide for his "comfort . . . on the 'home' question" whenever she traveled. Now, her travels would take her very far afield indeed. Explaining the puzzling turn of events, Hilles betrayed her weary difference of opinion with Vernon. Whereas Vernon stuck to the NWP line that "the President could get [Willard] Saulsbury's vote for suffrage immediately, with a word, if he wanted to," Hilles averred that she "would not leave" if she felt she could do anything "further during the present session of Congress." Suffragists "will either get" the necessary two senatorial votes "or wait until another session." In the meantime, she would sail for France. She did not return until September.[71]

Hilles's departure deprived the Delaware NWP of its most visible leader. It also coincided with the waning of the national NWP's organized attacks on Woodrow Wilson, and the growing agreement with Hilles's assessment among suffragists at large that they must concentrate on getting the suffrage amendment through the incoming Sixty-sixth Congress, still not scheduled to convene until December. To be sure, when the Delaware General Assembly met in January 1919, both the NWP and the Delaware Equal Suffrage Association were fanning the hopeful ember that a positive vote in the U.S. Senate might yet send the amendment to Dover for ratification before the legislature's sixty-day session ended. Accordingly, both groups pressed state legislators for resolutions urging Saulsbury and fellow senator Josiah Wolcott to change their "no" votes. Anti-suffrage leader Mary Wilson Thompson warned suffragists that, with the world in a period of postwar reconstruction, Senate passage of a suffrage amendment to the U.S. Constitution would be "a dangerous experiment."[72]

Alice Paul remained unwilling to accept the emerging consensus. She would not let the Senate hold the amendment up yet again. On February 9, a day before the scheduled vote, Paul reached into her tactical workbox and pulled out a final new exploit. Once again, NWP members, including Arniel, marched from the group's headquarters to the White House; Wilson was not yet back from Europe. On the sidewalk, they burned, not Wilson's words this time, but an effigy of the president himself. Reaction from the press "ranged from scorn to apathy," noted two of Alice Paul's biographers, but within the NWP, there was concern that the deed had been a "'grave mistake.'" Some two dozen members of the party resigned. "'It approaches so terribly to lynching,'" longtime member Lavinia Dock wrote to Paul. Still, Paul's most devoted followers within the party confronted Wilson when his ship arrived in Boston in late February and again when he spoke in New York on March 4, but by then the NWP's implements no longer cut as deeply as they once had. Equally important, other suffragists put the blame for the Senate's negative vote not on Wilson but on the Woman's Party. Terming the February 9 demonstration "disgraceful," Delaware Equal Suffrage Association President Eva Robin excoriated the NWP while underlining her organization's firm opposition to the party's "methods."[73]

Once the old Congress ended, suffrage leaders began to look to the new, Republican-controlled Congress for final passage of the Nineteenth Amendment. By March, when it was clear that the president would call a special congressional session in order to consider appropriations bills and other crucial national business, suffragists were ready. The special session of the new Sixty-sixth Congress met on May 19, 1919. On May 21, the new House of Representatives passed the Nineteenth Amendment; on June 4, the Senate followed suit. The amendment then went to the states for ratification.[74]

Conclusion

Delaware suffragists' wartime activism had made them sharply alert to questions of democratic citizenship and its elements. Having contributed actively to the war's prosecution as the nation's "second line of defense," to use historian Lynn Dumenil's phrase, both Black and white suffragists enlisted patriotic ideals and patriotic service as arguments and justifications for their right to vote.[75] Yet whatever role the war may have had in "accelerating the passage of the Nineteenth Amendment," by war's end, Delaware's suffragists had already largely abandoned the position, adopted most consistently by NAWSA, that "votes for women" should be granted as a necessary "war measure." In the 1918 election campaign, even the most ardent devotees of the notion that while politics required partisanship, women should strive to be non-partisan, had adopted the stance that in a democracy women should vote and make their political ideas heard. If nothing else, the National Woman's Party, with its pickets, watch fires, and banners, had brought to the fore the contradictions between the ideals for which Americans believed they fought the war and the exclusion of women from democratic practices.

By war's end, too, the Delaware Equal Suffrage Association was a transformed organization. Having bolstered their portfolios and learned some basic political lessons, including the necessity of alliance-building, the limits of petitioning, and the grubby realities of partisan politics, as well as the importance of vibrant leadership, its members were well positioned to work for ratification once Congress sent the federal amendment on its way. No longer would they seek to have suffrage *granted* to them; they planned to *win* what was rightfully theirs.

Similarly transformed was the Delaware Association Opposed to Woman Suffrage, whose leaders had learned valuable organizing skills and accumulated substantial political capital through their relentless emphasis on service, not suffrage, as the desire of true women. In the ratification battle ahead, they would be formidable opponents.

CHAPTER 4

Delaware
The Final State?

On June 26, 1919, the Delaware Equal Suffrage Association held a lively "Victory Luncheon" at Wilmington's Hotel Du Pont. Just a fortnight earlier, on June 4, the U.S. Congress had sent the Nineteenth Amendment to the states for ratification.[1] Several states, starting in the Midwest on June 10, quickly ratified, but Delaware's legislature was not in session and not scheduled to return to Dover until early 1921. If suffragists could persuade Governor Townsend to call a special session for 1920, Delaware might move the amendment on to victory. At the luncheon, the organization's longtime secretary, Mary de Vou, urged members to "put the will in Wilmington . . . and putting it in Wilmington put it into Delaware." "A Vote for Every Woman by 1920," read the banquet's slogan, echoed in an address by the group's "brilliant and witty" president, Eva Halpern Robin. "Prepare yourselves to be voters," exhorted Ida Perkins Ball, the vice-president. "Delaware can do what other states can do," dauntless advocate Emalea Pusey Warner assured her colleagues.[2]

The members could hardly know how much Warner's—and their—confidence would be tested over the following year. In spring 1920, when Delaware had the chance to become the final state to ratify the amendment, and thus enshrine it in the U.S. Constitution, they and their allies never faltered in expressing (outwardly, at least) their faith that the legislature, called into special session, would come through. In the end, although the State Senate voted to ratify the amendment on May 5, 1920, the House of Representatives abruptly adjourned on June 2 without taking a crucial planned vote. Delaware did not put the amendment over the top. That distinction fell upon Tennessee, whose legislature ratified the amendment by one vote on August 18, 1920.[3] Once the U.S. Secretary of State certified the results on August 26, eligible Delaware women could indeed prepare themselves to be voters.

For Delaware's suffragists, the General Assembly's failure to ratify wrote a frustratingly unsatisfactory conclusion to a story that was decades in the making. During the legislative session, the urgency of the moment was greater than it had been at any time during their decades of organizing and advocating for their rights to full citizenship. If the Nineteenth Amendment failed to achieve ratification in 1920, no one had a clear idea of how much longer the amendment's approval might take. Scarcely a year after their hopeful "Victory Luncheon," Delaware suffragists faced the prospect that, in the 1920 elections, women in the full- and presidential-suffrage states would be voters, but they would not. Women's right to vote would continue to depend on the randomness of their state residence. Scalded, they realized that it was Delaware's anti-suffragists who could claim the moment's victory. Having successfully defeated state-level suffrage in 1913, 1915, and 1917, now, in 1920, the antis had vanquished the suffragists in the most consequential contest of all.

By most political calculations, Delaware's legislature should have supported ratification. With a pro-suffrage Republican governor and Republican control of both houses of the legislature, Delaware fit the profile of states marked by an "alignment of interests between elected politicians and suffragists," where political competition between the two parties was high. Explaining why it did not become the final ratifying state requires placing the story within a larger set of political considerations, both national and statewide. For although that story was in part a tale of women—suffragists and anti-suffragists—facing off with each other over competing visions of womanhood and citizenship, it was never merely that. Instead, the struggle over "votes for women" was enmeshed in long-standing and intractable political divisions within the state's political parties and its legislature, divisions etched deep into Delaware's political history. It was also carried out on a political field whose boundaries had been set by longtime apportionment practices, providing substantial advantages to some members of the General Assembly over others. In Delaware in 1920, all legislative seats—and all votes—were not created equal. Suffrage advocates could hardly escape being ensnared in the state's political history during the special legislative session. Although staggered in June by their loss, once the amendment achieved ratification in August and they finally became voters, they were ready to use the power of their votes to write a new history. The November elections provided the pen, ink, and paper.[4]

A Special Legislative Session, 1919–1920

The Nineteenth Amendment moved rapidly through its first set of ratifications. By the time of DESA's victory luncheon, eight state legislatures had approved ratification. Even before Delaware's Governor John G. Townsend received the amendment officially from Washington, D.C., the Equal Suffrage Association's executive committee had begun discussing the call for a special session of the General Assembly to consider ratification, and a member from Kent County had asked the governor point-blank whether he favored the idea.[5]

Although Townsend was pro-suffrage, he was inclined to do nothing until the General Assembly next met in regular session—in 1921. The recently ended 1919 session had been bruising, largely because of a major revision to the state's school code, initiated as a way to deal with Delaware's poorly funded and scattershot approach to schooling its youngsters. With over four hundred school districts for a population of about 220,000, there was little uniformity in policy or practice, even in the number of school days per year, let alone standards for teacher certification or pay. Most egregious of all, however, was the neglect of African American children's education in a segregated state where, aside from a general state appropriation for education, local school taxes were apportioned by race. White residents' taxes supported white schools, and Black residents' taxes went to Black schools. It could surprise no one, then, that attendance and facilities in schools serving African American children were abysmal, or that teachers struggled to secure basic resources on a daily basis. Backed by the state's most illustrious social reformers and economic leaders, particularly industrialist Pierre S. du Pont, and designed to address the most glaring deficiencies in the educational system, the 1919 code was nevertheless deeply divisive, passing the General Assembly by thin margins. In the House, the bill's fate depended upon "the altered vote of one man," Wilmington Democrat

John Edward "Bull" McNabb, who switched to vote "yes" at a crucial moment. McNabb might not be so generous to Townsend's ambitions in the future. The new code "became law on April 14, 1919," noted its historian, "but the opposition was just beginning." By June, as challenges to the code mounted, Townsend no doubt hoped to stretch out the time before the General Assembly tackled school issues again. If he called a special session, he could not limit its scope to considering the Nineteenth Amendment alone. Under the state constitution, he had the power to call a special session, but not to set its agenda.[6]

The Delaware Equal Suffrage Association decided against making an immediate and direct demand for a special session. Instead, they first began to create the scaffolding necessary to support the work they would need to do to convince the governor to call the session, a process that lasted through the summer and autumn of 1919. The group already had in place key underpinnings, including help (and prodding) from NAWSA's organizer in both Kent and Sussex counties, an "energetic" Dover branch, a fundraising operation, and a substantial group of supporters who had, during wartime Red Cross and Liberty Loan campaigns, acquired layers of knowledge and experience to add to their existing talents. At the June 26 Victory Luncheon, DESA members mixed discussions of the practical steps necessary to secure their desired goal with celebration and reminiscence. Sentimental speeches by beloved older figures such as Martha Churchman Cranston ("the little grandmother of Delaware suffragists") and Emma Worrell reminded them of their lengthy common struggle, while renewing the members' determination to forge ahead.

Mabel Lloyd Ridgely, now widely known for her leadership in the Liberty Loan campaigns, offered several politically savvy suggestions about next steps, including mounting a statewide operation to educate the public on suffrage and "get public sentiment strong for ratification" so that legislators "would be in no doubt as to how their constituents expected them to vote." The recent school code debacle, she stressed, was an "object lesson" in "the futility of putting things through" without strong public demand behind them. "Interview the legislators who live in your district," she concluded, noting that numbers of them could be found during the summer at the Rehoboth Beach seaside. Four days later, the association named a powerhouse ratification committee, including: Ridgely as chair for Kent County; veteran suffragist Margaret White Houston of Georgetown as chair for Sussex County; Wilmington's

Emalea Pusey Warner as chair for rural New Castle County; and DESA President Eva Halpern Robin as chair for Wilmington as well as over-all state supervisor. Together, the women had decades of experience in suffrage advocacy and in knowing how to get things done in Delaware. They represented some of the best-connected, most "prominent" (to use a favored adjective) women in the state.[7]

At a July strategy meeting, the group strengthened the ratification scaffold with several additional supports. First, they appointed a state Legislative Chairman, Leah Burton of Lewes, another vigorous Liberty Loan organizer. Burton's name resonated in Delaware and especially in Sussex County; her widowed father, suffragist Dr. Hiram Burton, had served two terms in the U.S. House as Delaware's at-large representa-tive. During that time, Leah had often accompanied him to the nation's capital, likely serving as his assistant and hostess. Early in her suffrage career, Burton, like Ridgely, had supported the Congressional Union (CU) and at one point served as a Delaware delegate to a CU conference. But she had turned away from militancy, gaining "exceedingly impor-tant" experience through wartime service, and was now fully committed to NAWSA's approach to winning suffrage. Perhaps most importantly, along with Margaret Houston, she could presume to speak for Sussex County's women and assert with conviction that, despite anti-suffragist claims, they did indeed want the right to vote.[8]

Three other decisions demonstrated the group's brick-by-brick approach to securing ratification in a special session. Following Ridge-ly's lead, the ratification committee agreed to conduct another "educa-tional campaign." In an alliance-building strategy designed to secure endorsements and sheer numbers, they planned outreach efforts to white women's organizations across the state, including the recently formed Wilmington Junior League, the Woman's Christian Temper-ance Union (WCTU), the Red Cross, and the women's club federation. Their NAWSA organizer Maria McMahon would be returning to assist with forming local suffrage clubs as well, with no membership dues required. Her way would be smoothed by the offer of an automobile and chauffeur from Alice Elsie du Pont, the wife of T. Coleman du Pont, retired president of the eponymous company and champion of a north-south road project (the DuPont Highway). Finally, the commit-tee approved a letter drafted by Eva Robin requesting "support for rati-fication work [from] . . . influential men and women in the State . . . and the use of their names on the committee." Once they had commitments in place, DESA could print new stationery framed by the names and hometowns of "influential" Delawareans from up and down the state. Support for suffrage in all three counties appeared to be overwhelming. Any legislator scanning letters written on the stationery would quickly find notable people from his district. Would he be likely to ignore such individuals who showed up to lobby for ratification? The DESA's secretary's note that "much enthusiasm was shown . . . in regard to ratification" reflected how far the organization had come from the preceding summer when the members could barely muster the time and energy to hold meetings.[9]

The group's plans for an orderly progression toward the special session were disrupted when the state's NWP branch announced that it was creating its own ratification committee and was sending a delegation, which included three picketing veterans, to meet with the governor. They would press the issue of a special session—or demand one, as the case might be. After a summer during which the Delaware NWP appeared to be on hiatus, it buzzed with activity during the first few days of August. Realizing that Florence Bayard Hilles's extended absence in France was depriving them of their accustomed leadership sparkplug, acting chair Martha Derickson Bringhurst shrewdly designated Hilles's nineteen year-old daughter Katherine to speak to Governor Townsend on their behalf. The NWP journal *The Suffragist* gushed that "everyone in Delaware knows and honors the name of Bayard." Townsend was courteous to the group, but stood firm in his view that unless "there is no doubt about the passage of the amendment," he would not call the General Assembly into session. In an implicit endorsement of the Equal Suffrage Association's educational strategy, Townsend signaled that peremptory demands would not work. Nevertheless, with practiced skill, the state NWP staged two attention-getting public events during two August weekends in Wilmington. First, on Sunday, August 3, at the centrally located Majestic Theatre, owned by stalwart NWP member Sallie Topkis Ginns's family, a packed crowd listened to speeches by two former pickets (Annie Arniel and Catherine Boyle) and other NWP members, all focusing on the benefits that suffrage would bring to Delaware women and pressing the urgency of their case. Then, the following Saturday, on the steps of the soon-to-be-demolished downtown courthouse, where the May 1914 procession had concluded, their NWP national organizer,

Jessie Hardy MacKaye, produced a "suffrage street pageant" of ratifying states (by that date, there were thirteen).[10]

Some of the NWP's accustomed tactics backfired, however, when Middletown's Marie Lockwood, chair of its ratification committee, followed up with a letter to Governor Townsend. Modeling it on the national NWP's approach to Woodrow Wilson, Lockwood sought, as the Delaware group's spokeswoman, to hold him responsible for foot-dragging on calling the General Assembly into conference and for the votes of members of his own party. While "professing to be in favor of [ratification] and eager for early action," she claimed, he was actually colluding with "his closest friends and supporters in the legislature" who opposed suffrage. "Such a situation is so unnatural," Lockwood noted, "that it cannot fail to give rise to suspicion among . . . friends of suffrage." Townsend must "shoulder full responsibility" if there was no vote on ratification in 1920. Stung by the letter's accusations, Townsend sent an acerbic reply. He resented both its tone and its insinuation that he was anything but supportive of the Nineteenth Amendment. The NWP's ratification chair had alienated a powerful ally.[11]

The NWP's maneuvering represented, for the Delaware Equal Suffrage Association, something of a replay of earlier events, when the local NWP had sewn confusion in news releases by presuming to speak for all suffragists in the state. This time, DESA was ready with a rapid response. Prompted by an article describing Lockwood as "chairman of the Delaware committee," the association required Wilmington's papers to print a disclaimer and clarification. We have "no connection with any group of women who have resorted to sensationalism, or to partisan attacks on either political party," Eva Robin and Leah Burton wrote in a joint statement. In internal minutes, a secretarial malapropism rendered the NWP as "militarists," but even without naming the militants, the association's public statements made the reference clear. Their organization did not indulge in theatrics, but instead sought to "create sentiment for suffrage by education and organization." In late September, DESA members officially endorsed the calling of a special session.[12]

By December 1919, the Equal Suffrage Association's makeover was complete. Its educational and organizational campaign had led to the formation of twenty-five new affiliates across the state and several hundred new members. At the group's annual convention, strategically meeting in Dover after an automobile parade through town, a friendly Governor

Townsend welcomed the two hundred delegates to the State House. Getting down to business, the women agreed to open a headquarters in the capital city (in anticipation of a 1920 legislative session) and selected a new slate of officers, headed by Mabel Lloyd Ridgely as president. New letterhead printed at around the same time was embellished with the names of "prominent" white women from all three counties. With a bank account holding $650, the group could afford not only new stationery but also the rent on a Dover headquarters and the cost of a secretary's salary. At a reception to open the new headquarters at 231 State Street officially, DESA's members brimmed with optimism about the impending ratification of the Nineteenth Amendment. Twenty-five states had now ratified; surely, women would soon be voting nationwide and selecting political party affiliations. For now, as Leah Burton reminded them, it was "Suffrage First."[13]

Still, there remained the task of convincing a reluctant governor to call the General Assembly into session. Regardless of his support for the Nineteenth Amendment, Townsend had serious doubts, as he confided to Republican Party Chairman Will Hays, that "a majority of our Legislature . . . are willing to vote for the Suffrage Amendment, and at the same time not take up any other legislation." Once called into session, legislators might consider "other legislation," such as revising the school code. Opposition from new school boards to the code's provisions for higher taxes and more bureaucratic oversight had been building since the end of the 1919 legislative session, reaching a crescendo in October and November. Townsend's own party was divided on the code, with at least one of the governor's rivals, Daniel Layton of Sussex County (son of Delaware's at-large congressman), scorning it as autocratic and un-American. Even the best efforts of the code's parent, P.S. du Pont, to sway the opposition by offering millions for new school facilities for white pupils, along with money to replace atrociously inadequate African American schools, could not placate most critics. African Americans were among the code's strongest supporters, but as W.C. Jason, president of Delaware State College in Dover put it on behalf of the state's Negro Civic League, they "have no voice in legislation" in an all-white legislature. It was unlikely that the suffrage amendment would be the sole agenda item if the General Assembly met in 1920.[14]

African American suffragists, largely excluded from the internecine squabbling between DESA and the Delaware NWP, on occasion found themselves included. In her role as ambassador to Wilmington's white clubwomen and suffragists, Blanche Williams Stubbs attended the Equal Suffrage Association's June 26 luncheon, the only African American in the audience. Alice Gertrude Baldwin, Howard High School pedagogy teacher and NAACP secretary, assumed a more visible public position when she participated as a speaker at the NWP gathering at the Majestic Theatre in early August. Fashioned along the lines of Chaucer's *Canterbury Tales*, the program featured short speeches by Annie Arniel ("the taxpayer's tale"), Marie Lockwood ("the nurse's tale"), and others. Baldwin spoke on "The Colored Teacher's Tale." Hers was a talk that highlighted the connection among three signal political issues: woman suffrage, the new school code, and racial segregation. If white suffragists anticipated using their votes to bring Delaware's social and educational institutions into line with those in other states, African American suffragists had higher hopes. With their votes, they expected to help realize—and secure—the school code's promises for African American communities, including equitable educational funding for curricular materials and teacher salaries. P.S. du Pont's pledge of funds for improved school buildings added yet another a hopeful note for the future.[15]

In the context of national events in 1919, however, their hopes remained buds that might never blossom. Almost every day brought reports of African American urban populations in places like East St. Louis and Chicago, Illinois, Knoxville, Tennessee, and Washington, D.C., being terrorized on a scale not seen since before the war. Fueled by resentment of Black wartime gains in jobs and pay, along with housing pressures brought on by the arrival of migrants from the South and fears of Black men in uniform, white rioting took a heavy toll in murder, physical destruction, and abject fear in African American communities. Historians estimate that in 1919 alone, there were twenty-five such incidents, most of them characterized by violent invasions of African American neighborhoods and efforts at community defense by local people, including returning armed veterans. Although Wilmington did not directly experience the "Red Summer" of 1919, the city's three daily newspapers ginned up white readers' fears with sensational reports on "riots" in other cities and regular race-baiting articles. Blanche Stubbs's family's personal experience of racial hostility warranted a small note in an evening paper: residents of the West Sixth Street neighborhood where her daughter Jean and her dentist husband Francis T. Jamison had been living "object[ed] to the occupancy of the house by Negroes" and sought to buy the couple out. As historian Chad L. Williams notes, "the explosion of racial violence" that year challenged African Americans to wonder about "the best strategy for obtaining social and political equality."[16]

Votes for women remained an important strategy for Wilmington's African American suffragists, not only because they sought to gain improvements in schools and schooling but also because they were moving steadily toward achieving the longtime goal of establishing an Industrial School for Colored Girls. Since 1897, educators such as Alice Baldwin and Edwina Kruse had been seeking to implement such a plan. In 1911, Stubbs found supportive white allies in the WCTU, and by September 1919, the Delaware Federation of Colored Women's Clubs, of which she was president, had assumed full responsibility for the planned school. They had a site in Marshallton, a fundraising program, an act of incorporation, a superintendent ready to go to work, and an advisory board that included Equal Suffrage Study Club members Alice Dunbar-Nelson and Mary J. Woodlen. The school would open in June 1920. The women clearly understood that, if they were able to vote, they would be able to lobby in Dover for state support of the school. It remained to be seen, however, whether white Delawareans would willingly see their school taxes go toward improving educational prospects and opportunities for their Black neighbors.[17]

Drama in Dover, 1920: Suffragists and Anti-Suffragists

On March 6, 1920, Governor Townsend did what had by now become expected: he called a special session of the General Assembly to convene on March 22. From the start, controversy and political wrangling were guaranteed. Not only would the legislature consider ratifying the Nineteenth Amendment during the session, but its members would also most certainly revisit the new school code and the revamped taxation system underpinning it. The two topics were hardly separate: supporters of ratification—women's club members, white and African American teachers and school administrators, progressive reformers—were exactly the same people who had advanced passage of the school code. In addition, the state's physicians and pharmacists were hoping the legislature would amend Delaware's alcohol laws to permit them to prescribe "whisky or brandy for medicinal purposes." A fourth matter to be considered, funding necessary bridge construction over the Brandywine River in Wilmington, was urgent, but not likely to bring the masses out to demonstrate on Dover's Green. Suffrage, school reform, taxes, and liquor laws were issues entwined with each other, particularly insofar as legislators associated Prohibition and school reform, like suffrage, with activist women in public arenas. As each new issue sprouted like a vine, ready to trip the unwary, the political stakes for winning suffrage rose.[18]

For months preceding the announcement of Townsend's decision, suffragists and their allies peppered him with letters, telegrams, and petitions pressing him to call the special session. A January handwritten petition from eleven Frankford women represented grassroots support; a letter from Democratic Party stalwart and former U.S. Secretary of State William Jennings Bryan demonstrated the national significance that the special session began to assume. The Delaware Equal Suffrage Association's leaders were confident that over many months they had laid down solid keel timbers that would send the ratification vessel sailing swiftly through the General Assembly. Interviews with "influential men" and women had produced a long list of endorsements, including, finally, one from the State Federation of Women's Clubs. From the "majority in both parties," including both the Democratic and Republican state committees, the women had received "assurances" that "their votes would be cast in favor of ratification." Having learned from NAWSA's "Front Door Lobby" the necessity for laying such groundwork, members of the ratification and legislative committees were conducting polls, securing pledges, strategizing, campaigning, vote-counting, rallying, and persuading, and then, finally, creating lists of legislators' potential votes. At the same time, Mary Wilson Thompson broadcast the "unanimous opinion" of Delaware's anti-suffragists that Delaware should "reject the Susan B. Anthony Amendment" and "stand by the Constitution of the United States."[19]

And so began a two-month period of high drama, the likes of which neither the General Assembly nor the residents of Dover had ever seen. By the time the special session began on March 22, 1920, two additional states, West Virginia and Washington, had ratified the suffrage amendment, bringing the count to thirty-five; one more state's ratification would complete the process. Why not "the little state of Delaware?" The "first state" and its capital became the focus of national coverage, with newspapers from Montana to Florida (and places in between) reporting breathlessly on the ins and outs of events in the State House and on the Dover Green. "Everybody and his mother and sister is heading for the State Capitol," reported the *Philadelphia Inquirer* on March 25. Hotels were packed. The "streets were jammed . . . while the corridors and meagre seating accommodations of the State House fairly groaned under the burden of interested humanity," as the Wilmington morning paper described the scene. The anti-suffragists vowed to "make the Dover green look like a red sea with their rose emblems," while the suffragists "will make the park look like a yellow ocean" of tulips and daffodils (jonquils), their chosen flower. "The situation in Delaware is as tense, taut and tight as it could be," editorialized Montana's *Anaconda Standard*; "the crisis is of national significance." Week after week, headlines following events in Dover lurched from confidence to despair and back again. "Delaware Doubtful," wrote the *Miami Herald*, on March 24, 1920; "Delaware Suffrage Placed in Friendly Hands," was the March 25 headline in the *Philadelphia Inquirer*. But then, "Delaware Fails of Being 36th Suffrage State," concluded the *Duluth News-Tribune* on April 2; and then again, "Women Still Hope for Victory in Delaware," reported the *Fort Wayne News-Sentinel* the very same day. From late March until early June, as the ratification seesaw pitched from side to side, those seeking the safe harbor of certainty experienced nothing but queasy vertigo.[20]

With so much at stake, the national organizations poured resources into the effort. From the start, NAWSA's Carrie Chapman Catt and Nettie Rogers Shuler, the group's publicity director, were frequent presences, until Catt left in mid-May for Geneva to preside over the International Woman Suffrage Association meeting. So too were Maria McMahon, who had helped to revitalize the Equal Suffrage Association, and the politically savvy Republican Women's National Committee representative, Betsy Edwards. The NWP's Alice Paul, having assumed an uncharacteristic pose as "the Betsy Ross of Suffrage," demurely stitching stars onto a ratification flag, was eager to fix the final star into place. To that end, she spent the first eight days of the legislative session in Dover and Wilmington, then returned several times in April and May for key debates, demonstrations, and votes. When the denouement came in early June, Paul was back in Washington, planning a major protest for the Republican Party's nominating convention in Chicago. They were the party in power now. The Woman's Party's day-to-day work was left largely to skilled organizers such as Pennsylvania's Dora Kelly Lewis, along with Mabel Vernon and Florence Bayard Hilles, although other well-known tacticians were present at various times. Both the NAWSA and the NWP workers sent regular dispatches to their respective newspapers, *The Woman Citizen* and *The Suffragist*, variously predicting final victory in the First State and ramping up anxiety about the outcome.[21]

After Mary Wilson Thompson consulted with them in New York, both the president, Mary Kilbreth, and the field secretary, Charlotte Rowe, of the National Association Opposed to Woman Suffrage traveled to Wilmington for a mass rally at the Hotel Du Pont on March 19. The hotel staff had scarcely a day to clean up from a similar event sponsored by the Delaware Equal Suffrage Association. Rowe then continued on to Dover, making it her base for frequent speeches and rallies, but more explicitly for a strong anti-suffrage lobbying effort. Rowe was not only an accomplished speaker and experienced debater, but she also had joined the truly oxymoronic Women Voters Anti-Suffrage Party in her native New York once the 1917 referendum succeeded there. Rowe would use her voting rights—to rescind women's right to vote. As associate editor of the antis' journal, *The Woman Patriot*, Rowe had additional resources at her disposal, rendering her a formidable opponent. Throughout the special session, the paper reprinted anti-suffrage editorials from newspapers, and praised "Splendid Delaware" and "Dauntless Delaware" for "standing firm" against pro-suffrage pressure and "defending her honor as a sovereign state." At one point in April, the editors splashed across the front page a 1916 letter from Woodrow Wilson to Thompson (her husband, Henry B. Thompson and Wilson were friendly fellow Princeton alumni), in which he assured her that he would never change his "well formed convictions" on "the suffrage question" merely to seek votes. It was a pointed commentary on the untrustworthiness of politicians.[22]

As before, the group assailed suffrage as contradictory to the needs and desires of Delaware women. Repeatedly, the group's leadership claimed that the vast majority of Delaware's female citizens did not need or want the vote. On occasion, they claimed to have polls to demonstrate that point. Even if enfranchised, most women would not vote, except, of course, for "colored women," who would turn out in great numbers and vote Republican as a bloc. As before, too, the antis evoked representations of white suffragists designed to paint them as harridans, hussies, ugly crones, discontented wives, worthless mothers, and ambitious careerists. They were, to use a favorite term of the era, "unsexed," and would, once provided with full citizenship, "unsex" the men in their lives. These arguments tapped into fears rising from the Great War's ashes that suffrage was the lever that would overturn and invert the accustomed gender order, and that men's and women's roles would no longer be clear or stable, as they had (presumably) been before the war.[23] Anti-suffrage cartoons reprinted in *The Woman Patriot* and in popular periodicals regularly evoked that theme, with sad sack men juggling babies, laundry, and cooking while their wives charged off to the polling place or the lecture stage.

Rowe's presence brought to the Delaware Association Opposed to Woman Suffrage the national anti-suffrage association's new, more strident line of attack, which it crafted in the aftermath of its 1917 New York loss, tying woman suffrage to "bolshevism" and "socialism" in an effort to link suffrage supporters to wartime charges of disloyalty and to the most radical elements in the Russian Revolution. The description of *The Woman Patriot* on its masthead made explicit connections between opposing suffrage and championing women's traditional roles. The journal was "dedicated to the defense of womanhood, motherhood, the family and the state, against suffragism, feminism, and socialism." Speaking in Wilmington on March 20, Rowe argued that suffrage was "accelerating Bolshevism and other isms more than anything else." Local anti-suffragists followed her path by reviving charges that suffrage leaders were unpatriotic. At a March 26 Dover hearing, Emily Bissell delivered "giant verbal dynamite," as a local reporter framed it, by accusing Carrie Chapman Catt of having been a pacifist during the war. Given the context of the times, in which pacifism had become associated with treason, the claim was indeed explosive.[24]

Bissell's bombshell claim represented her acceptance of the antis' postwar rhetoric. Earlier, her arguments had stressed both how little need she had for voting rights and also the potential of suffrage to destroy "sex harmony" between women and men. Her experiences working with suffragists in the Red Cross and through other wartime volunteerism seem not to have altered her views on suffrage, but only encouraged in her the kind of hyper-patriotism that suffused the air in 1919 and 1920. In adopting that stance, she continued to walk in step with Mary Wilson Thompson. Unlike Thompson, however, who was married to a wealthy cotton manufacturer and employed French governesses and nurses for her five children, Bissell was a single professional woman who earned her own living as a social worker and author. Still, she and Thompson had more in common than the superficial dissimilarity of marital status indicated. Bissell came from a family of bankers and investors, was educated in private schools, and was accustomed to the presence of live-in servants (in 1920, the household in which she lived with her sister and brother-in-law had a cook and a housemaid). Like Thompson and New York's Josephine Jewell Dodge, she had reasons to think that she had little personal need for voting rights. Her family's connections to Delaware's political and social elites meant that she was in a position to call upon governors, senators, and judges at will. When she did, her calls were returned. Bissell's friendship with Delaware's Democratic Senator Willard Saulsbury (she addressed him as "Cousin Plantagenet" and he wrote to her as "Miss Cherrie") and his anti-suffragist wife May du Pont Saulsbury enabled her to tap his help regularly for her Red Cross and anti-tuberculosis work.

Thompson was brash and confident enough to ask Saulsbury to use his congressional franking privilege to officially mail out reams of anti-suffrage literature for free (to his credit, Saulsbury declined the request). Surely, when Bissell and Thompson claimed that women did not want the right to vote, would not use it, and as non-partisan non-voters, had as much influence as they wished, they looked at "women" through the myopic lens of their own elite status and their own experience in getting things done. Accusations of disloyalty against suffragists propped up the anti-suffragists' platform by shaping it into a pedestal on which only they could stand.[25]

The other women whose names appeared on the letterhead of the Delaware Association Opposed to Woman Suffrage were exactly as the Equal Suffrage Association's longtime secretary Mary de Vou characterized them: "well known women of social prominence." To be sure, a few suffragists fit that mold as well, but for the antis, it was solely their "access to money, leisure, and extensive social networks" that facilitated their political activities and shaped their anti-suffragism. Aside from Bissell and Ethel Pyle, the daughter of a leather manufacturer who in 1913 married Eugene I. du Pont, none was a working woman or had the experience of supporting herself. Indeed, in 1920, only three (11.5 percent) of the twenty-six officers and directors were single women, and one of those, Delaware City's Florence C. Hall, a clubwoman and president of her Presbyterian Church's missionary society, appears to have done little for the cause aside from lending her name. Among the wives, several were, like May du Pont Saulsbury, married to high-ranking Delaware lawyers and political figures. They included Elizabeth du Pont Bayard (wife of Thomas F.) and Eliza Corbit Lea (widowed second wife of former governor Preston Lea), as well as Alice Hazel Pennewill, whose husband James was Chief Justice of the Delaware Supreme Court. Others had husbands who were bankers, executives, lawyers, judges, and manufacturers. The women were connected through their marriages and moved in the same elite social circles; their daughters "came out" into society as debutantes at lavish parties. To a woman, they were Protestant; many lived near each other in Wilmington's seventh ward, and most attended the same fashionable Episcopal churches, either Trinity in Wilmington or Christ Church in Greenville. Bissell and Ethel du Pont attended Westminster Presbyterian.

They were patrons of the arts and supported local charitable causes, particularly those serving children or fundraising for health care institutions. Their names appeared on the same membership lists of cultural, social, and heraldic societies, such as the Colonial Dames, the Daughters of the American Revolution (DAR), and agencies dedicated to historic preservation. In those commitments, as well as in their support for the Red Cross and membership in women's clubs, especially the Wilmington New Century Club, they regularly crossed paths with their white middle-class and elite suffragist counterparts. And of course, some encountered—or avoided—suffrage advocates at family gatherings and on ceremonial occasions, for there were Bayards and du Ponts on both sides of the suffrage divide, and observing the niceties of etiquette required inviting political enemies to important social events. Among the five hundred people attending Katherine Lee Bayard Hilles's debut party at the Hotel Du Pont in November 1919 were daughters of three anti-suffrage leaders, including Mary Wilson Thompson's daughter Elinor.[26]

As the political conflict of "antis" versus "suffs" played out in Dover, participants and observers presented it variously as a high-stakes endgame, a melodrama, a comedy of errors, or a tragedy. For much of the press, it was most attention-grabbing as a fight among white women for or against their own voting rights. Not surprisingly, press reports reveled in writing stories filled with imagery of pugilism and warfare, representing the spectacle of women battling each other over the right to vote, with male allies lined up in supportive bastions. And indeed, both pro- and anti-suffrage advocates took pains to demonstrate the strength of their cause's support from men. Largely lost in the narrative was the long-standing strife between the Delaware Equal Suffrage Association and the state's National Woman's Party branch. In later years, Mary de Vou remembered that during that spring ratification campaign, "we all worked together again."[27]

But there are reasons to wonder whether time had dropped fuzzy filters over de Vou's recollections. After several years of rancor between the two organizations, there were visible raw edges that would need smoothing if they were to work together toward their common goal. The NWP established its Dover anchor at the Capitol Hotel. During the legislative session, their captain, Florence Bayard Hilles, was highly visible as a speaker for the suffrage cause, along with Mabel Vernon, but so were Mabel Ridgely and Carrie Chapman Catt. Alice Paul generally kept a low profile. Still, she routinely represented Ridgely's DESA and Catt's NAWSA as having done "little work" in advance of the special session. Although Annie Arniel was in Dover during the legislative session, the NWP seems not to have called upon any of its working-class supporters to represent it in public. The two groups jockeyed to take credit for the work being done and reporters routinely confused readers by variously describing either Hilles or Ridgely as the central figure in the effort. The Equal Suffrage Association had the advantage of a fleet of workers and on-the-ground resources, as well as an established headquarters office. Ridgely lived in her family's historic home on Dover's Green, a short walk from the statehouse. Along with other Dover residents, she was well positioned to buttonhole legislators—literally, with flowers for their lapels—as they traveled around town and in and out of the train station. The NWP had the advantage of Hilles's constant presence and willingness to give the press well-turned quotes.

Yet ratification advocates faced stiff opposition. "Only a political miracle can avert defeat," commented a supportive Wilmington newspaper as the legislative session got under way, noting that a score of House members had signed onto a "round robin" pledging to defeat the ratification bill. Moreover, the moment was one of extreme urgency; where would national suffrage leaders turn if Delaware refused to ratify? Coming face-to-face with the powerful organized opposition may have helped the members of the Equal Suffrage Association and National Women's Party local branches concentrate on finding ways to work together.[28]

In the suffragists' contest with the anti-suffragists, and occasionally in internecine disputes among suffragists, African American suffragists once again found themselves invoked as emblems of the dangers of equal suffrage. As during earlier efforts to amend the state constitution, anti-suffragists resurrected the argument that woman suffrage would expand African American suffrage at the expense of white voters. (The rationale was the same as before: that Black women would turn out in droves to vote Republican, while white women would never vote in proportion to African Americans' numbers and would be as likely to vote Democratic as Republican.) "The crux of the suffrage issue," noted a letter to the consistently anti-suffrage Democratic paper, the Wilmington *Every Evening*, was that it "would add at least 10,000 votes to the Republican Party from colored women, who . . . would vote as the colored men vote." No "true Democrat," the writer concluded, would "vote for such a measure." Woman suffrage, argued *Every Evening* editorialist Merris Taylor, just as he had in 1913 and 1915, would lead to "complete Negro domination." Anti-suffrage appeals asserting that suffrage would be "forced in States that do not wish it," called attention to the amendment's second clause, which conferred enforcement powers on Congress. Such appeals to states' rights framed the Nineteenth Amendment as the sort of "force bill" that would permit federal supervision of elections in order to protect African American voting rights. Democratic Representative "Bull" McNabb from Wilmington dispensed with any niceties of language in making his argument. Flinging a common slur for African Americans around the House chamber, he deplored the ratification process, claiming that if women won the right to vote, "Democrats will never elect another Representative to the Legislature from Wilmington." Lobbing the slur a second time, he advocated taking away voting rights from Black men, as well.[29]

Difficult as it may have been for African American suffragists to read such assaults on their characters, they took measures in defense of themselves. Within a few days of McNabb's speech, Wilmington's Sunday newspaper, the *Star*, carried a letter from Emma Gibson Sykes, founding vice-president of the Equal Suffrage Study Club. In it, she assailed McNabb by name as "a disgrace" and instructed him to find "a more reasonable . . . excuse" to oppose ratification than needless attacks on "[N]egro women." These women have, she asserted, "enough burdens to bear" without such "unnecessary ones." It should be "plain" that Black women's votes could never numerically dominate elections; moreover, where African American women were already voting, they voted "to the satisfaction of all and for the benefit of all." Shifting gears, Sykes reminded readers of the wartime sacrifices of Black soldiers who "gave up their lives for Delaware," but whose "mothers and sisters" were now being made "objects of ridicule." And in a final riposte, she offered praise for "noble suffragists" such as Hilles and Catt, who, in her telling, had made common cause with Black women in pursuit of suffrage. In something of a stretch in the face of the historical record, she lauded Delaware's white suffragists for refusing any suffrage plan that excluded Black women. In this way, Sykes sought to situate discussions of African American women's suffrage firmly within the constellation of pro-suffrage arguments that emphasized the clear and simple justice of all women's entitlement to "the privileges of citizens."[30]

African American suffragists contended with familiar anti-suffrage affronts, but they also dealt with suffragists' skittishness over cross-racial alliances. To anyone who knew Florence Bayard Hilles's checkered history in invoking racially tinged arguments, let alone the numerous compromises that Carrie Chapman Catt made with southern white suffragists, Emma Sykes's praise for white allies would have appeared overly generous. But Sykes's compliment may have been strategic, and Hilles's relationships with African American suffragists were complex. In 1914, Sykes had marched with the Equal Suffrage Study Club in the Hilles-organized Wilmington suffrage parade, which created one of the first tentative lines of connection between the club and the Congressional Union. Other club members, particularly Blanche Williams Stubbs and Alice Dunbar-Nelson, associated with Hilles and the CU by accepting invitations to CU-sponsored events, such as luncheons and conventions. The women returned the favor, opening the Garrett Settlement House for a CU meeting in 1916 at which Stubbs sat in the presiding chair and, in 1918, inviting Hilles to speak on suffrage at the annual meeting of the Delaware Association of Colored Women's Clubs, of which Stubbs was president. At the moment when Sykes was responding to "Bull" McNabb's racial diatribes in the General Assembly, an Equal Suffrage Study Club meeting heard Hilles urge the members to affiliate with the NWP. The women responded with a resolution urging the legislature to ratify the Nineteenth Amendment and pledging to send a copy of the resolution to every member of the legislature. Dunbar-Nelson then undertook joint speaking engagements with Hilles in Wilmington and Delaware City designed "to arouse the colored women in the city and to secure their aid in winning the battle."[31]

With Black women's potential as voters being deployed in Dover as a threat or "a boogie," to use Josephine du Pont's language, in order to deter legislators from supporting ratification, it is hardly surprising that members of the Equal Suffrage Study Club preferred to spend their time in community meetings rather than at Dover rallies. Even so, they were no doubt aware of NWP organizers' anxiety and dismay about Hilles's overtures, particularly her encouragement to Black suffragists to attend a rally in Smyrna scheduled for April 14, at which she and du Pont would speak. Because the rented event space, the local Century Club building, was segregated, the anti-suffrage cohort seized the opportunity to call attention to suffragists' seeming embrace of racial equality—and once more to haunt the legislature with the specter of the "colored women's vote." According to Philadelphia's Dora Kelly Lewis, in Dover as an NWP organizer, antis had "gone all about in Smyrna seeing the negroes . . . & telling them that Mrs. Hilles wants them all to come" to the event. In the end, the antis did not get the spectacle they hoped for. Some four hundred white suffragists (and some antis) turned out to hear the local suffrage club president, Marjorie Josephs Speakman, and the scheduled speakers, both of whom were white, stress the perennial pro-suffrage argument that their cause was one of "justice only," as du Pont had put it in an earlier speech.[32]

African American suffragists were deeply familiar with the anti-suffragists' repeated and unapologetic use of racially charged visual materials and texts, particularly in the Jim Crow states. (Black women antis were as rare as water lilies in a desert.) But the Smyrna event is an indicator of the extent to which both NAWSA and the NWP were willing to accept Black disfranchisement as the price for achieving ratification in those states.[33] Dora Lewis's position was fairly typical of that taken by leaders of the two national suffrage organizations: don't raise the "race question," but when the antis do, deflect if possible. By April 1920, the fifty-seven year-old Lewis was a seasoned NWP organizer who had earned her stripes as a picketer, watch fire starter, and hunger striker. Recounting Hilles's meetings with African American suffragists, she asserted the NWP's position: "I tried to tell her how we have always (with great difficulty) kept ourselves clear of the negro question but she didn't like me saying anything that implied the least criticism of her action." At that historical moment, she believed, "The injection of the negro question could easily wreck all our hopes." Added to her frustration was her exasperation with Hilles, whom she considered both "indiscreet" and "difficult to manage." (Hilles herself might not have disputed the characterization.) Caught between anti-suffragists' blatant racism and white suffragists' deflection strategies, African American suffragists looked toward a better future. They understood that, if women's voting rights became enshrined in the Constitution, the antis in Delaware would lose the effort to keep African American women from the polls, and the Republican Party would be happy to tap into their voting power.[34]

Drama in Dover, 1920: The General Assembly

In the end, the ratification struggle came down not to a contest between pro- and anti-suffrage women, let alone to compelling arguments on the two sides, but to a political contest among male politicians, editors, industrialists, agriculturalists, and businessmen. Despite months of organizing, list-checking, rallying, petitioning, buttonholing and the rest, suffragists were, as Mary de Vou sighed, "little prepared for the weeks of intrigue and double dealing into which they were thrust immediately upon the convening of the Legislature." By 1920, historian Carol Hoffecker reminds us, "the arguments and tactics on both sides . . . were not only well-established but also well-known." The only "unknown element" was "the most crucial—the legislature." Given Republican Party control of the governorship and of both houses of the legislature—in the Senate, they held twelve of the seventeen seats; in the House, twenty-three of thirty-five—an observer might be forgiven for assuming that the amendment would win easy passage. But the Republicans were riven by factional disputes, with Governor Townsend at the center of more than one, and a number of legislators from both parties were still smarting over the new school code. Indeed, some of them, particularly those from Sussex County where both woman suffrage and the code were deeply unpopular, were looking to "lick Governor Townsend" on the suffrage issue and find ways to undo the work of the 1919 legislative session. Added to the toxic atmosphere, the Eighteenth Amendment, establishing national Prohibition, was now in effect (via the Volstead Act); its unpopularity in parts of the state bled over into opposition to woman suffrage, as anti-Prohibition legislators blamed women as a group for supporting the measure, and doctors and druggists were still seeking access to medicinal alcohol. If women voted, who knew what other abhorrent legislation they might support?[35]

The weeks between March 22 and June 2 witnessed an extraordinary series of highs and lows, with dramatic turns that fascinated chroniclers, most of whom focused on two groups of players: pro- and anti-suffrage legislators. As they took their places center stage, all the action initially followed decorous standard procedures. Suffrage supporters introduced the ratification bill with hard-won political aplomb. First, the governor framed the matter as no less than "a world wide question of right and wrong." Then, in the General Assembly, a Republican from Hockessin, Senator John M. Walker, and a Democrat from Townsend, Representative Walter Hart, prepared to place the bill in the hopper. In the House, a familiar round of hearings followed, with pro- and anti-suffrage supporters each allotted the standard two hours for presentations, then thirty minutes for rebuttals. The House leadership scheduled a vote for six days later, March 31.

Decorum soon disappeared, as legislators on both sides found themselves subjects of intense lobbying from national political figures, leaders of their own parties, and constituents. In the hothouse atmosphere of the State House, even the hardiest workers on both sides began to wilt. Representative Hart, the suffrage resolution's sponsor and the only Democrat in the House to declare publicly in its favor, after promising to bring up the resolution for a vote, "mysteriously disappeared" from Dover, likely hoping to postpone a seemingly inevitable defeat. Reports had it that he "was spirited out of the House by one of the woman suffragist leaders [from Connecticut] . . . taking the resolution with him" to his Townsend home, "so it could not be forced to a vote."[36] Accusations of kidnapping flew, as the anti-suffrage legislators made plans either to send the "Sergeant at arms to go to his home and bring him to Dover" or to prepare an "identical resolution" for consideration. Not to be detoured from her chosen path, Mary Wilson Thompson pursued Hart and "secured . . . his written consent" (in other words, a proxy) for the resolution to be called up the following day "in case of his absence." He arrived back that morning, April 1, conveyed by Florence Bayard Hilles "in her machine on her way to Dover." The House defeated ratification by a vote of nine affirmative to twenty-two negative. Of the assembly's nineteen Republicans

Table 1. Vote in Delaware House, April 1, 1920, by County and Party Affiliation

County	Vote: Yes	Vote: No	Not Voting	Absent
New Castle	7 (6R 1D)	6 (D)	1 (R)	1 (R)
Kent	2 (R)	8 (3R 5D)	0	0
Sussex	0	8 (7 R 1D)	2 (R)	0
Totals	9	22	3	1
Totals by Party	8 (R), 1 (D)	10 (R), 12 (D)	3 (R)	1 (R)

Source: "Line-Up on Suffrage Vote," Wilmington *Morning News*, April 2, 1920, 1.

present, only eight supported the measure. All Democrats but Hart voted in opposition. A clear geographical pattern was evident. To a man, every single representative from Sussex County—one Democrat and seven Republicans—opposed the measure (see Table 1).[37]

Covering the reactions of the women in the arena, press reports described scenes of jubilation and dejection. "Some of the antis' leaders shouted and sang," crowding around Thompson to congratulate her "for the great fight she made" as their captain, wrote the *Evening Journal*. Suffragists "looked very downhearted," but vowed to "continue their fight to keep the suffrage issue alive." The pro-suffrage Wilmington *Morning News* offered a vivid portrait of anti-suffragists rushing into the "sacred legislative confines" to congratulate their "champions," then "hoist[ing]" Mary Wilson Thompson to a chair "amidst riotous cheering." From an "improvised rostrum," her deputy, Mrs. Henry P. (Virginia McChesney) Scott "expressed her thanks for the loyalty of the 'boys' who had supported the anti-suffrage position." Both women's husbands provided the papers with quotable comments, praising the "loyal women who had advocated a righteous cause." And Hilles's brother, Thomas F. Bayard, was on hand to laud the antis' states-rights advocacy, and by implication denigrate his famous sister. Her only retort: "He who laughs last, laughs best." In a tactical maneuver, the hapless Hart and two other House suffrage supporters changed their votes to "nay" in order to be able to move later for a reconsideration of the resolution. The House then recessed until April 5.[38]

Promising to stage a second act, suffragists began their campaign again. For a time, they remained away from Dover, undertaking new efforts in Sussex County, in hopes of convincing that county's Republican House members to change their votes. Holding rallies, parades, and band concerts, and collecting petition signatures, they also hoped that a positive Senate vote would lead to a reconsideration by the House. Local papers printed their press releases, which found "a deep interest in suffrage in lower Delaware towns" and particularly highlighted the names and photographs of white suffragists from prominent Sussex County families, including Margaret White Houston and her daughter Elizabeth. During the "respite from lobbying" in the state capital, suffragists focused on rallying to their side the constituents of House members who had voted in the negative. Her voice "quiver[ing] with excitement," Margaret Houston reported encountering "astonishing sentiment for suffrage" in her home county. To be sure, at many turns, suffragists found their heels dogged by anti-suffrage women, who disputed the idea that suffrage enjoyed any support in Sussex County at all. It was "suffragists who do not live in Delaware but are members of a paid lobby doing propaganda work" who were behind any suffrage support in the county, argued Mrs. George (Mary Donnell) Marshall in an April 16 letter to the anti-suffrage editor of the *Every Evening*. But with buoyant optimism, Houston was convinced that Republican House members from her county were "now released" from the anti-suffrage "round robin" pledge they had signed earlier, and were "free to vote which ever way they desire[d]." Surely, they would be willing to reconsider their negative votes.[39]

At the same time, with some hopes of pressing one or two of New Castle County's Irish-American Democratic legislators to change their votes, suffragists promoted early April speeches in Dover and Wilmington by Eamon de Valera, president of the provisional Irish Republic. Irish feminists had won voting rights in 1918 for those aged thirty and older. By tying the cause of Irish independence (a matter close to the hearts of many Irish-Americans) to universal suffrage, Delaware's suffragists sought support for women's voting rights on this side of the Atlantic. De Valera returned to Wilmington on May 17, where he met with three anti-suffrage House Democrats, including "Bull" McNabb. His plea centered on "the prestige it would give the Irish cause should the votes of Irish-Americans in the Delaware Legislature be the direct means of giving the ballot to millions of women." McNabb and the others remained implacable.[40]

Now began the second act of the amendment battle drama. Suffragists returned to Dover on April 20 with a massive daylong rally that capped their efforts at convincing House members to support ratification. Timed to coincide with the Republican Party's state convention and pulled together by the Delaware Equal Suffrage Association's leadership, the event saw "every road . . . ablaze with automobiles decorated with suffrage colors," suffrage banners and flags "being used all over the town," "speeches . . . all day" on Dover Green, and a "crowning feature of the day": a parade of suffragist children, designed to counter the "moth-eaten argument that suffragists do not have children." The signatures of some twenty thousand Delaware suffrage supporters embellished a lengthy set of petition sheets to be presented to the legislature. To the *Every Evening* reporter, it was "an effort to stampede the Republican State Convention." To the *Morning News*, it was a "picturesque and colorful human spectacle," designed to "impress upon Republican[s] that ratification is the desire of the majority" of Delawareans. The convention delegates claimed the Nineteenth Amendment as "an achievement of the Republican party" and "urged their fellows in the legislature to vote to ratify."[41]

When the Senate handed the suffrage forces a key victory on May 5, with a vote of eleven in favor (ten Republicans, one Democrat) versus six opposed (two Republicans, four Democrats) to ratification, the narrative arc seemed to be turning. Moreover, positive votes came from all three counties (five from New Castle and three each from Kent and Sussex) (see Table 2).[42] Perhaps the legislature's Republican members were coming to their senses, suffragists thought. The question now could return to the House for a new vote, bringing the drama to a close. But with a potential defeat still looming over them, pro-suffrage legislators bought time by "forcing an adjournment" until May 17. In the meantime, the Senate's leadership, worried about what might happen in the interim, "placed [the ratification bill] under lock and key" in the Senate office, "for in Delaware bills were known to have been stolen." Once again, suffragists mustered forces numbering in the hundreds to lobby in Dover, targeting House members such as Wilmington Democrat "Bull" McNabb, who claimed that his constituents were overwhelmingly opposed to woman suffrage. In a stunt worthy of their counterparts in the National Woman's Party, Mary Clare Brassington, past president of DESA, and Jane White Pennewill, a Wilmington businesswoman, delivered to "Mr. McNabb's desk in the House chamber" a five-yard-long petition containing over five hundred signatures from constituents—specified as "white women only," likely in a retort to his earlier racial slurs—urging him to support the amendment. Given that it had taken seventeen women, including Annie Arniel, only two hours to collect the signatures, the presentation appeared to rattle a "noticeably nervous" McNabb. Mustering his accustomed bluster, he stammered that "there were not enough women in his district to defeat him and that he expected to be elected" to a seat in the State Senate in the fall.[43]

The third and final act of the drama commenced after the mid-May adjournment. Already, before the break, McNabb had pointed verbal projectiles at suffragists, accusing them of being willing to "buy, bribe, bulldoze, or intimidate members." The bribery charge had been bandied about since April Fools' Day, when Sussex County Republican anti-suffrage Representative James E. Lloyd reported receiving a joke note offering him "a Ford sedan if you will vote for suffrage." The accusation continued to be heard in anti-suffrage circles, and when another House member called upon McNabb to provide specifics as to who was doing the bribing, the usually genteel Mary Wilson Thompson was heard to shout from behind him, "tell them, tell them." The Republican floor leader hushed her. She later admitted that it was all "wild rumors." The Republican and Democratic national and state committees were urging a positive vote, and President Wilson sent a specific message urging "every Democrat in the Delaware Legislature [to] vote for" the suffrage amendment. Nevertheless, it was evident that the ratification effort in Delaware was in dire straits. No House member really budged from his original position, and the national organizations' lobbyists were packing up and moving on. On June 2, an effort to bring the Senate bill up for a vote in the House evaporated into thin air. By a vote of "24 nays to 10 yeas," with one member absent, the House turned it back. The lineup remained in virtual lockstep with the April 1 vote; one Republican from New Castle County shifted from "yea" to "nay." The outcome provoked "wild applause" from the small group of anti-suffragists in the gallery. "I was picked up bodily and set upon a table . . . [and] forced to make a speech," recalled Thompson. The special session then ended, as Hoffecker describes the denouement, not with a bang "but with the proverbial whimper." Red rose petals fluttered in the departing legislators' wake.[44]

Table 2. Vote in Delaware Senate, May 5, 1920, by
County and Party Affiliation

County	Vote: Yes	Vote: No
New Castle	5 (R)	2 (D)
Kent	2 (R), 1 (D)	2 (D)
Sussex	3 (R)	2 (R)
Totals	11	6

Source: "How Senators Voted on the Greatest Issue of the Day,"
Wilmington *Morning News*, May 6, 1920, 1.

In the end, the crucial action occurred backstage. A *Philadelphia Inquirer* reporter had been prescient when he wrote, soon after the House's negative vote, that the naysaying Sussex County Republican legislators had been determined to "lick Governor Townsend." Peering ahead, he predicted that newspaper owner Alfred I. du Pont's actions would be crucial to the eventual outcome.[45] He was correct on the first count. While most Delawareans were watching the dramatic contest between "suffs" and "antis" in April and May, the suffrage bill's fate was being shaped by disputes among male politicians and jockeying by their powerful allies within the state's business, farming, and newspaper worlds. Hostility toward the governor and opposition to woman suffrage from Democratic legislators was to be expected. But why would Republicans oppose Townsend on this matter, especially if they believed Democratic propaganda that "votes for women" would transport their party—and Delaware—to a Shangri-la of Republican political dominance for eons to come?

To begin with, Townsend was unpopular with men from his own party. Some of the dislike, particularly in Sussex County (Townsend's home county), derived from the 1919 struggle over the school code. But Townsend was also ensnared in political dramas affecting two powerful Delaware families. One, the Laytons of Sussex County, counted among their members Delaware's lone representative in the U.S. House, Caleb R. Layton, and his son, Daniel J., the Republican Party's state chairman. Caleb was a suffragist, as was Daniel's wife Laura Schimpf Layton. But when Daniel took an anti-suffrage stance, in part over the school code, in part over personal ambition, his influence as party chairman undercut

Townsend's power to sway legislators' votes. Moreover, Daniel Layton's ambition to be chosen as one of the two Sussex County delegates to the Republican National Convention, scheduled to meet in Chicago in June, became the source of an "open fight" in Sussex County "in an effort to defeat" Townsend in his desire for the same appointment. Townsend was pledged to support T. Coleman du Pont for national committeeman. After the April 1 negative House vote on the amendment, rumors spread that Layton had a "written memorandum" from Sussex County members "pledg[ing] themselves to vote for suffrage" if Townsend agreed to give up the delegate race. At the end of March, he offered to do so, but his Sussex County opponents remained unmoved.[46]

At the same time, in an "only in Delaware" scenario, Townsend's allegiance to Coleman du Pont (of the DuPont Highway plan) meant that he was caught in long-standing infighting within the state's most prominent family. Pierre S. du Pont, the philanthropic school reformer and patron of the new school code, had been feuding with his cousins, Coleman and Alfred I. du Pont. At one time, the three men had run the family business together, but now they were bitterly divided over the control of its stock and its future, and over political matters, particularly a 1919 bill to amend the state's corporate law. All three men were Republicans, and both Coleman and Alfred owned local Wilmington newspapers (the *Evening Journal* and the *Morning News*, respectively). In the 1918 elections, they had forged a "unity" agreement that led to the party's control of both houses of the General Assembly, but by 1920, "unity" was nowhere to be found. Daniel Layton was one of Alfred du Pont's minions, while Townsend was affiliated with Coleman du Pont. When it became known that Alfred's *Morning News* had endorsed ratification, and that he "might confer" with his cousin Coleman in an effort "to have the suffrage amendment ratified," some believed that he could sway legislators' votes. In fact, no votes were swayed.[47]

There were other backstage players, as well. Contemporaries and historians echoed the argument of suffragists themselves that "the liquor interest" spent lavishly to defeat suffrage. In Delaware, where the governor was a prohibitionist, that argument was occasionally repeated during the ratification struggle, despite the fact that the Eighteenth Amendment had already been federally ratified in January 1919, and the Volstead Act, enabling its enforcement, had gone into effect a year later. Moreover, the state's two lower counties had enacted local option laws in 1907, leaving

Wilmington "a wet island in a dry sea." To be sure, the state's Woman's Christian Temperance Union members were a significant element in the Delaware Equal Suffrage Association from the start, and the state WCTU furnished a key bloc in the political coalition of suffrage supporters. But once Martha Cranston stepped down as WCTU president in 1915, and especially once the state legislature had ratified the Eighteenth Amendment in 1918 and then passed strict alcohol restrictions in 1919, the temperance-suffrage nexus lost its salience. By early 1919, the leadership overlap between the state WCTU and DESA had largely vanished; unlike Cranston, her successor, Sussex Countian Lena Messick, took no official part in state suffrage organizations. During the 1920 special session, physicians and druggists lobbied for an exception to the 1919 restrictions (the "Klair Law") in order to acquire liquor for "medicinal purposes," but they were unsuccessful. Whether "Bull" McNabb's support for their plea bore a connection with his opposition to suffrage is impossible to establish.[48]

Equally difficult to pin down is the claim that various business interests, especially the railroads, opposed ratification of the Nineteenth Amendment. The Pennsylvania Railroad and its subsidiaries were powerful entities in Delaware. As one of the state's largest property owners, hence one of the largest taxpayers, the railway experienced new obligations under the 1919 school code. Perhaps, too, like downstate commercial farmers and Wilmington leather and textile manufacturers, its managers feared that women voters would support Progressive-Era legislation creating new workplace protections for women and child workers. Such concerns affected legislators' votes insofar as they projected into the future their assumptions about how women would vote, and which party women voters would support. Those assumptions, like others about women's possible voting patterns, depended upon which "women" they had in mind when they imagined women at the polls: their wives and mothers; office secretaries and stenographers; African American maids, cooks, and laundresses; or women toiling in the state's fruit and vegetable fields, canneries, and textile mills.[49]

In the ins and outs of the ratification struggle in Dover, however, the backstage element that deserved the spotlight most and got it the least was the extreme malapportionment of General Assembly seats. An artifact of Delaware's vanishing agrarian past in an era of increased commercial farming (Townsend made his money in banking and in the

lumber, truck farming, and canning businesses) and growing manufacturing strength, as well as its long history of political corruption, the
distribution of legislative seats in the 1897 state constitution weakened
considerably the votes of New Castle County representatives relative to
population, and bolstered those of both Sussex and Kent Counties. In
1920, New Castle County was home to about two-thirds (66.4 percent)
of the state's population (Wilmington alone constituted almost half of
the state's population), but the county's elected representatives held only
about two-fifths (42.8 percent) of the seats in the Delaware House. By
contrast, Sussex and Kent Counties, with 19.6 and 13.9 percent of the
state's population, respectively, each possessed 28.5 percent of the House
seats. Each representative from New Castle County stood for almost ten
thousand constituents, while each representative from Sussex County
served around forty-four hundred. Wilmington's five representatives
had over twenty-two thousand constituents each (see Table 3). Given that
over a third (35.4 percent) of Delaware's African American population
lived in Wilmington, the apportionment system severely diluted Black
voting strength, just as it watered down the influence of all of New Castle
County's voters. When anti-suffragist leader Mary Wilson Thompson
reminded Governor Townsend of "the menace of the negro vote," and
when anti-suffragist newspaper editors stoked similar fears about African American women's votes, they handily ignored basic math in favor
of fear-mongering.[50]

Given the reality of the apportionment system, it is understandable
that both suffragists and anti-suffragists would deploy so much attention to lower Delaware, attempting to change or nail down votes after
the House's April rejection of the Nineteenth Amendment. But, in combination with the political infighting afflicting Sussex County Republicans, the suffragists' longer-term approaches to organizing the county
undoubtedly had a negative impact. As late as November 1916, the
Delaware Equal Suffrage Association leadership threw up its collective
hands about "the two lower counties" (Kent and Sussex), sighing that "on
account of lack of local support," they could be written off. Yet an experienced NAWSA organizer who spent five weeks in the state in early 1917
managed to recruit three affiliated clubs in Sussex County alone. The
state's NWP workers made a number of valiant efforts to recruit in the
lower counties, beginning in summer 1914, recording some successes,
but those appeared to be temporary, as one year's county organizer

Table 3. Apportionment of Seats in Delaware House of Representatives, by County and Population, 1920

DE pop. in 1920: N=223,003	County pop. as % of state pop.	House Seats as % of all seats	# of people served by each House member
New Castle	N=148,239 66.4%	N=15 42.8%	9,882.6
Kent	N=31,023 13.9%	N=10 28.5%	3,102.3
Sussex	N=43,741 19.6%	N=10 28.5%	4,374.1

Sources: H. Clay Reed, ed., *Delaware: A History of the First State*, 2 vols. (New York: Lewis Publishing Company, 1947), II: 976; John A. Munroe, History of Delaware, 3rd edition (Newark: University of Delaware Press, 1993), 156–89.

might have moved by the next year. During the crucial weeks after the House's initial negative vote, the shards remaining from the broken alliance between DESA and the Delaware NWP remained jagged; it would be difficult to fit them together into one common endeavor. The groups tried, holding some joint rallies in Dover and in Sussex County. Yet each established its own court in the capital city, and the national leaders that they hosted studiously ignored each other's presence. For their part, the anti-suffragists focused their labors on "'missionary' work among the legislators personally," in other words, on political lobbying. Following the April 1 House vote, National Association Opposed to Woman Suffrage national organizer Charlotte Rowe gave speeches in Kent and Sussex Counties, and organized a few anti-suffrage clubs, but the state's anti-suffrage leaders knew that their task was merely to hold the line and prevent House members from changing their votes.[51]

The results of the special session were deeply disappointing to the suffragists from both national and state organizations who had poured so much effort and hope into the Delaware legislature. The inability to get the suffrage amendment ratified rattled Governor Townsend as well. A cartoon published in Alfred du Pont's *Morning News* summed up the truck farmer governor's experience with the session: "I thought I had planted a flower bush," ran the caption, "and behold – 'tis a lemon tree." Not only had he not been able to win ratification for the amendment, but the session had produced other bitter fruits, including a second school code fight in which a bill to repeal the entire code came close to winning in the House. He did not seek another term as governor. For their part, suffrage organizers took their bitter Delaware defeat and moved on to Tennessee, where in August the legislature provided the final ratifying vote needed to add the Nineteenth Amendment to the Constitution.[52]

Delaware Women Vote

With the Nineteenth Amendment ratified, Delaware's suffragists turned to another set of tasks: organizing new voters to register and choose political affiliations, educating them on the issues, informing them about the mechanics of voting, and getting them to the polls in November. Their suffrage experiences had prepared them well for the moment. Indeed, even before the U.S. Secretary of State had certified the amendment on August 26, Alice Dunbar-Nelson gave a local reporter a preview of African American women's plans to exercise "the highest privilege of a citizen . . . cast[ing] a free and untrammelled (sic) ballot." Black women, she reminded him, "are in a very favorable position . . . because they have so many organizations of a fraternal and semi-fraternal nature," and through the Equal Suffrage Club, which had been "studying municipal affairs, and party organization," they would be spreading the word on registration and voting. By early September, the club's members had transformed the group into the Committee of Colored Republican Women and "blocked out the city into workable districts" for voter registration and education efforts. In Bridgeville, Sussex County, a local teacher and clubwoman, Sadie B. Monroe Waters, whose father had been a drummer boy with the storied 54th Massachusetts Volunteer Infantry Regiment in the Civil War, sponsored a rally and candidate forum for African American voters, at which Black women's allegiance to the Republican Party was clearly evident.

The Delaware League of Women Voters, organized on August 27, with Mabel Lloyd Ridgely in the president's chair, and populated by former white suffragists who pledged non-partisanship, was similarly prepared to get women registered in time. Alarmist headlines from local papers warned that women voters had only a small window in which to register, but when registration opened, steady streams of newly enfranchised women arrived at the first hour. "Women at Booths to Register Early; Reveal Ages, Too" ran one headline, revealing the reporter's assumption

Figure 12. "I thought I had planted a flower bush and Behold – 'Tis a Lemon Tree." Political cartoonist George T. Maxwell created this image for the Wilmington *Morning News*. In it, he depicted the 1920 General Assembly's special session as one that bore only bitter fruit for Governor John G. Townsend, Jr. Credit: Wilmington *Morning News*, May 7, 1920.

that women's vanity about age might keep them away. In Milton, theater owner Ida Fox, sustained by sandwiches and a thermos, camped out at the registration office in the early morning hours, "determined" to be the first woman to register in Delaware. Comments on women registrants' "surprising knowledge of the procedure," reports of both white and Black women registering, and statements on women's support for a variety of political parties challenged earlier anti-suffrage arguments that enfranchised women would be "slackers" or would support only one party.[53]

Newly empowered by their voting rights, some former suffragists did more than help others get registered. Delaware's fall elections offered the opportunity for payback against state legislators who had doomed ratification earlier in the year. Perhaps most notably, both Black and white Wilmingtonians targeted Democratic candidate for the State Senate, "Bull" McNabb, for defeat. Not only had he, as a member of the state House, spewed casual racial slurs during legislative debates, as Emma Gibson Sykes pointed out, but he had also used his power in the legislature to undermine support for suffrage by introducing issues considered toxic to women's voting rights, such as lenient liquor laws. Wilmington businesswoman Jane Pennewill headed up the effort against McNabb, announcing it to all and sundry in late October. She had support from African American women in the Republican Party and the womanpower of over one hundred canvassers who "telephoned every woman [who had a phone] in Mr. McNabb's district, made a personal house to house canvass, and held meetings to tell the voters why he should be defeated." McNabb was only the most visible sputtering legislator to face angry women voters. Earlier, during the primaries, a bipartisan group of Sussex County suffragists, led by Seaford Democrat Mary Phillips Eskridge and Republican Anna Fisher Morse, helped defeat Sussex County Representatives James E. Lloyd (a Republican from Blades) and Joseph B. Lord (a Republican from heavily Democratic Seaford), both of whom had allied themselves with McNabb in "firm" opposition to ratifying the Nineteenth Amendment.[54]

The path to the polls was not always easy, particularly outside of New Castle County, and particularly for African American Republican women. What Dunbar-Nelson termed the "Democratic State Machine" sought to intimidate or defraud individuals out of their constitutional right to vote "because of their color or their sex or both." That effort continued during the 1920 campaign. Mincing no words in a long letter to Wilmington's Sunday newspaper, Dunbar-Nelson quoted the state's former U.S. senator, Democrat Willard Saulsbury, who termed African Americans "a dense mass of black ignorance." Recalling the recent sacrifices of Black Delawareans, she pointedly reminded readers that "our colored citizens during the war were considered very desirable, very useful, and very patriotic by the Democratic leaders who now would disfranchise them." The threat of intimidation was not an empty one.

Dunbar-Nelson's letter was written in direct response to two recent events. First, her friend (and sometime rival) and past National

Association of Colored Women president Mary Church Terrell, on her way to make speeches in Dover and Wilmington, was arrested at the Dover railway station, charged with "disorderly conduct." Her offense? Asking the station agent to assist her in finding her Dover host's telephone number. Her "tone," the agent averred, was "far from courteous." Terrell made it to her Wilmington appointment, where a capacity crowd at the National Theatre, outraged at the insult to this leading national clubwoman and suffragist, passed resolutions protesting her arrest and pledging an investigation. Then, on the heels of Terrell's ordeal, the Democratic State Chairman, Henry R. Isaacs, received space in the Wilmington *Every Evening* (whose editor had consistently taken race-baiting anti-suffrage positions) to make an overt threat to all African American voters, women as well as men: they should be prepared to be arrested at the polls if they tried to bypass state election requirements. On the final weekend of voter registration, Isaacs carried out the threat, targeting four African American Wilmingtonians who were fully eligible to register. The arrest warrants were quickly invalidated, but Isaacs got the effect he sought: publicity that would depress registration and turnout among the city's Black voters.[55]

Regardless of the alarms and difficulties raised, NAACP Secretary Alice G. Baldwin reported to the association's New York office that Election Day November 2, 1920, "passed off . . . very nicely and peaceably." "Many women" voted, "and thanks to the instructions given before hand—they voted intelligently and honestly." Jane Pennewill echoed Baldwin's remark, albeit rather condescendingly, noting that "colored women" had "conducted themselves in an extremely creditable manner." Local reporters indulged in the usual smirking comments about husbands needing to stay at home with babies while their wives went off to vote, but by far the most dramatic election outcome was the resounding defeat of candidate "Bull" McNabb. "Badly beaten" in his bid to move to a State Senate seat, McNabb understood that Pennewill and her coworkers had "helped to bring about the result." One day in downtown Wilmington, as Pennewill stood chatting with friends, McNabb drove by. He jumped out of his automobile, grabbed her arm, and excoriated her: "You keep your tongue out of my business!" The Democratic donkey on his lapel pin was a "jackass," McNabb told Pennewill, apparently seeking to add the insult of inappropriate language to the injury of manhandling her. She had a retort ready: "Well, don't make one of your self!"[56]

As in many other states, Delaware's women voters turned out in solid numbers but in somewhat smaller proportions than men. Exactly what the figures were is difficult to pin down, but when registration ended on October 16, around 40 percent of Delaware's 103,000 registered voters were women. Turnout of eligible voters on Election Day appears to have been startlingly high (88 to 93 percent of those registered). By most accounts, women constituted about 42 percent of the day's 96,000 voters. Compared with women in other states and in the context of a long-term downward slide in voter participation that had begun in the late nineteenth century, Delaware women voters' turnout was fairly robust. As scholars have demonstrated, even as states introduced measures to limit access to voting or simply to disfranchise whole categories of citizens, turnout remained high in states where legal barriers to registering and voting were few, elections were close, and parties were competitive. The 1920 election in Delaware fit that mold. Wilmington's anti-suffrage editorialist, Merris Taylor, was left to explain women's enthusiasm for voting, given that his cohort had consistently maintained that nine-tenths of white Delaware women did not want voting rights. Clearly, he concluded, "women who protested against suffrage" decided "prudently and wisely" to accept "the responsibilities thrust upon them" and go to the polls. Perhaps, but Mary Wilson Thompson remained unyielding. "I have always opposed votes for women," she wrote in her 1937 memoir. Indeed, "after more than fifteen years . . . what has been accomplished? The cheapening of womanhood."[57]

As elsewhere, too, political parties took notice of women voters' new electoral significance by appointing them to positions on party committees. Beginning in fall 1920, former suffragists could be found serving on both state and national committees. In October, for instance, Wilmingtonians Annie Arniel and Alice Dunbar-Nelson, and Georgetown's Margaret Houston, accepted appointments to the Women's Republican State Committee. Seaford's Mary Eskridge became a member of the Democratic State Committee and in 1928 was the state's national committeewoman and an advocate for Alfred E. Smith's election to the presidency. Townsend's Anna Reynolds became chairman of the New Castle County Democratic Women's Club in 1922, with the purpose of "arous[ing] the interest of the Democratic women," and bringing women "of the rural districts" into the party's orbit. Like their counterparts in other states, many such women carried out their partisan activities while also participating in the state's women's club federations. The new League of Women Voters maintained the determinedly nonpartisan stance of its predecessor, the National American Woman Suffrage Association, all the while attracting the allegiance of former suffragists from both political affiliations, such as Democrat Mabel Ridgely and Republican Marjorie Josephs Speakman.[58]

Conclusion

A short fifteen months had taken Delaware's suffrage activists from a victory luncheon to a victory . . . but in Tennessee, not Delaware. It had been an extraordinary journey, beginning with the hope that Delaware could be the final state needed to ratify the Nineteenth Amendment, and then terminating in defeat. In the end, it remained unclear what it would have taken for suffrage to win ratification in the "First State." The state had two well-organized pro-suffrage branches of national organizations, national organizers who spent months lobbying in Dover and elsewhere, a well-connected group of anti-suffrage stalwarts, a pro-suffrage governor whose party controlled both houses of the legislature, and a competitive political landscape. Neither the National Woman's Party's storied flamboyant tactics nor the Delaware Equal Suffrage Association's relentless organizing and lobbying, nor a combination of the two, was able to win the day. The tale of Delaware's failure to ratify is a reminder that the specifics of history, locale, personnel, racial politics, demographic gerrymandering, and even personal grudges and pique can matter enough to shape an important historical moment. And such factors can matter more than reasonable argumentation, rational calculation, organizational talent, and passionate advocacy.

Epilogue
After Suffrage

The telegram was urgent. Alice Dunbar-Nelson sent it off to Washington, D.C., late on the evening of February 8, 1921. Its message was simple. She and five other members of the Wilmington League of Colored Republican Women would be in the capital in time to join a "deputation" of sixty African American suffragists who would "wait upon" Alice Paul, chairman of the National Woman's Party (NWP), on February 12. "Waiting upon" was a polite term for the delegation's purpose: to confront Paul regarding her and, by extension, the NWP's unwillingness to defend the voting rights of Black women by pressing Congress for federal enforcement of women's enfranchisement, as provided in the Nineteenth Amendment's second clause. In a similar move at the 1921 League of Women Voters meeting, African American women took the floor with their concerns, but received little satisfaction from other delegates. At stake was the question of whether African American women would enjoy the full citizenship that both white and Black women envisioned for themselves as an outcome of the Nineteenth Amendment's ratification.[1]

Throughout the country, African American suffragists had organized in order to register, educate, encourage, and protect women voters, particularly in states such as Delaware, where women were new voters in 1920. In the Southern states, they met massive resistance by registrars and other public officials determined to impose as complete a disfranchisement on Black women as they had engineered against Black men since the 1890s.[2] With the voting rights of a significant group of women under threat, the leadership of the NAACP and the National Association of Colored Women (NACW) hoped that African American members of the NWP could prevail upon their organization to help ameliorate that threat. At the NWP's convention, white ally Ella Rush Murray supported the African American suffragists' resolution, requesting a congressional investigation of "violations of the intent and purposes" of the Nineteenth Amendment during the 1920 elections. "Unless we of the Woman's Party went on record with a protest against disfranchisement," she wrote in describing her stance, "we could never consider that our work for the 19th Amendment had been finally achieved." Delawareans Dunbar-Nelson, Blanche W. Stubbs, Mary J. Woodlen, Elsie B. Walker, Elmyra [or Elmira] M. Hall, and Cecilia Sterrett Dorrell concurred. There is no evidence that white Delaware delegates in attendance, such as Florence Bayard Hilles, Mabel Vernon, and Annie Arniel, were disposed to support their colleagues, although during the decade, Dunbar-Nelson remained an active NWP supporter and Stubbs participated in some NWP events.[3]

Alice Paul's response was "thoroughly hostile," according to Addie Hunton, the NAACP's field secretary; indeed, she made the delegation wait "until she had time" to see them. Then, Paul dismissed the delegation's concerns, arguing that disfranchisement was a "race" not a "sex" issue. Although the resolution on the floor received some discussion at the NWP convention, it was voted down. The Wilmington delegation returned home, but not until some of the group had attended the dedication of a statue that the NWP was donating to Congress, the very event for which their League of Colored Republican Women had taken up a collection. Commemorating the work of three early suffragists—Elizabeth Cady Stanton, Susan B. Anthony, and Lucretia Mott—the dazzlingly white marble sculpture seemed physically to embody the exclusion of African American suffragists from the story that the NWP's leadership had begun to tell about their movement.[4]

Once back in Delaware, the six women, along with their coworkers in clubs, in the local NAACP chapter, and in churches and community organizations, redoubled their efforts to ensure that in their home state, at least, voting rights would continue to be safeguarded and used by African Americans as well as whites. More to the point, they used their voting rights to place their concerns into the state's public arena. These were concerns that they had pursued throughout the pre-1920 era and that reflected a broad racial justice agenda. Now, as voters, these women could do something about them. The League of Colored Republican Women, for example, conducted ward-level organizing in advance of elections and campaigned for one of Wilmington's handful of Black physicians, Conwell Banton, to sit on the city's new seven-member Board of Education (he had served on the old school board). His would be a voice seeking equity within the city's segregated school system. As members of the Delaware Federation of Colored Women's Clubs, energized Black women voters successfully lobbied in 1921 for state funding for the Industrial School for Colored Girls, then astutely named a building at the school for the state's supportive new governor, William Denney. The school's sound financial footing meant providing a stable mechanism for the federation members' vision of managing "delinquent" girls, while creating professional opportunities for the middle-class women who served as teachers, matrons, and social workers. (Dunbar-Nelson taught at the school throughout the 1920s.)

Federation members also took the lead in pressing Delaware's congressional delegation on a major anti-lynching bill, and in opposing any attempts by the revived "infamous Ku Klux Klan" to organize in the "fair State of Delaware" or hold meetings in public spaces. (The new Klan was not only racist but also anti-Semitic, and anti-Catholic.) A proposed 1923 Klan meeting on the steps of the Wilmington municipal building at Tenth and King Streets, a literal stone's throw from "Teacher's Row," might incite "riotous acts," argued a group that included women from the federation and the NAACP, Blanche Stubbs and Dunbar-Nelson among them. They won, and the meeting was prevented. In claiming their right to use public spaces, and to be safe while doing so, Black women voters refused to back down when threatened. In 1927, in her capacity as director of the Garrett Settlement House, Stubbs lodged a formal complaint with Wilmington's Park Commission over an incident that occurred when she took a group of her students, aged three to twelve, to use playground equipment at a local park. They were denied access. Her action sparked a major NAACP-led protest against African Americans' exclusion from public parks.[5]

The experiences of Delaware's African American suffragists during the 1920s offer an entry point for considering the opportunities and challenges afforded to all Delaware women voters in the wake of the Nineteenth Amendment's ratification. Although the uses to which women put their voting rights were a constant source of public discussion, argument, and contestation during the 1920s, they did not vote as a bloc, as many observers predicted, nor did they uniformly support proposals framed as "women's issues," such as a federal child labor amendment. Insofar as scanty available information enables scholars to draw any conclusions, it appears that women's and men's vote choices followed "generally similar patterns." That is, women made decisions based on social experience and values, just as men did. In 1920s Delaware, former suffragists could be found registering as Republicans and Democrats, or affiliating with the Progressive Party, the Socialist Party, or the Prohibition Party (former DESA president Martha Cranston, aged seventy-four, ran for presidential elector on the 1920 Prohibition ticket). NWP activists Mary E. Brown and Elizabeth Stirlith, along with Arden suffragists Donald and Frank Stephens, organized votes for a Liberal Party candidate in 1922, then for the Progressive Party ticket in 1924.[6] Women voters in general, and presumably in Delaware too, voted in somewhat lower percentages than men did, but overall voter participation had been declining for two decades before 1920. In Delaware, as elsewhere, there were women voters, but there was no "women's vote."

There was, however, a Black women's vote.[7] In 1920, the Republican Party still commanded the votes of African Americans—of those who were not disfranchised, that is. As pundits had predicted, Delaware's African American women registered and voted enthusiastically for Republican candidates. Their support helped to elect Warren G. Harding to the presidency and William Denney to succeed John Townsend as governor, and to reelect Caleb R. Layton to the state's at-large seat in the U.S. House. But as Layton soon learned, African American women's fidelity to the party of Lincoln rested upon the expectation that Republican elected officials would stand with them on a broad platform of equality and racial justice. When Layton failed to support the Dyer Anti-Lynching Bill in Congress, the Delaware State Federation of Colored Women's Clubs passed a resolution pledging to support only "those who are our friends" in the fall 1922 elections. Led by the local branch of the NAACP and by Alice Dunbar-Nelson, who chaired the federation's legislation committee, a coalition of activists registered thousands of new voters who, in turn, voted for Layton's Democratic opponent. Layton lost. To be sure, it was still anomalous for Black Delawareans to vote for a Democrat, and few African Americans willingly questioned what one national clubwoman termed their "superstitious loyalty" to the Republicans.

Layton's fate was a warning sign that the solid wall of African American support for his party could be breached. Organized clubwomen were helping to wield the chisels and hammers. As yet, few followed up by registering as Democrats. But Dunbar-Nelson did, announcing "why I am a Democrat in 1924," and signing on as director of the "colored division" of the Democratic National Committee. Four years later, along with her husband, Robert Nelson, she canvassed for the Democratic presidential candidate Alfred E. Smith, the first Catholic to secure a major party's nomination for the office. A vote for Smith was a vote against the lynchers and the Ku Klux Klan, she argued. She and other Black Democrats may have been denounced as "traitors to the party that gave them the right to vote," but in their willingness to support Smith, as historian Lisa Materson has demonstrated, they became the leading edge of a political realignment that saw the emergence, in the 1930s, of a Democratic Party that drew the allegiance of both Northern African Americans and Southern white supremacists.[8]

For their part, Delaware's white former suffragists moved smoothly into the political spaces their votes afforded them. Unlike their African American counterparts, they chose disparate party affiliations; like them, they looked to influence state legislators through party apparatuses. But a number also joined the new League of Women Voters, the officially nonpartisan—but unabashedly political—successor organization to the National American Woman Suffrage Association (NAWSA). Under its umbrella, they carried out voter education and Americanization projects while strategically identifying women voters' priorities, thereby tapping into legislators' assumptions about a "women's vote." The vehicle for moving sponsored legislation onto the General Assembly floor was the Women's Joint Legislative Committee, a coalition of white women's groups, including the Delaware State Federation of Women's Clubs, the state teachers' association, the Consumers' League, the Woman's Christian Temperance Union, and the women's committees of the state's two main political parties. Mabel Lloyd Ridgely led both the League of Women Voters and the Joint Legislative Committee, whose membership lists were filled with the names of suffrage leaders.

When the state's General Assembly met in 1921, those names were familiar to returning members. The skills the women had honed during their long years of suffrage and wartime organizing meant that they were ready with a set of priorities and suggestions for model legislation, and armed with know-how in lobbying for their proposals. Throughout the 1920s, those proposals included another revision of the school code, improved school funding, legislation designed to improve the health and welfare of women and children, protections for working women and children, consumer legislation, and juvenile justice reform—all in conformance with Delaware's segregation laws. The Delaware League of Women Voters also took positions on issues facing Congress, including disarmament, ending sex discrimination in the federal civil service, and restoring the citizenship of American-born women who married foreign-born men. On occasion, their presence in the State House brought up echoes of the past, such as when the suffragists' old foe, the Wilmington *Every Evening*, penned stinging critiques of their "conduct." Predicated on ideas about how proper middle-class white women should comport themselves, such complaints sought to limit women's public activism by defining it as outside the pale of respectability.[9]

Though the Joint Legislative Committee supported separate funding for African American schools and institutions, white women did give heft to some of the priorities of their Black counterparts. They did not, however, share African American women's vision of an expansive canvas on which to situate Black voting rights. A proposal that white women's club members support abolition of the use of the whipping post, a barbaric criminal punishment that fell heavily on the state's African American men, got nowhere. Only toward the end of the decade did Delaware witness the development of tentative cooperative efforts across racial lines, this time over the appalling housing conditions that Wilmington's Black population endured, an issue that Alice Dunbar-Nelson had first highlighted in her 1914 investigative reports for the *Star* newspaper.[10]

Former anti-suffragists, too, chose their political affiliations and made decisions about which state and federal policies they would support. Nationally, former anti-suffragists formed the core of a highly conservative group of voters and politicians, their stances shaped by their endorsement during the Great War and the postwar "Red Scare" of attacks on radicals, socialists, and others smeared as disloyal. Led by Mary Kilbreth, president of the National Association Opposed to Woman Suffrage and boosted by the organization's journal, *The Woman Patriot*, anti-suffragists for a time continued efforts to undo the Nineteenth

Amendment's ratification, insisting that it was illegal or (oddly) unconstitutional. The Supreme Court settled the issue in a unanimous 1922 decision (*Leser v. Garnett*) confirming the amendment's constitutionality. Nevertheless, Kilbreth and the *Woman Patriot* labored to tar the activities of clubwomen and members of the League of Women Voters, the WCTU, the YWCA, and the Women's Trade Union League with the brush of radicalism, describing them as "tools" of "International Socialism," entwined in a "spider web" network of "socialist-pacifist" organizations. At the national level, the former antis remained a reliable font of critique and nay-saying. Their activities testified to the nonexistence of any women's voting bloc.[11]

In Delaware, as on the national stage, a major piece of federal legislation brought former anti-suffragists' views into open discussion: the Sheppard-Towner Act of 1921. Aimed at reducing the United States's alarmingly high rates of infant and maternal mortality, the law provided matching funds to states for prenatal and well-baby clinics. Delaware quickly accepted the money; the clinics' success reduced the state's infant mortality rate (in the first year of life) from one hundred deaths per one thousand live births in 1923 to eighty-one per one thousand in 1929. Former anti-suffragists denounced the law as a "socialistic" intrusion on America's families and "an invasion of states' rights." Once again, Florence Bayard Hilles was on the opposite side of an issue from her brother, Thomas F. Bayard, who in 1922 won a special election for U.S. senator. In 1926, he read into the *Congressional Record* a thirty-six page petition from the former anti-suffragists affiliated with *The Woman Patriot*, adding his view that Sheppard-Towner "conform[ed] to Bolshevik ideas coming out of Russia." Other former Delaware antis were a milder bunch, generally refusing to adopt such alarmist rhetoric and tactics. Most gave their energies to their clubs, charities, arts associations, and social events in the post-suffrage years. For her part, Mary Wilson Thompson, who had strewn the State House with red rose petals in 1920, preferred cultivating her garden and fundraising for a local charity. As late as 1937, she confidently asserted that "the country has certainly not benefited by the women's vote."[12]

The post-suffrage decade witnessed a series of "firsts" in Delaware, including the first two (white) women to gain admittance to the Delaware Bar in 1923: Sybil Ward and Evangelyn Barsky, both of whom had graduated from the University of Pennsylvania Law School. The same year, Elizabeth Tatnall became the first woman elected to the Wilmington School Board. The first Delaware woman juror in a federal court case, Helen Garrett, got newspaper coverage, as did the "first woman notary," Loretta B. Smith, who worked in the law office of Florence Bayard Hilles's husband William, and the first woman to serve on a grand jury, Bridgeville's Lena Messick, a "well-known club worker and prohibitionist." Soon enough, however, the novelty wore off, and by the time that Roxana Arsht was admitted to the Delaware Bar in 1941, she was only the fifth woman—all of them white—to achieve that distinction. A few notable white women won seats in the General Assembly, but not until 1971 was there a Black woman legislator, when Henrietta Johnson took her seat.[13]

Successes by professional women in arenas previously barred to them were a particular interest of Delaware's NWP cohort, who continued the party's work in Delaware while also joining in activities of the Women's Joint Legislative Committee. Although the NWP, with Alice Paul as chairman, saw its numbers shrink substantially after 1920, the core membership of the Delaware group, led by Florence Bayard Hilles, were stalwarts who remained connected to the party for decades. Bonded by their experience of picketing and protesting, the coterie of perhaps twelve women could be found traveling together to Washington, D.C., when NWP events called. They carried flags at the NWP memorial service for Emmeline Pankhurst in 1929, and participated as Woman's Party "escorts of honor" at Alva Vanderbilt Belmont's lavish funeral in 1933 (Belmont had been a generous financial supporter of the NWP).[14]

As time went on, the funerals of old comrades became occasions for meeting and reminiscing, and for bringing suffrage-hued flowers to graves. Upon Annie McGee's passing in 1934, Hilles and Mary E. Brown were there with bouquets. Brown's own funeral in 1948 induced Mabel Vernon to visit Delaware from her home in Washington, D.C. Brown had served for decades as vice-president and then treasurer of the Delaware branch. Saddest of all was the death by suicide of Annie Arniel in 1924. The most self-sacrificing of the Delaware NWP contingent, with her eight arrests and 103 days spent in jails and workhouses, Arniel was beset by health troubles in the post-suffrage years, including a "nervous breakdown" that required several months' hospitalization under a physician's care. Released to her Wilmington apartment on a Saturday afternoon, that evening she wrote a note to her daughter Rebecca, a graduate nurse studying in Philadelphia, signing it "Goodbye, daughter." Her death certificate gave the cause of death as "asphyxiated by illuminating gas."[15]

As the only extant suffrage organization after the Nineteenth Amendment's certification, the NWP now assumed two roles: curating the narrative of suffrage history; and devising an agenda that might unite former suffragists into a new feminist vanguard. At the white marble sculpture's 1921 dedication ceremony, the NWP claimed for itself the mantle of Seneca Falls. Afterward, the group held commemorative events there and regularly placed wreaths on Susan B. Anthony's grave in nearby Rochester, New York. (It mattered not a whit that Anthony had not attended the 1848 Seneca Falls Convention.) The more daunting task of defining how women might achieve full citizenship became the NWP's post-suffrage *raison d'être*. Led by Paul, as single-minded as ever in her pursuit of political goals, the group followed their charismatic leader as she proposed and planned a strategy. To complete the work left undone by the Nineteenth Amendment and press forward toward Paul's vision of women's full citizenship, in 1923 she proposed a new constitutional amendment, an Equal Rights Amendment (ERA), which the group soon christened the "Lucretia Mott Amendment." However broad a path to full citizenship the amendment seemed to promise, in Paul's interpretation, it was in reality a narrow trail with one signpost: legal equality. Other definitions of equal rights were left by the wayside, whether they involved personal and sexual rights, as some NWP birth control advocates wished, or, more important, advanced an ideal of equality that took into account women's different historical and social experiences from those of men, and the different experiences of women from varied ethnic and racial backgrounds.

The singularity of Paul's and the NWP's vision meant that the group's size shrank considerably, particularly as African American members departed, along with white feminists whose conception of women's future was considerably more expansive, and emancipatory, than Paul's. Rather than uniting, the ERA proposal divided NWP members and other former suffragists along bitterly contested lines. Nevertheless, in 1923, Alice Dunbar-Nelson, following her contrarian instincts, convinced the Delaware Federation of Colored Women's Clubs to endorse a resolution "favoring the passage in Congress of the proposed Equal Rights Amendment, which will give women absolute equality with men before the law."[16]

Others might have departed, but Hilles rededicated herself to the NWP and its perspective on citizenship and equality. For the rest of her life, and with magnetic focus after her husband's death in 1928, Hilles was a passionate advocate for an ERA, giving speech after speech, challenging opponents in debates, and learning to cite chapter and verse on the ways in which state laws discriminated on the basis of sex. Described as "one of the most popular speakers in the Woman's Party," she traveled, spoke, and wrote regularly on the need for an ERA, particularly with regard to women's economic rights. She vigorously opposed all protective labor legislation for women workers and championed the value of women's unpaid labor in the home. From 1933 through 1938, she served as the party's national chairman, and later as honorary chairman. In 1943, the NWP dedicated the new library at its headquarters in Washington, D.C., in her name. Throughout, as Delaware and Wilmington changed, Hilles gave time to other commitments, including the Wilmington Business and Professional Women's Club and the city's Birth Control League, but she remained as committed to the NWP as she had become in 1913, when an encounter with Mabel Vernon at the Delaware State Fair changed the course of her life.[17]

In 2019, one hundred years after the U.S. Congress sent the Nineteenth Amendment to the states for ratification, the Delaware General Assembly wrote something of a coda to its own history by inscribing an Equal Rights Amendment into the state constitution. When in 1955, Delaware's Democratic United States Senator Harris McDowell had agreed to cosponsor an ERA in the Eighty-fourth Congress, he paid explicit tribute to Florence Bayard Hilles, who had died the year before. In his remarks, McDowell framed the amendment as a weapon in the Cold War, one that "will give the Communists a clear answer to their propaganda" about American women's subservience to men. By then, both political parties had endorsed an ERA in their national platforms—the Republicans in 1940, the Democrats in 1944. In 1945, the amendment first made it to the floor of Congress for consideration. Not until the 1960s, however, did the ERA return to the national debate stage for serious consideration. Endorsed by the recently formed feminist organization, the National Organization for Women (NOW) in 1967, a reworded version was introduced to the House in 1969 by the newly elected Shirley Chisholm of New York, the first African American woman to serve in Congress. In 1972, when both houses of Congress passed it by the requisite majorities, then sent it to the states for ratification, Delaware and New Hampshire became the third and fourth states to ratify on March 23, 1972. A fierce backlash against feminist gains manifested itself in opposition to the amendment, however, which went down to defeat in 1982, three states short of the number needed to ratify.[18]

Clearly, Delaware's politics had changed. During the 1960s, court-ordered reapportionment of the General Assembly created legislative districts that were finally equally apportioned, and the legislature now met yearly. By 2015, with women winning state offices, a female governor who had served from 2001 to 2009, support from male elected officials, and a renewed interest in women's rights nationally, Delaware women, led by State Senator Karen Peterson and Suzanne Moore, head of ERANow, worked to revive interest in a federal amendment, an effort that is continuing. With other states amending their constitutions to guarantee women's equal rights, an Equal Rights Amendment to Delaware's constitution seemed a logical step. Shepherded through the General Assembly by Representative Valerie Longhurst and others, and passed in two successive legislative sessions, the amendment entered the state constitution in January, 2019.[19]

Appendix A
Delaware Suffrage Leaders

Delaware suffrage leaders profiled in the *Online Biographical Dictionary of the Woman Suffrage Movement in the United States* https://documents.alexanderstreet.com/VOTESforWOMEN

I. National Woman's Party Suffragists ("militants")

Annie Melvin Arniel 1870–1924

Naomi Schopfer Barrett 1899–1993

Catherine Thornton Boyle [Mrs. Thomas Boyle] 1879–1955

Martha Penny Derickson Bringhurst [Mrs. Frederick Bringhurst] 1876–1957

Mary E. Crossley Valentine Brown [Mrs. John L. Brown] 1867–1948

Josephine Anderson du Pont [Mrs. Victor du Pont] 1853–1943

Sallie Topkis Ginns [Mrs. James Ginns] 1880–1976

Florence Bayard Hilles [Mrs. William S. Hilles] 1865–1954

Marie T. Lockwood 1872–1956

Annie Stirlith McGee [Mrs. Thomas McGee] 1873–1973

Alice Eugenie du Pont Ortiz [Mrs. Julian Ortiz] 1876–1940

Adelina Piunti 1902–1992

Elizabeth Bussier Stirlith [Mrs. Frank Stirlith] 1878–1974

Mabel Vernon 1883–1975

II. Wilmington Equal Suffrage Study Club Suffragists (African American)

Helen Wormley Anderson [Mrs. George Anderson] 1877–1962

Alice Gertrude Baldwin 1859–1943

Bessie Spence Dorrell [Mrs. Frederick Dorrell] 1875–1945

Alice Ruth Moore Dunbar-Nelson 1875–1935

Fannie Hopkins Hamilton [Mrs. George Hamilton, Jr.] 1882–1964

Susie Estella Palmer Hamilton [Mrs. Snowden Hamilton] 1864–1942

Nellie B. Nicholson [Mrs. William H. Taylor] 1888–1965

Blanche Williams Stubbs [Mrs. J. B. Stubbs] 1872–1952

Emma Belle Gibson Sykes [Mrs. George J. Sykes] 1885–1970

Sarah E. Tate 1872–1965

Mary Ellen Taylor 1858–1918

Caroline B. Williams 1875–1971

Mary J. Johnson Woodlen [Mrs. John H. Woodlen] 1870–1933

III. Sussex County African American Suffragist

Sadie B. Monroe Waters [Mrs. George L.Waters] 1872–1971

IV. Delaware Equal Suffrage Association Suffragists

Anna Cootsman Bach [Mrs. Frederick E. Bach] 1858–1931

Ida Perkins Ball [Mrs. J. Frank Ball] 1859–1929

Mary Richardson Bancroft [Mrs. Samuel Bancroft] 1847–1933

Mary Clare Laurence Brassington [Mrs. John W. Brassington] 1872–1966

Emma Jester Burnett [Mrs. Philip Burnet, Sr.] 1853–1929

Leah Burton 1878–1971

Martha Churchman Cranston [Mrs. John Cranston] 1846–1927

Dr. Josephine White De Lacour 1849–1929

Mary de Vou 1868–1949

Mabel F. Donahoe Derby [Mrs. Marshall C. Derby] 1877–1953

Agnes Y. Downey 1871–1945

Rose Lippincott Hizar Duggin [Mrs. William L. Duggin] 1884–1918

Mary Seward Phillips Eskridge [Mrs. John Eskridge] 1883–1967

Ethel Millington Hammond [Mrs. Rosewell Hammond] 1884–1945

Lillian Woolson Hayward [Mrs. Harry Hayward] 1868–1938

Margaret Burton White Houston [Mrs. Robert G. Houston] 1864–1937

Caroline Taylor Hughes [Mrs. James Hughes] 1881–1959

Ella W. Johnson 1869–1959

Anna Brown Jones [Mrs. Don P. Jones] 1871–1956

Margaret Harrigan Kent [Mrs. Benjamin Lundy Kent] 1858–1941

Emma Maria Lore [Mother Mary Cecelia, OSU] 1869–1939

Mary H. Askew Mather 1860–1925

Mary E. Marchand Milligan [Mrs. Joseph H. Milligan] 1852–1915

Winifred Morris 1887–1960

Anna Fisher Morse [Mrs. Willard S. Morse] 1857–1956

Gertrude Fulton Nields [Mrs. Benjamin Nields] 1842–1929

Mary Alexandra Ospina 1879–1925

Jane White Pennewill 1866–1929

May Price Phillips [Mrs. J. Ernest Phillips] 1863–1927

Adda Gould Quigley [Mrs. Winfield Quigley] 1864–1920

Mabel Lloyd Fisher Ridgely [Mrs. Henry Ridgely] 1872–1962

Anna Beauchamp Reynolds [Mrs. W. Harman Reynolds] 1884–1970

Eva Halpern Robin [Mrs. Albert Robin] 1876–1969

Willabelle Shurter 1882–1969

Marjorie Willoughby Josephs Speakman [Mrs. Cummins Speakman]
    1889–1978

Margaret Jones Spicer [Mrs. R. Barclay Spicer] 1875–1952

Alice Lightbown Steinlein [Mrs. Fred Steinlein] 1880–1965

Emalea Pusey Warner [Mrs. Alfred D. Warner] 1853–1948

Emma Worrell 1834–1930

Appendix B
Delaware Women's Suffrage Timeline

Nov. 12, 1869	Wilmington's first women's rights convention. Delaware Suffrage Association founded. It affiliates with the American Woman Suffrage Association (AWSA).
1870s	Married women in Delaware receive the right to make wills, own property, and control their earnings.
1878	Mary Ann Sorden Stuart, the Delaware representative for the National Woman Suffrage Association (NWSA), led by Elizabeth Cady Stanton and Susan B. Anthony, testifies before the U.S. Senate Judiciary Committee in favor of women's suffrage.
1881	Stuart, Stanton, and Anthony address the Delaware General Assembly in an attempt to amend the state constitution to allow women's suffrage.
1884	Belva Lockwood, the "woman's rights candidate for president," speaks at Delaware College in Newark.
1888	Delaware Woman's Christian Temperance Union (WCTU) endorses women's suffrage.

1890	The AWSA and NWSA unite to form the National American Woman Suffrage Association (NAWSA).
June 1895	Commencement exercises at Wilmington's Howard High School feature a debate on woman suffrage and an address by Mary Church Terrell, first president of the National Association of Colored Women (NACW).
1895	Wilmington Equal Suffrage Club (or Association) organized. Delaware Equal Suffrage Association (DESA) founded, affiliated with the National American Woman Suffrage Association (NAWSA).
Dec. 1896	Delaware State Grange endorses woman suffrage.
Jan. 13, 1897	Carrie Chapman Catt, Martha Churchman Cranston, Emalea Pusey Warner, Margaret White Houston, and Emma Worrell address hearing at Delaware constitutional convention in favor of suffrage. The Committee on Elections votes against women's suffrage.
1900	Eligible women paying real estate tax in Delaware granted the ability to vote for school commissioners. Wilmington's Emily Bissell testifies before U.S. House and Senate committees opposing woman suffrage.
1909	DESA signs on to help NAWSA's "great petition drive" for a federal suffrage amendment.
1911	Josephine White De Lacour, M.D., runs for election to the Wilmington school board for the second time; she is supported by the Wilmington Equal Suffrage Association.
1912	Led by Frank Stephens, the Arden single-tax colony forms a suffrage club, affiliated with DESA. Alice Paul becomes chair of the Congressional Committee of NAWSA, which demands a suffrage amendment to the United States Constitution.

1913	Equal suffrage amendment to state constitution fails in Delaware General Assembly.
Feb. 1913	"General" Rosalie Gardiner Jones and her group of "suffrage pilgrims" walk through Delaware on their way to the March 3 national suffrage parade in Washington, D.C.
Mar. 3, 1913	Delaware suffragists participate in national suffrage parade in Washington, D.C., planned and carried out by NAWSA's Congressional Committee, led by Alice Paul. Spectators mob the suffragists.
Apr. 1913	Paul forms the Congressional Union (CU), affiliated with NAWSA but run separately, and focused on a national amendment.
Summer 1913	Wilmington's Mabel Vernon hired as a CU organizer for Delaware; holds a series of suffrage meetings, including street-corner speeches and rallies.
Sept. 1913	Florence Bayard Hilles hears Vernon speak at DESA's suffrage tent at the State Fair in Wilmington and is converted to the suffrage cause.
Nov. 23, 1913	Emmeline Pankhurst, noted English suffragette, speaks in Wilmington.
Dec. 1913	Emily Bissell speaks before the U.S. House Rules Committee as President of the Delaware Association Opposed to Woman Suffrage.
Mar. 19, 1914	Led by Alice Moore Dunbar (later Dunbar-Nelson), Emma Gibson Sykes, Blanche Williams Stubbs, Mary J. Woodlen, Alice Gertrude Baldwin, and others, African American suffragists organize the Equal Suffrage Study Club.
Mar. 1914	Hilles becomes Delaware chair of the CU; begins to plan suffrage parade in Wilmington for May 2.
May 2, 1914	Large suffrage parade in Wilmington.
May 9, 1914	Some Wilmington suffragists travel to Washington, D.C., to participate in national parade.

Summer 1914	Hilles and Elsie Hill speak in seven towns on a two-day tour of Delaware.
Jan.-Feb. 1915	In support of an equal suffrage amendment to state constitution, the "Votes for Women Flyer," Hilles's gaily decorated car, tours the state, taking the suffrage message to many small towns.
Feb. 1915	Paul rebrands the federal suffrage amendment as the "Susan B. Anthony" amendment to differentiate it from other proposals.
Feb.-Mar. 1915	Stubbs and Woodlen publish letters in Wilmington newspapers criticizing racist opposition to African American women's quest for voting rights.
Mar. 1915	Equal suffrage amendment to state constitution fails in Delaware General Assembly.
June 1915	DESA and CU split, with DESA moving out of joint headquarters n Wilmington.
July-Nov. 1915	Dunbar travels throughout Pennsylvania encouraging voters to support woman suffrage in their November referendum. The referendum fails.
Sept. 25, 1915	Hilles and Bissell debate woman suffrage at a local Methodist church.
Nov. 1915	Cranston retires as DESA President after twenty years of service, by which time the organization has 270 dues-paying members.
Apr. 1916	Hilles joins CU-sponsored "Suffrage Special" train trip through full-suffrage states.
June 1916	CU becomes National Woman's Party, completing its split from DESA. DESA President Mary Clare Brassington attends both political party conventions to lobby for suffrage planks in party platforms.
July 4, 1916	Vernon heckles President Woodrow Wilson from the platform at an event in Washington.

July 1916	Alice Dunbar-Nelson attends the Delaware CU convention as a "fraternal delegate" from the Garrett Settlement House.
Aug. 1916	Delaware Federation of Colored Women's Clubs forms, with Stubbs as president.
Oct. 23, 1916	DESA sponsors "Federal Amendment Day" in Wilmington.
Nov. 1916	Jeannette Rankin (R-Montana), becomes the first woman elected to serve in the U.S. Congress. As a NAWSA organizer, she had visited Delaware in 1913.
Dec. 1916	Delaware CU claims thirty-six branch organizations. Vernon and Hilles are in a group that unfurls a suffrage banner in Congress during a speech by Woodrow Wilson.
Jan. 1917	John G. Townsend, Jr., inaugurated as Delaware's governor; declares his support for suffrage.
Jan. 10, 1917	NWP "Silent Sentinels" begin to picket the White House.
Feb. 3, 1917	Hilles (pro) and Mary Wilson Thompson (anti) issue statements on the equal suffrage amendment being introduced to the Delaware General Assembly; the amendment fails in late February.
Feb. 18, 1917	Fifteen "wage-earning women" from Delaware, including Annie Arniel, Mary E. Brown, and Agnes Yerger and her daughter Naomi Schopfer, go to Washington to do NWP picket duty at the White House. The Delaware Association Opposed to Woman Suffrage goes to Dover for a General Assembly hearing.
Mar. 1, 1917	Delaware Day: all White House pickets, led by Vernon, are from Delaware.

Apr. 6, 1917	Congress officially declares war on Germany. NAWSA and NWP take different positions on pursuing suffrage during wartime.
June 25, 1917	Twelve suffrage pickets arrested, including Vernon and Arniel, on charge of "obstructing traffic," and sentenced to three days in the District of Columbia jail.
July 14, 1917	Sixteen women, including Hilles, arrested at the White House and sentenced to sixty days in the Occoquan Workhouse in Virginia, then pardoned by President Wilson after serving three days of their sentence.
Nov. 5, 1917	Some jailed suffragists, including Paul, begin hunger strikes in a bid to be considered political prisoners.
Nov. 6, 1917	New York women win the right to vote through a referendum.
Nov. 7, 1917	Josephine Anderson du Pont holds a reception for Arniel, just released from the Occoquan Workhouse after serving sixty-three days.
Nov. 23, 1917	DESA goes on record as opposing picketing.
Jan. 10, 1918	The U.S. House passes the suffrage amendment, and sends it to the Senate.
Mar. 1918	The Washington Court of Appeals declares all suffrage arrests, trials, and punishments illegal.
June 1918	A group of suffragist munitions workers from Delaware, led by Hilles, waits at the White House for two weeks in a futile effort to see Wilson.
Aug. 6, 1918	Arrests of White House pickets resume.
Aug. 1918	Dunbar-Nelson begins serving as a field representative for the Woman's Committee of the Council of National Defense.

Oct. 1, 1918	The U.S. Senate (Sixty-fifth Congress) defeats the suffrage amendment; both Delaware senators vote against it.
Fall 1918	Eva Halpern Robin becomes DESA President.
Nov. 1918	DESA collects over eleven thousand signatures on a suffrage petition to Delaware's senators; members hand out suffrage literature at the polls.
Nov. 11, 1918	The Armistice ends the Great War.
Dec. 2, 1918	Wilson urges the new Sixty-sixth Congress to pass the suffrage amendment when it convenes.
Dec. 16, 1918	Suffragists begin to burn Wilson's words in watch fires in front of the White House.
Jan. 1–20, 1919	Perpetual watch fires lit at the White House. Delaware suffragists Arniel, Brown, Catherine Boyle, Annie McGee, Adelina Piunti, Naomi Schopfer Barrett, and others participate. Several arrested.
Jan. 3, 1919	Eighteenth Amendment (Prohibition) ratified.
Feb. 9, 1919	Wilson burned in effigy at the White House.
Feb. 10, 1919	U.S. Senate (Sixty-fifth Congress) defeats suffrage amendment. Both Delaware senators vote no.
May 19, 1919	Wilson calls new Sixty-sixth Congress into special session.
May 21, 1919	U.S. House (Sixty-sixth Congress) passes suffrage amendment.
June 4,1919	U.S. Senate (Sixty-sixth Congress) approves suffrage amendment. Thirty-six states are needed to ratify.
June 26, 1919	DESA holds "Victory Luncheon" in Wilmington; makes plans for Delaware ratification push.
Summer 1919	DESA and NWP lobby Governor Townsend to call a special session of the General Assembly to consider ratification.

Aug. 3, 1919	NWP ratification rally in Wilmington. Baldwin speaks on "The Colored Teacher's Tale."
Nov. 1919	DESA votes to open a headquarters in Dover in anticipation of a special session being called; elects Dover's Mabel Lloyd Ridgely as president.
Mar. 22–June 2, 1920	Special session of Delaware General Assembly held, including consideration of suffrage amendment. Pro and anti forces mobilize for a big fight. If successful, Delaware would be the final state needed to ratify. Senate ratifies; House does not.
Apr. 1920	Dunbar-Nelson and Hilles together address gatherings of Delaware African American suffragists.
Apr. 5, 1920	Emma Gibson Sykes publishes letter in Sunday *Star* criticizing racist opposition to woman suffrage.
Apr. 20, 1920	Large suffrage rally held in Dover.
June 2, 1920	Delaware General Assembly adjourns without ratifying the amendment.
Aug. 18, 1920	Tennessee becomes the final state to ratify the Nineteenth Amendment.
Aug. 26, 1920	The Nineteenth Amendment is certified, becoming part of the United States Constitution.
Aug.–Nov. 1920	Delaware women organize, register, and go to the polls. DESA regroups as the League of Women Voters (LWV).
1923	The Delaware General Assembly ratifies the Nineteenth Amendment.
2019	The Delaware General Assembly passes an Equal Rights Amendment to the state constitution.

Notes

Introduction

1. Carol E. Hoffecker, "Delaware's Woman Suffrage Campaign," *Delaware History* 20, no. 3 (Spring-Summer 1983): 149–67; Elaine Weiss, *The Women's Hour: The Great Fight to Win the Vote* (New York: Viking, 2018); Eleanor Flexner, *Century of Struggle: The Woman's Rights Movement in the United States* (Cambridge, MA: Harvard University Press, 1959), 321–24; Ellen Carol DuBois, *Suffrage: Women's Long Battle for the Vote* (New York: Simon & Schuster, 2020), 255–77.

2. Alice Dunbar-Nelson, "These 'Colored' United States: No. 16—DELAWARE: A Jewel of Inconsistencies," *The Messenger* 6, no. 8 (August 1924): 244.

3. John A. Munroe, *History of Delaware*, 3rd edition (Newark: University of Delaware Press, 1993), 154–72; H. Clay Reed and Marion Björnson Reed, *Delaware: A History of the First State*, 2 vols. (New York: Lewis Publishing Company, 1947).

4. "Delaware Suffragists have Waged 21 Year Fight for the Ballot," *Sunday Morning Star*, July 27, 1913, 9.

5. Munroe, *History of Delaware*, 171–72; "Equal Suffrage Convention," Wilmington *Daily Republican*, April 23, 1898, 1.

6. Doris Stevens, *Jailed for Freedom* (New York: Boni and Liveright, 1920), 354. "Watch fire" protests took place in 1918 and early 1919; suffragists marched near the White House with burning torches and, in small urns, set fire to Woodrow Wilson's printed speeches. See Chapter 3 below.

7. See Martha S. Jones, "The Politics of Black Womanhood, 1848–2008," in *Votes for Women! A Portrait of Persistence*, ed. Kate Clark Lemay (Princeton, NJ: Princeton University Press for the Smithsonian Institution, 2019), 29–47.

8. Nancy F. Cott, "Marriage and Women's Citizenship in the United States, 1830–1934," *American Historical Review* 103, no. 5 (December 1998): 1440–75; J.D. Zahniser and Amelia Fry, *Alice Paul: Claiming Power* (New York: Oxford University Press, 2014), 1; Susan E. Marshall, *Splintered Sisterhood: Gender and Class in the*

Campaign against Woman Suffrage (Madison: University of Wisconsin Press, 1997), 93–140; Alexander Keyssar, *The Right to Vote: The Contested History of Democracy in the United States* (New York: Basic Books, 2000), 208, 220; Lori D. Ginzberg, "Radical Imaginings: The View from Atop a Slippery Slope," *Journal of Women's History* 32, no. 1 (Spring 2020): 14–22.

9. Susan Ware, *Why They Marched: Untold Stories of the Women Who Fought for the Right to Vote* (Cambridge, MA: Harvard University Press, 2019); DuBois, *Suffrage*, 5.

10. Anne M. Boylan, *Women's Rights in the United States: A History in Documents* (New York: Oxford University Press, 2016), 3–7, 246; "With Senate Vote, Del. ERA Gets Final Okay," *The News Journal*, January 17, 2019, A7.

11. Paula Giddings, *When and Where I Enter: The Impact of Black Women on Race and Sex in America* (New York: William Morrow, 1984), 164–70; Sarah Wilkerson-Freeman, "The Second Battle for Woman Suffrage: Alabama White Women, the Poll Tax, and V.O. Key's Master Narrative of Southern Politics," *Journal of Southern History* 68, no. 2 (May 2002): 333–74; Candice Bredbenner, *A Nationality of Her Own: Women, Marriage, and the Law of Citizenship* (Berkeley: University of California Press, 1998).

12. "Ex-Councilman J. O. Hopkins Dies," Wilmington *Morning News*, March 12, 1956, 4.

13. *Online Biographical Dictionary of the Woman Suffrage Movement in the United States*, eds., Thomas Dublin and Kathryn Kish Sklar (Alexandria, VA: Alexander Street, 2015–) accessed online at https://documents.alexanderstreet.com/VOTESforWOMEN.

Chapter 1

1. Larry Gara, "Garrett, Thomas 1789–1871, Abolitionist and Underground Railroad Activist" *American National Biography*, February 1, 2000, accessed online at https://www-anb-org.udel.idm.oclc.org/view/10.1093/anb/9780198606697.001.0001/anb-9780198606697-e-1500255; "2 Women to Join Del. Hall of Fame," Wilmington *News Journal*, March 28, 1990, 4; Mary R. de Vou, "The Woman Suffrage Movement in Delaware," in *Delaware: A History of the First State*, eds. H. Clay Reed and Marion Bjornson Reed, 2 vols. (New York: Lewis Historical Publishing Company, 1947), I: 349–53.

2. For a useful, but incomplete, retrospective summary of Delaware's suffrage history, see "Delaware Suffragists have Waged 21 Year Fight for Ballot," and "Suffrage Advocates to Urge Congress to Action," Wilmington *Sunday Morning Star*, July 27, 1913, 9–10 (title varies, hereafter *Star*).

3. Ellen Carol DuBois, *Suffrage: Women's Long Battle for the Vote* (New York: Simon & Schuster, 2020), 6–61; Eleanor Flexner, *Century of Struggle: The Woman's Rights Movement in the United States* (Cambridge, MA: Harvard University Press, 1959); Lori D. Ginzberg, *Untidy Origins: A Story of Woman's Rights in Antebellum New York* (Chapel Hill: University of North Carolina Press, 2005); Judith Wellman, *The Road to Seneca Falls* (Urbana: University of Illinois Press, 2004); Anne M. Boylan, *Women's Rights in the United States: A History in Documents* (New York: Oxford University Press, 2016), 96–117.

4. Faye Dudden, *Fighting Chance: The Struggle over Woman Suffrage and Black Suffrage in Reconstruction America* (New York: Oxford University Press, 2011), 188–207; DuBois, *Suffrage*, 61–83.

5. John Cameron, "Letter from Delaware," *Woman's Journal* 1, no. 14 (April 9, 1870): 107.

6. Mary Ann Sorden Stuart testimony, *History of Woman Suffrage*, eds. Elizabeth Cady Stanton, Susan B. Anthony, et al., 6 vols. (Rochester, NY: various, 1889–1922), III: 95, 158 (hereafter *HWS*).

7. *HWS* II: 353–82; Lori D. Ginzberg, *Elizabeth Cady Stanton: An American Life* (New York: Hill & Wang, 2009), 127–28; DuBois, *Suffrage*, 71–78.

8. Frances Ellen Watkins Harper, "We Are All Bound Up Together," in *Proceedings of the Eleventh Woman's Rights Convention* (New York: Robert J. Johnston, 1866); *HWS* II: 152–56; Ginzberg, *Elizabeth Cady Stanton*, 119–22; Rosalyn Terborg-Penn, *African American Women in the Struggle for the Vote, 1850–1920* (Bloomington: Indiana University Press, 1998), 24–45.

9. Terborg-Penn, *African American Women in the Struggle for the Vote*, 40–41; "Women Who Went to the Polls, 1868 to 1873," *The Selected Papers of Elizabeth Cady Stanton and Susan B. Anthony*, ed. Ann D. Gordon, 6 vols. (New Brunswick, NJ: Rutgers University Press, 1997–2013), II: 645–54, xxiv; *HWS* III: 159 (Mary Ann Stuart's statement); Jane Rhodes, *Mary Ann Shadd Cary: The Black Press and Protest in the Nineteenth Century* (Bloomington: Indiana University Press, 1999), 195–97; Dudden, *Fighting Chance*, 188–91; DuBois, *Suffrage*, 85–86, 104–5; *Minor v. Happersett*, 88 U.S. 162 (1875). On Stuart's local attempt to vote, see "She Tried to Vote," Wilmington *Morning News*, November 23, 1888, 2 (hereafter *MN*).

10. Flexner, *Century of Struggle*, 164–78; DuBois, *Suffrage*, 79–83; Sally G. McMillan, *Lucy Stone: An Unapologetic Life* (New York: Oxford University Press, 2015).

11. John A. Munroe, *History of Delaware*, Third Edition (Newark: University of Delaware Press, 1993), 169–72; "Big Week's Work," Wilmington *Evening Journal*, March 9, 1889, 2 (hereafter *EJ*); Constance J Cooper, "Biographical Sketch of Josephine M. R. White De Lacour," *Online Biographical Dictionary of the Woman Suffrage Movement in the United States*, accessed online at https://documents. alexanderstreet.com/d/1010111665 (hereafter *OBD*); Deanna Lewis, "Biographical Sketch of Ella Weldin Johnson," *OBD*, accessed online at https://documents.alexanderstreet.com/d/1010111719. The towns were Milford, Newark, Townsend, and Wyoming.

12. *HWS* III: 158–59; Wilmington *Every Evening*, January 21, 1881, 2 (hereafter *EE*); Wilmington *Daily Republican*, January 26, 1881, 4; *Delaware State Journal*, January 27, 1881, 2; "She Tried to Vote," 2.

13. The national Grange endorsed woman suffrage in 1893; the Delaware Grange in 1896. *Delaware Gazette and State Journal*, October 30, 1884, 2; Carol E. Hoffecker, *Beneath Thy Guiding Hand: A History of Women at the University of Delaware* (Newark: University of Delaware, 1994), 6–15 (9); "Delaware Suffragists Have Waged 21 Year Fight for Ballot," 9; Jennifer Schneider, "Biographical Sketch of Martha Churchman Cranston," *OBD*, accessed online at https://documents.alexanderstreet. com/d/1009657349.

14. Hoffecker, *Beneath Thy Guiding Hand*, 15.

15. Normal schools offered the alternative of a teaching credential without a degree. Sussex County Delaware suffrage leader Margaret White Houston, for instance, graduated from the short-lived, co-educational Normal Department of the Academy of Newark in 1887. See "Newark Academy Commencement," *MN*, June 18, 1887, 1; and

Anne M. Boylan, "Biographical Sketch of Margaret Burton White Houston," *OBD*, accessed online at https://documents.alexanderstreet.com/d/1009859941.

16. Delaware State University, "History," accessed online at https://www.desu.edu/about/history.

17. "Equal Suffrage Association," *Delaware Gazette and State Journal*, November 21, 1895, 1; "An Interesting Meeting," *Wilmington Daily Republican*, December 18, 1895, 1; "For Equal Suffrage," *MN*, February 4, 1896, 1; "Woman's Suffrage Convention," *Delaware Gazette & State Journal*, April 30, 1896, 2; "Equal Suffrage," *Delaware Gazette & State Journal*, May 7, 1896, 3; "Delaware Notes," *Woman's Journal* 27, no. 20 (May 16, 1896): 160; "Delaware Annual Meeting," *Woman's Journal* 27, no. 50 (December 12, 1896): 399; "For Equal Suffrage," 1; *HWS* IV: 563–64; de Vou, "Woman Suffrage in Delaware," 353.

18. *Debates and Proceedings of the Constitutional Convention of the State of Delaware . . . Commencing December 1, 1896*, 5 vols. (Milford, DE: Milford Chronicle Publishing Co., 1958), I: 417–40; "Woman Suffrage Discussed," *EJ*, January 14, 1897, 6, rendered Catt's name as "Caroline Chapman Catts"; Boylan, "Margaret Burton White Houston"; Boylan, "Biographical Sketch of Emma Worrell," *OBD*, accessed online at https://documents.alexanderstreet.com/d/1009859945; Emily A. Watson Ley, "Biographical Sketch of Emalea P. Warner," *OBD*, accessed online at https://documents.alexanderstreet.com/d/1009656532; Alexander Keyssar, *The Right to Vote: The Contested History of Democracy in the United States* (New York: Basic, 2000), 201.

19. The eventual vote was seven to seventeen, with six members absent.

20. "Women Will Not Vote," *Daily Republican*, February 11, 1897, 1.

21. Munroe, *History of Delaware*, 168.

22. "Don't Be Partisan; Women's Warning," *MN*, September 25, 1920, 5.

23. For Delaware WCTU pro-suffrage resolutions, see *Report of the Twelfth Annual Convention . . . 1891* (Smyrna, DE: n.p., 1891), 24; and *Report of the Seventeenth Annual Convention . . . 1896* (New Castle, DE: n.p., 1896), 31. Martha Cranston headed up the state WCTU's Franchise Department; annual conventions routinely passed pro-suffrage resolutions. See also Janet Zollinger Giele, *Two Paths to Women's Equality: Temperance, Suffrage, and the Origins of Modern Feminism* (New York: Twayne, 1995), 105–6.

24. Gail Stanislow, "Domestic Feminism in Wilmington: The New Century Club, 1889–1917," *Delaware History* 22, no. 3 (Spring 1987): 158–85; Karen Blair, *The Clubwoman as Feminist: True Womanhood Redefined, 1868–1914* (New York: Holmes & Meier, 1980), 111–14; Anne M. Boylan, "Biographical Sketch of Mary Seward Phillips (Mrs. John R.) Eskridge," *OBD*, accessed online at https://documents.alexanderstreet.com/d/1010111651.

25. "Against Woman Suffrage," *EE*, February 20, 1900, 6; Emily P. Bissell, "Woman's Progress Versus Woman's Suffrage," *EE*, March 6, 1900, 4. See also Anne Firor Scott, *Natural Allies: Women's Associations in American History* (Urbana: University of Illinois Press, 1991), 146–65.

26. Dorothy B. Salem, *To Better Our World: Black Women in Organized Reform, 1890–1920* (Brooklyn: Carlson Publishing, 1990), 130–44; Linda Gordon, "Black and White Visions of Welfare: Women's Welfare Activism, 1890–1945," *Journal of American History* 78, no. 2 (September, 1991): 559–90; Judith Weisenfeld, *African American Women and Christian Activism: New York's Black YWCA, 1905–1945* (Cambridge, MA:

Harvard University Press, 1997), 10–11; Adrienne Lash Jones, "Struggle among Saints: African American Women and the YWCA, 1870–1920," in *Men and Women Adrift: The YMCA and the YWCA in the City*, eds. Nina Mjagkij and Margaret Spratt (New York: New York University Press, 1997), 161; Laura M. Pierson, *The Young Women's Christian Association of Wilmington, Delaware: "That They Might Live More Abundantly," History, 1895–1945* (Wilmington: YWCA, 1945); Thomas Dublin and Angela Scheuerer, "Why Did African American Women Join the Woman's Christian Temperance Union, 1880 to 1900," *Women and Social Movements in the United States, 1600 to 2000* (Binghamton, NY: State University of New York at Binghamton, 2000), accessed online at https://documents-alexanderstreet-com.udel.idm.oclc.org/c/1000636143; Rhodes, *Mary Ann Shadd Cary*, 197–200. On Delaware's "no. 2 unions," see *Report of the Twenty-Eighth Annual Convention Delaware Woman's Christian Temperance Union, held in Laurel, Delaware, October 16–18, 1907* (Smyrna: np, 1907).

27. Carol A. Scott, "Biographical Sketch of Blanche William Stubbs," *OBD*, accessed online at https://documents.alexanderstreet.com/d/1009054791; "And Now for Vacation," *EJ*, June 26, 1895, 1; Elizabeth Lindsay Davis, *Lifting as They Climb* (1933; New York: G.K. Hall & Co., 1966), 11, 33; Anne M. Boylan, "Introduction: Delaware's African American Suffragists," *Delaware History* 35, no. 2 (Fall-Winter 2019–2020): 106–16.

28. "Colored Folks Speak," *MN*, January 2, 1897, 2; "Booker T. Washington," *EE*, September 12, 1902, 2; *Give Us Each Day: The Diary of Alice Dunbar-Nelson*, ed. Gloria Hull (New York: Norton), 13–16. See also Salem, *To Better Our World*, 40–43.

29. J. Morgan Kousser, *The Shaping of Southern Politics: Suffrage Restriction and the Establishment of the One-Party South, 1880–1910* (New Haven, CT: Yale University Press, 1974); Rebecca Edwards, *Angels in the Machinery: Gender in American Party Politics from the Civil War to the Progressive Era* (New York: Oxford University Press, 1997), 135–45; Treva B. Lindsay, *Colored No More: Reinventing Black Womanhood in Washington, D.C.* (Urbana: University of Illinois Press, 2017), 96–100; Lisa Materson, *For the Freedom of Her Race: Black Women and Electoral Politics in Illinois, 1877–1932* (Chapel Hill: University of North Carolina Press, 2009), 44–45.

30. Patricia Schechter, *Ida B. Wells-Barnett and American Reform, 1880–1930* (Chapel Hill: University of North Carolina Press, 2001); Dennis B. Downey, "'Mercy Master, Mercy: Racial Politics and the Lynching of George White," *Delaware History* 30, no. 3 (Spring/Summer, 2003): 189–210. In an 1898 speech to a suffrage convention, Mary Church Terrell reframed the WCTU "home protection" argument by reminding her audience of the NACW's commitment to "homes, more homes, better homes, purer homes." Terrell, *The Progress of Colored Women: An Address Delivered before the National American Woman Suffrage Association* (Washington, D.C. Smith Brothers, 1898).

31. Glenda Gilmore, *Gender and Jim Crow: Women and the Politics of White Supremacy in North Carolina, 1890–1920* (Chapel Hill: University of North Carolina Press, 1996); Evelyn Brooks Higginbotham, *Righteous Discontent: The Women's Movement in the Black Baptist Church, 1880–1920* (Cambridge, MA: Harvard University Press, 2003); Salem, *To Better Our World*; Stephanie J. Shaw, *What a Woman Ought to Be and to Do: Black Professional Women Workers during the Jim Crow Era* (Chicago: University of Chicago Press, 1996); Cheryl D. Hicks, *Talk With You Like A Woman: African American Women, Justice, and Reform in New York, 1890–1935* (Chapel Hill:

University of North Carolina Press, 2010), 9–10; Brittney C. Cooper, *Beyond Respectability: The Intellectual Thought of Race Women* (Urbana: University of Illinois Press, 2017), 43–55. See also Weisenfeld, *African American Women and Christian Activism*, 83–90.

32. On Wilmington's African American middle class and the East Side neighborhood, see Annette Woolard-Provine, *Integrating Delaware: The Reddings of Wilmington* (Newark: University of Delaware Press, 2004), 32–36 (39–40); and Carol E. Hoffecker, *Corporate Capital: Wilmington in the Twentieth Century* (Philadelphia: Temple University Press, 1983), 28, 94–96. See also Scott, "Blanche Williams Stubbs"; Alison Lewis, "Biographical Sketch of Alice Gertrude Baldwin," *OBD*, accessed online at https://documents.alexanderstreet.com/d/1009054793; Alanna Gordon, "Biographical Sketch of Emma Belle Gibson Sykes," *OBD*, accessed online at https://documents.alexanderstreet.com/d/1009054792; Stephanie Clampitt, "Biographical Sketch of Caroline B. Williams," *OBD*, accessed online at https://documents.alexanderstreet.com/d/1009594393; Helene Carey, "Biographical Sketch of Nellie B. Nicholson (Taylor)," *OBD*, accessed online at https://documents.alexanderstreet.com/d/1009595399; Anne M. Boylan, "Biographical Sketch of Helen Wormley Anderson (Webb)," *OBD*, accessed online at https://documents.alexanderstreet.com/d/1009805437, and Boylan, "Biographical Sketch of Fannie Hopkins Hamilton," *OBD*, accessed online at https://documents.alexanderstreet.com/d/1009594397. On Edwina Kruse and the community of Howard School teachers and students, see Alice Dunbar-Nelson's sketch, "Pioneer in Work for Colored Schools Celebrates Birthday," *Star*, February 22, 1920, 22; and Kruse's letters to Dunbar in the Alice Dunbar-Nelson Papers, MSS 133, University of Delaware Library Special Collections, Boxes 8 and 9. See also Thelma Young Papers, Delaware Historical Society. Oral history interviews conducted in the 1970s with Dunbar-Nelson's niece, Pauline A. Young, and Newark activist George Wilson, include unsparing details about life in segregated Delaware. See Robert H. Richards, Jr., Delaware Oral History Collection, University of Delaware Library Special Collections: https://library.udel.edu/special/findaids/view?docId=ead/mss0179.xml.

33. [Alice Moore Dunbar,] "Health and Welfare of Negroes a Serious Problem," *Star*, February 15, 1914, 11. Concern about "moral contagion" affecting unprotected African American girls was another theme in middle-class reformers' writings; see Weisenfeld, *African American Women and Christian Activism*, 77–78. See also Edwina Kruse's letters to Alice Dunbar in the Alice Dunbar-Nelson Papers, University of Delaware Library Special Collections.

34. "W.C.T.U. Institute," *EJ*, March 31, 1911, 2; "Work Among Negroes Given in Able Report: Mrs. J. Bacon Stubbs, a Member of the Race, Points out Urgent Needs," *MN*, April 19, 1912, 11; Minutes of the New Castle County Woman's Christian Temperance Union, 1912–1920, entry of May 23, 1912, Woman's Christian Temperance Union Collection, Accession 73.35, Delaware Historical Society, Box 1, Folder 27. For earlier discussions of a "colored" industrial school, see "In the Interest of Colored Girls," *Wilmington Daily Republican*, May 13, 1897, 2; "Home for Wayward Girls," *EJ*, November 9, 1899, 1; "Colored Industrial School," *EJ*, November 24, 1899, 2.

35. For background on the WCTU's racial terrain, see Betty Livingston Adams, *Black Women's Christian Activism: Seeking Social Justice in a Northern Suburb* (New York: New York University Press, 2016), 46–55.

36. "WCTU Institute"; "WCTU Workers Report of Work," *EJ*, May 23, 1912, 2; "For Negro Settlement," *EJ*, April 12, 1913, 8; "Need $3350 For the Colored Settlement," *EJ*, June 12, 1913, 5; "Settlement Dedication," *EJ*, January 10, 1914, 12. Blanche Stubbs to Helen Garrett, undated note [c. 1913] found in Helen Garrett Scrapbook, Delaware Historical Society.

37. "Negro Women to Study Suffrage," *MN*, March 21, 1914, 2; Anne M. Boylan, "Biographical Sketch of Fannie Hopkins Hamilton," *OBD*, accessed online at https:// documents.alexanderstreet.com/d/1009594397; "Ex-Councilman J.O. Hopkins Dies," *MN*, March 12, 1956, 4. Both Alice Dunbar and Edwina Kruse were clients of Fannie Hamilton's dressmaking establishment.

38. Woolard-Provine, *Integrating Delaware*, 43–45; NAACP Papers, Library of Congress, Washington, D.C., microfilm edition, Part 12: Selected Branch Files, 1913–1939, Part B: The Northeast, Reel #1; Anne M. Boylan, "Biographical Sketch of Gertrude W. Nields," *OBD*, accessed online at https://documents.alexanderstreet. com/d/1010111652. On women's leadership in the early years of the NAACP, see Salem, *To Better Our World*, 155–79. Among the key leaders was Alice Gertrude Baldwin's sister, Maria Baldwin, principal of the Agassiz School in Cambridge, Massachusetts.

39. Belle Kearney, "The South and Woman Suffrage," *Woman's Journal* 34, no. 14 (April 4, 1903): 106; *HWS* V: 59–60; Marjorie Spruill Wheeler, *New Women of the New South: The Leaders of the Woman Suffrage Movement in the Southern States* (New York: Oxford University Press, 1993), 113–25, 135–57; DuBois, *Suffrage*, 152–54.

40. "Equal Suffrage Convention," Wilmington *Daily Republican*, April 23, 1898, 1; Trisha Franzen, *Anna Howard Shaw: The Work of Woman Suffrage* (Urbana: University of Illinois Press, 2014), 2, 92. See also "Woman's Suffrage Number," *The Crisis* 10, no. 5 (September 1912).

41. Hoffecker, *Beneath Thy Guiding Hand*, 19–32 (26); Emalea Pusey Warner, Women's College Scrapbook #1, University of Delaware Archives, Newark, Delaware.

42. "Suffrage Hikers Reach This City," *MN*, February 19, 1913, 1–2; "Votes for Women Receive Attention," *Newark Post*, February 26, 1913, 1, 5; "The Suffragists Leave Delaware: They Received a Hearty Welcome at Newark and Elkton," *MN*, February 21, 1913, 8; Shredded Wheat Advertisement, *EJ*, March 6, 1913, 3; Jerron John, "Biographical Sketch of Rosalie Gardiner Jones," *OBD*, accessed online at https://documents.alexanderstreet.com/d/1009656480. See also Mark Taylor, "Utopia by Taxation: Frank Stephens and the Single Tax Community of Arden, Delaware," *Pennsylvania Magazine of History and Biography* 126, no. 2 (April 2002): 305–25.

43. See Nancy F. Cott, *The Grounding of Modern Feminism* (New Haven, CT: Yale University Press, 1987), 16–22.

44. On Arden suffragists, see Frank Stephens Correspondence, Folder 7, Arden-Stephens Papers, Accession #1992.30, Delaware Historical Society. On Delaware's Progressive Republicans (Bull Moose Party), led by Robert G. Houston, see "Progressives Plan Campaign at Dover Meet," *EJ*, August 16, 1912, 2, and "Suffragists Shy at Platform of Progressives," *EJ*, September 24, 1912, 12.

45. "Delaware Suffragists have Waged 21 Year Fight for the Ballot," 9–10 (10); W. David Lewis, "Bissell, Emily Perkins" *Notable American Women, 1607–1950*, 3 vols. (Cambridge, MA: Harvard University Press, 1971), I: 152–53; "Hearing on Equal Suffrage Bill Today," *MN*, February 26, 1913, 12; "Women Ask Legislature for Ballot," *EJ*,

February 27, 1913, 5; Anthony Higgins, ed., "Mary Wilson Thompson Memoir (Part Four)," *Delaware History* 18, no. 4 (Fall-Winter 1979): 251–53.

46. De Vou, "Woman Suffrage Movement in Delaware," 358; Carrie Chapman Catt and Nettie Rogers Shuler, *Woman Suffrage and Politics: The Inner Story of the Suffrage Movement* (New York: Scribner's, 1926), 235–36; "Mrs. Lake to Speak for W.C.T.U.," *EJ*, March 4, 1909, 5; "Hissing of Taft Was Unfortunate," *EJ*, April 27, 1910, 5; *New York Times*, March 17, 1910, 8.

47. "Delaware Suffragists Have Waged 21 Year Fight for Ballot," 10. See also "Women Ask Legislature for Ballot," 5; and "Open Fight for Suffrage Amendment," *EJ*, March 14, 1913, 1–2.

Chapter 2

1. "Suffrage Parade Striking Success," Wilmington *Sunday Morning Star*, May 3, 1914, 1, 23 (title varies; hereafter *Star*); see also the press release prepared by Mary de Vou, Corresponding Secretary of the Delaware Equal Suffrage Association, on which the newspaper relied heavily: Emalea Pusey Warner Papers, VB87A, Folder #4, Delaware Historical Society.

2. "Cheers this Time Instead of Hisses," *Star*, May 10, 1914, 1; "Washington Mob Fights Suffragists," *Evening Journal* (hereafter *EJ*), March 4, 1913, 2, 8; "Suffragists Return Home Looking Well," Wilmington *Morning News* (hereafter *MN*), March 6, 1913, 5; "Parade Struggles to Victory despite Disgraceful Scenes," *Woman's Journal and Suffrage News* 44, no. 10 (March 8, 1913): 73, 78; J.D. Zahniser and Amelia R. Fry, *Alice Paul: Claiming Power* (New York: Oxford University Press, 2014), 146–49.

3. Doris Stevens, *Jailed for Freedom* (New York: Boni and Liveright, 1920), 3.

4. "Delaware Women in Suffrage Line," *EJ*, March 4, 1913, 4; "Mrs. Cranston Marches Today in Suffrage Parade," *EJ*, April 7, 1913, 10; Zahniser and Fry, *Alice Paul*, 52–101, 139–50, 160–65; Christine Lunardini, *From Equal Suffrage to Equal Rights: Alice Paul and the National Woman's Party, 1910–1928* (New York: New York University Press, 1986), 14–16, 34. On the British suffragettes, see Laura Nym Mayhall, *The Militant Suffrage Movement: Citizenship and Resistance in Britain, 1860–1930* (New York: Oxford University Press, 2003).

5. Lisa G. Materson, *For the Freedom of Her Race: Black Women and Electoral Politics in Illinois, 1877–1932* (Chapel Hill: University of North Carolina Press, 2009), 44–45, 229; Paula Giddings, *When and Where I Enter: The Impact of Black Women on Race and Sex in America* (New York: William Morrow, 1984), 127–28; "Marches in Parade Despite Protests," *Chicago Defender*, March 8, 1913, 1; "The Equal Suffrage Parade was Viewed by Many Thousand People from All Parts of the United States," *The Broad Ax* [Chicago], March 8, 1913, 1.

6. Eleanor Flexner, *Century of Struggle: The Woman's Rights Movement in the United States* (Cambridge, MA: Harvard University Press, 1959), 263–64; Marjorie Spruill Wheeler, *New Women of the New South: The Leaders of the Woman Suffrage Movement in the Southern States* (New York: Oxford University Press, 1993), 100–32; DuBois, *Suffrage*, 187–201. See also Belinda A. Stillion Southard, *Militant Citizenship: Rhetorical Strategies of the National Woman's Party, 1913–1930* (College Station: Texas A&M University Press, 2011), 53–89.

7. Wage Earners League for Woman Suffrage Leaflet, March 22, 1911, Leonora O'Reilly Papers, A-39, folder, 111, Schlesinger Library, Radcliffe Institute, Harvard

University; DuBois, *Suffrage*, 173–84. See also Annelise Orleck, *Common Sense and a Little Fire: Women and Working-Class Politics in the United States, 1900–1965* (Chapel Hill: University of North Carolina Press, 1995), 96–100; and Rebecca J. Mead, *How the Vote Was Won: Woman Suffrage in the Western United States, 1868–1914* (New York: New York University Press, 2004), 135–42.

8. Mary R. de Vou to Henry Clay Reed, undated postscript, and letter of September 8, 1946, H. Clay Reed Papers, Special Collections, University of Delaware Library, MSS 0499, Box 4, Folder 66; "City Suffragists Continue Activities," *EJ*, March 10, 1913, 5; "Suffragists at State Fair," *EJ*, April 15, 1913, 12. In 1913, the Delaware State Fair was held in Wilmington in Wawaset Park, off Woodlawn Avenue; Kent and Sussex Counties held a separate, joint fair in Harrington. Lucy Eve Kerman, "Vernon, Mabel," *Notable American Women: The Modern Period*, eds. Barbara Sicherman and Carol Hurd Green (Cambridge, MA: Harvard University Press, 1980), 711–12; "Society in Washington," *New York Times*, March 21, 1890, 1; "In Washington," *New York Times*, June 5, 1892, 10; Madison Heitz, Mia Cimino, and Jessica Sharp, "Biographical Sketch of Florence Bayard Hilles," *Online Biographical Dictionary of the Woman Suffrage Movement in the United States*, eds., Thomas Dublin and Kathryn Kish Sklar (Alexandria, VA: Alexander Street, 2015–) (hereafter *OBD*), accessed online at https://documents.alexanderstreet.com/d/1008342612; Alexandra Nickliss, *Phoebe Apperson Hearst: A Life of Power and Politics* (Lincoln: University of Nebraska Press, 2018), 113–24. See also Amelia Fry's interview with Mabel Vernon, describing the Hilles encounter, in the Suffragist Oral History Project, Bancroft Library, University of California at Berkeley, http://bancroft.berkeley.edu/ROHO/projects/suffragist/, and Florence Bayard's 1890 letters to Hearst in the George and Phoebe Apperson Hearst Papers, Bancroft Library, University of California at Berkeley, available in digital form at https://oac.cdlib.org/ark:/13030/hb0r29n68n/?order=15&brand=oac4.

9. "Wilmington Girl Heads Suffrage Cohort's Active Campaign Here: Miss Mabel Vernon Speaks at Votes for Women Meeting at Court House," *Star*, July 29, 1913, 9–10; "Suffrage Meeting at Fair," 8; "Suffragists Say Their Cause is Winning Friends," *EJ.*, October 13, 1913, 7; "Suffragist Cause before Saturday Crowd," *Star*, October 19, 1913, 1, 6; "Votes for Women War Opens Here," *EJ* September 19, 1913, 1; "Local Suffragists Bar Mrs. Pankhurst," *MN*, October 20, 1913, 1, 9; "Mrs. Pankhurst to Visit Wilmington," Wilmington *Every Evening*, October 22, 1913, 1 (hereafter *EE*); "Mrs. Pankhurst Talks to Local Suffragists," *EE*, November 24, 1913, 2; Fry, Mabel Vernon interview, Suffragist Oral History Project; Flexner, *Century of Struggle*, 264–65. See also Carol E. Hoffecker, "Delaware's Woman Suffrage Campaign," *Delaware History* 20, no. 3 (Spring-Summer 1983): 152–55; and Mayhall, *The Militant Suffrage Movement*, introduction.

10. "New Committee for Suffrage Work at Home," *EJ*, March 4, 1914, 1.

11. Heitz, et al., "Florence Bayard Hilles," *OBD*; Lunardini, *From Equal Suffrage to Equal Rights*, 34–40. See also Florence Bayard Hilles's letter to Alice Paul and Lucy Burns, May 15, 1914, National Woman's Party Records, Library of Congress, Microfilm Edition, Box I:17, Reel 10.

12. "Constance J. Cooper, "Biographical Sketch of Mary R. de Vou," *OBD*, accessed online at https://documents.alexanderstreet.com/d/1010111666; Mary R. de Vou, "The Woman Suffrage Movement in Delaware," in *Delaware: A History of the First State*, eds. H. Clay Reed and Marion Björnson Reed, 2 vols. (New York: Lewis Historical

Publishing Company, 1947), I: 349–70; Fry, Mabel Vernon interview, Suffragist Oral History Project; Mary de Vou letter to Alice Paul, May 7, 1914, National Woman's Party Records, Library of Congress, Microfilm Edition, Box I:17, Reel 10.

13. Mark Taylor, "Utopia by Taxation: Frank Stephens and the Single Tax Community of Arden, Delaware," *Pennsylvania Magazine of History and Biography* 126, no. 2 (April 2002): 305–25.

14. Anne M. Boylan, "Biographical Sketch of Annie Melvin Arniel [Arneil]," *OBD*, accessed online at https://documents.alexanderstreet.com/d/1009054733; and Gabriella Di Marco and Maeve Shields, "Biographical Sketch of Annie J. Magee [or McGee],"*OBD*, accessed online at https://documents.alexanderstreet.com/d/1009054724. On the Arden suffragists, see the Arden-Stephens Papers, Delaware Historical Society, Accession #1992.30. Elenor Getty and Frank Stephens married in 1905; his first wife, Caroline Eakins, had died in 1889. Mayme Statnekoo became a local teacher and principal; her family later shortened their name to Stat. In 1929, she married Benjamin Frank, brother of the legendary Delaware newspaper reporter Bill Frank.

15. "Ex-Sen. Washburn to Talk on Suffrage," *Star*, June 7, 1914, 14; Annette Woolard-Provine, *Integrating Delaware: The Reddings of Wilmington* (Newark: University of Delaware Press, 2003), 30–45; Giddings, *When and Where I Enter*, 95–117.

16. For the Seventeenth Amendment's "profound" impact on Delaware politics, see Carol E. Hoffecker, *Democracy in Delaware: The Story of the First State's General Assembly* (New Castle, DE: Cedar Tree Press, 2004), 150. See also Richard Evans, *The Feminists: Women's Emancipation Movements in Europe, America, and Australia, 1840–1920* (London: Croom Helm, 1977); and Dawn Langan Teele, *Forging the Franchise: The Political Origins of the Women's Vote* (Princeton, NJ: Princeton University Press, 2018), 3–6.

17. "Women Seekers of Ballot in Session," *EJ*, October 30, 1914, 1–2.

18. "Suffragists Re-Elect Officers: Will Urge New Legislature to Amend Constitution in their Favor," *EJ*, October 31, 1914, 7; Lunardini, *From Equal Suffrage to Equal Rights*, 71, 82–87; Flexner, *Century of Struggle*, 279–82.

19. "'Suffrage Flier' to Tour State," *MN*, January 26, 1915, 7; "'Suffrage Flier' Returns From Trip," *MN*, February, 22, 1915, 6; "Equal Suffragists Storm the Capitol," *EE*, January 5, 1915, 1; "Suffrage Forces Invade Dover," *MN*, January 6, 1915, 5, 9; "Suffrage Day," *MN*, March 9, 1915, 1; "'Votes' Luncheon at Hotel Du Pont," *MN*, March 11, 1915, 7.

20. "Suffrage Headquarters on Delaware Avenue," *EE*, June 20, 1914, 11; "Suffragists Drag in Broom to Help in Fight for Vote," *EJ*, June 26, 1914, 7; "Delaware Congressional Union Outgrows Present Headquarters," *The Suffragist* 2, no. 23 (June 6, 1914): 7.

21. "Parlor Meeting for Suffrage," *EE*, January 24, 1914, 13; "Sign Recruits for Suffragist Parade," *MN*, March 6, 1914, 6; "Voiceless Speech," *MN*, July 18, 1914, 5. "The Little Yellow Rose of Equal Suffrage," sheet music, lyrics by Mary H. Askew Mather, Delaware Historical Society Collections. On these points, see Jessica Ellen Sewell, *Women and the Everyday City: Public Space in San Francisco, 1890–1915* (Minneapolis: University of Minnesota Press, 2011), 127–68, esp. 144–48 on the choice of yellow as a signature suffrage color; and Mary Chapman, *Making Noise, Making News: Suffrage Print Culture and U.S. Modernism* (New York: Oxford University Press, 2014), 54–85.

On racial passing, see Allyson Hobbs, *A Chosen Exile: A History of Racial Passing in American Life* (Cambridge, MA: Harvard University Press, 2014).

22. "Fraternal Parade a Brilliant Spectacle," *EJ*, October 15, 1914, 2; "Suffrage Movement Part of State's History," *EJ*, May 2, 1914, 14 (photos); "Campaign Through the Country: Delaware," *The Suffragist* 32, no. 2 (August 8, 1914): 7 (the photo was cropped for publication); Virginia Scharff, *Taking the Wheel: Women and the Coming of the Motor Age* (New York: Free Press, 1991), 79–88; Sewell, *Women and the Everyday City*, 144.

23. Anne McCue, "The Ballot from a Factory Girl's Point of View," *The Suffragist* 2, no. 23 (June 6, 1914): 6; "Women and Children in Industry," *The Suffragist* 2, no. 31 (August 1, 1914): 4.

24. "Factory Workers Hear Suffrage," *EJ*, July 7, 1914, 6; "Suffrage Meetings," *MN*, July 7, 1914, 12; "Why They Should Have the Ballot," *MN*, July 9, 1914, 7; "Central Body Favors Votes for Women," *EJ*, February 4, 1914, 1; "Central Labor Union Meeting," *MN*, April 22, 1914, 14. See also Orleck, *Common Sense and a Little Fire*, 53–113; and Ellen Carol DuBois, *Harriot Stanton Blatch and the Winning of Woman Suffrage* (New Haven, CT: Yale University Press, 1997), 94–101, 133–37.

25. "Many Women Ask Equal Suffrage," *MN*, February 3, 1914, 1; Charles Schopferer obituary, *EJ*, June 30, 1906, 5; Boylan, "Annie Melvin Arniel," Maayme Agyemang and Maggie Inglis, "Biographical Sketch of Naomi Schopfer Barrett (Bennett)," *OBD*, accessed online at https://documents.alexanderstreet.com/d/1009054725; Di Marco and Shields, "Annie J. Magee"; "Local Suffragists March in Parade," *MN*, October 13, 1915, 12; "Campaign Through the Country," *The Suffragist* 3, no. 33 (August 14, 1915): 7. See also, Sewell, *Women and the Everyday City*, 163–65.

26. "Mrs. Hilles Heads State Suffragists," *EJ*, May 15, 1915, 7; "Suffrage Lines Hold Full Sway," *MN*, May 14, 1915, 1; "Suffragists End Their Convention," *MN*, May 15, 1915, 5; See also Constance J. Cooper, "Biographical Sketch of Josephine M. R. White De Lacour," *OBD*, accessed online at https://documents.alexanderstreet.com/d/1010111665, and Meghan Willis, "Biographical Sketch of Mabel Lloyd Fisher Ridgely," *OBD*, accessed online at https://documents.alexanderstreet.com/d/1009656548. On the use of Anthony's name for the amendment and the misleading nature of that naming, see DuBois, *Harriot Stanton Blatch*, 248–50; and Lisa Tetrault, *The Myth of Seneca Falls: Memory and the Women's Suffrage Movement, 1848–1898* (Chapel Hill: University of North Carolina Press, 2014), 185–87. NAWSA briefly endorsed the alternate Shafroth-Palmer Amendment, which would have made suffrage a states' rights matter. It would have triggered a suffrage referendum whenever eight percent of a state's active voters signed a petition requesting that the issue be placed on the state ballot. See Lunardini, *From Equal Suffrage to Equal Rights*, 55.

27. "Suffrage Executive Committee Meets," *MN*, November 27, 1915, 5; "Suffrage Day at Panama Exposition," *EJ*, September 14, 1915, 8; Delaware Equal Suffrage Association, Executive Committee Minutes, November 11, 1915, Ridgely Collection, Delaware Public Archives, #9200 R09, 002 1 box (hereafter DESA Minutes); Martha C. Cranston to Anna Howard Shaw, May 15, 1915, NAWSA Records, Library of Congress, microfilm edition, Box 48, Reel 33; "Dr. Anna Howard Shaw Talks to Suffragists," *MN*, November 12, 1915, 1, 7–8; *History of Woman Suffrage*, eds. Elizabeth Cady Stanton, Susan B. Anthony, et al., 6 vols. (Rochester, NY: various, 1889–1922), VI: 91 (hereafter

HWS). See also "The Suffrage Booth at the Panama-Pacific Exposition," *The Suffragist* 3, no. 16 (April 17, 1915): 6.

28. Alice Paul, "Salutatory," *The Suffragist* 1, no. 1 (November 15, 1913): 4; Zahniser and Fry, *Alice Paul*, 193–209.

29. *HWS* V, 377–81, 453–55, 675–77; DuBois, *Suffrage*, 207–10; Lunardini, *From Equal Suffrage to Equal Rights*, 78–79; Zahniser and Fry, *Alice Paul*, 178–91; Flexner, *Century of Struggle*, 266–67; Jacqueline Van Voris, *Carrie Chapman Catt: A Public Life* (New York: Feminist Press, 1987). See also Trisha Franzen, *Anna Howard Shaw: The Work of Woman Suffrage* (Urbana: University of Illinois Press, 2014), 141–63.

30. "Stand Against Woman Suffrage," *EE*, June 12, 1914, 1, 5; "'Antis' Ask Legislature Not to Give Women the Vote," *EJ*, January 21, 1915, 12; "Anti-Suffrage Tent at the State Fair," *EE*, September 4, 1915, 11; "Judges Decide in 'Votes' Favor," *MN*, September 25, 1915, 2. See also Susan Goodier, *No Votes for Women: The New York State Anti-Suffrage Movement* (Urbana: University of Illinois Press, 2013); Thomas J. Jablonsky, *The Home, Heaven, and Mother Party: Female Anti-Suffragists in the United States, 1868–1920* (New York: Carlson, 1994), 31–50; Jane Jerome Camhi, *Women Against Women: American Anti-Suffragism, 1880–1920* (New York: Carlson, 1994), 5–37.

31. "Sen. DuPont Receives the Suffragists," *EJ*, January 30, 1914, 1, 15.

32. W. David Lewis, "Bissell, Emily Perkins," *Notable American: A Biographical Dictionary*, eds. Edward T. James, Janet Wilson James, and Paul S. Boyer, 3 vols. (Cambridge, MA: Harvard University Press, 1971), I: 152–53; "Tent Colony Now," *MN*, July 12, 1906, 1; "Plans are Ready," *MN*, January 3, 1909, 1. See also Bissell's correspondence with Delaware's Democratic Senator Willard Saulsbury, Jr., Saulsbury Papers, University of Delaware Special Collections, Mss #331, Box 57, Folder 27; and Mary de Vou's May 7, 1914, letter to Alice Paul, lamenting Bissell's influence, "especially with club women in our state," National Woman's Party Records, Library of Congress, Microfilm Edition, Box I:17, Reel 10. African American Delawareans cobbled together the resources to found Edgewood Sanatorium in 1914 and acquire state funding; see Andrea Marth, "The Fruits of Jim Crow: The Edgewood Sanatorium and African American Institution Building in Wilmington, Delaware, 1900–1940" (MA Thesis, University of Delaware, 1994), 92–99.

33. Editorial: "Woman's Suffrage in Delaware," *EE*, February 3, 1913, 4; Editorial: "Partisanship and Equal Suffrage," *EE*, February 18, 1915, 4; Anthony Higgins, ed., "Mary Wilson Thompson Memoir (Part Four)," *Delaware History* 18, no. 4 (Fall-Winter 1979): 251. See also J. Morgan Kousser, *The Shaping of Southern Politics: Suffrage Restriction and the Establishment of the One-Party South, 1880–1910* (New Haven, CT: Yale University Press, 1974).

34. "Suffrage Forces Invade Dover," *MN*, January 6, 1915, 9; "Grant Lone Woman Papers as Citizen," *EJ*, July 6, 1915, 1; Mary Ospina, letter to the editor, *EE*, July 6, 1915, 8; Anne M. Boylan, "Biographical Sketch of Mary A. Ospina," *OBD*, accessed online at https://documents.alexanderstreet.com/d/1010111653.

35. "Suffrage Forces Invade Dover," 9; "Lawmakers Hear Strong Pleas of the Suffragists," *EJ*, January 21, 1915, 1–2; Anti-Suffragists Write to Legislature," *MN*, January 21, 1915, 7. On anti-suffragists and the "race issue," see Suzanne Lebsock, "Woman Suffrage and White Supremacy: A Virginia Case Study," in *Visible Women: New Essays on American Activism*, eds. Nancy A. Hewitt and Suzanne Lebsock (Urbana: University of Illinois Press, 1993), 62–100.

36. Editorial: "Partisanship and Equal Suffrage"; Mary J. Woodlen, letter to the editor, February 27, *EE*, March 1, 1914, 4.

37. Blanche W. Stubbs, letter to the editor, *EJ*, February 23, 1915, 6. See also Deborah Gray White, *Too Heavy a Load: Black Women in Defense of Themselves, 1894–1994* (New York: Norton, 1999), 36–51.

38. On the rejected version, the Shafroth-Palmer proposal, see note 25 above and Lunardini, *From Equal Suffrage to Equal Rights*, 55–59; and Flexner, *Century of Struggle*, 267–72. "Suffragists at Farewell Luncheon," *EJ*, March 11, 1915, 7. On African American suffragists' strategies for dealing with white racism, see Rosalyn Terborg-Penn, *African American Women in the Struggle for the Vote, 1850–1920* (Bloomington: Indiana University Press, 1998), 107–35; and Julie A. Gallagher, *Black Women and Politics in New York City* (Urbana: University of Illinois Press, 2012), 24–25. See also Hobbs, *A Chosen Exile*. At least one Delaware suffragist had relatives who crossed over the color line and became white: Anne M. Boylan, "Biographical Sketch of Helen W. Anderson (Webb)," *OBD*, accessed online at https://documents.alexanderstreet.com/d/1009805437.

39. Alice Dunbar-Nelson Suffrage Scrapbook, University of Delaware Special Collections, Collection #113, Series II, Box 12, Scrapbook #3, accessible online at https://udspace.udel.edu/handle/19716/24348. Quotations are from: "Negro Poet's Widow to Devote Herself to Suffrage Cause," Philadelphia *Evening Ledger*, August 7, 1915; "Local Colored People Organize for Woman Suffrage," *Lansdowne News*, July 30, 1915, quoted in *Swarthmore News*, July 30, 1915; "Women Ask for 'Square Deal,'" *York Daily*, November 2, 1915, 3; *Masterpieces of Negro Eloquence*, ed. Alice Moore Dunbar (New York: Bookery, 1914). See also Ellen Gruber Garvey, "Alice Moore Dunbar-Nelson: The View from Her Scrapbook," *Legacy* 33, no. 2 (2016): 310–35. A columnist for the *Williamsport Sun*, August 14, 1915, claimed to have learned that her marriage to Dunbar constituted "the happiest years of her life." See also Gloria [Akasha] Hull, *Color, Sex and Poetry: Three Women Writers of the Harlem Renaissance* (Bloomington: Indiana University Press, 1987), 42–43; and Brittney Cooper, *Beyond Respectability: The Intellectual Thought of Race Women* (Urbana: University of Illinois Press, 2017), 78–80.

40. Dunbar-Nelson Suffrage Scrapbook; Garvey, "Alice Moore Dunbar-Nelson," 323–24; "Women Here Slow to Get the Vote," Philadelphia *Evening Ledger*, August 7, 1915; Mrs. Paul Laurence Dunbar, "The Colored Working Woman," in Reports of Annual Convention, Baltimore, 1914, NAACP Papers, Library of Congress, Microfilm Edition, Part 1, Reel 8; "Betterment of the Negro Woman Advocated," *Chester Times*, July 14, 1915, 1; "Nixon's Injunction Made Permanent by Judge Reid," *Pittsburg Press*, September 3, 1915; "Women's Clubs: Mrs. Dunbar at Loendi Club," *Pittsburgh Dispatch*, October 24, 1915; "Mrs. Dunbar at Wesley Church," *Harrisburg Advocate-Verdict*, October 30, 1915. See also "Votes for Women: A Symposium," *The Crisis* 10 (August 1915): 184–92; and Treva B. Lindsey, *Colored No More: Reinventing Black Womanhood in Washington, D.C.* (Urbana: University of Illinois Press, 2017), 109–10.

41. "Suffragists in Convention Here Plan Campaign: Congressional Union, at Hotel du Pont, Welcomed by Governor," *EE*, July 8, 1916, 5; "Want Suffrage Amendment Passed," *MN*, July 10, 1916, 7; "To Organize City for Suffrage Cause," *EJ*, July 19, 1916, 1; "Women Organize Five City Wards," *EJ*, July 24, 1916, 1; "To Widen Work at Settlement for Negro Race," *EE*, October 6, 1916, 8; "Annual Convention of the Delaware Congressional Union," *The Suffragist* 4, no. 30 (July 22, 1916): 4.

42. National American Woman Suffrage Association, *Victory, How Women Won It: A Centennial Symposium, 1840–1940* (New York: H.W. Wilson, 1940), 161–64; DuBois, *Harriot Stanton Blatch*, 205–6; DuBois, *Suffrage*, 184–85.

43. "Suffrage Meeting Tonight," *MN*, January 31, 1916, 2; "Two Day Suffrage Convention Planned," *EJ*, February 19, 1916, 9; "Suffragists Postpone Convention Meeting," *EJ*, February 26, 1916, 7; "Suffragists Will Celebrate Tonight," *MN*, October 21, 1916, 5; "Federal Amendment Day Celebrated," *EE*, October 23, 1916, 3; DESA Minutes, March 31, July 28, August 18, October 30, November 10, 1916, Ridgely Collection.

44. Florence Bayard Hilles to Phoebe Apperson Hearst, 10 March 1916, Hearst Papers, Bancroft Library, University of California, accessed online at https://oac.cdlib.org/ark:/13030/hb4q2nb2kc/?order=25&brand=oac4; "Suffragists Delighted," *MN*, January 31, 1916, 7; "Suffragists Ready for State Convention," *EE*, March 3, 1916, 6; Grace Simmons and Sophia Giannetta, "Biographical Sketch of Josephine Anderson (Mrs. Victor) du Pont," *OBD*, accessed online at https://documents.alexanderstreet.com/d/1008342645; Willis, "Mabel Lloyd Fisher Ridgely," and Julia Rizzo, Laura Stankewicz, and Colleen Hall, "Biographical Sketch of Leah Burton (Paynter)," *OBD*, accessed online at https://documents.alexanderstreet.com/d/1010596163.

45. "New Castle Suffragists Name Miss Speakman Chairman; Women Predict Victory," *EJ*, March 4, 1916, 7; "Suffragists Ready for State Conference," 6; "Want Suffrage Amendment Passed; Action Taken at First Annual Meeting of Delaware Congressional Union," *MN*, July 10, 1916, 7; "Organizing in the Constituencies," *The Suffragist* 4, no. 11 (March 11, 1916): 9. On the strategic uses of apparent (not actual) local support in suffrage organizing, see Amy Aronson, *Crystal Eastman: A Revolutionary Life* (New York: Oxford University Press, 2020), 106. Phyllis Mason moved to New Castle County to teach, leaving Sussex County without a CU organizer until she moved back in time for the 1920 ratification effort.

46. "New Castle Suffragists Name Miss Speakman," 7; Florence Bayard Hilles, "Letter to the Editor: The National Woman's Party," *MN*, July 26, 1916, 6; Zahniser and Fry, *Alice Paul*, 239–45; Lunardini, *From Equal Suffrage to Equal Rights*, 85–89.

47. Lunardini, *From Equal Suffrage to Equal Rights*, 87–88; "Suffrage Invasion a 'Wonderful Success,'" *EJ*, May 4, 1916, 1; "Suffragists to Welcome Mrs. Hilles, *EJ*, May 17, 1916, 12; "Suffragists in Capitol," *New York Times*, May 17, 1916, 11; Zahniser and Fry, *Alice Paul*, 237–38.

48. DESA Minutes, April 28, July 7, July 28, November 11, 1916, Ridgely Collection; "Off for Chicago," *MN*, June 6, 1916, 7; "Federal Amendment Day Celebrated," *EE*, October 23, 1916, 3; "Favors Suffrage Plank in Platform," *MN*, August 15, 1916, 6; "Suffragists in Annual Session," *MN*, November 11, 1916, 11; Mary A. Ospina to Willard Saulsbury, Jr., October 5, 1916, Willard Saulsbury, Jr., Papers, Mss. 331, Box 44, Folder 51, University of Delaware Library Special Collections; Zahniser and Fry, *Alice Paul*, 242.

49. "John G. Townsend Inaugurated Governor; Declares for Woman Suffrage," *EJ*, January 16, 1917, 1; Hoffecker, *Democracy in Delaware*, 162; Richard B. Carter, *Clearing New Ground: The Life of John G. Townsend Jr.* (Wilmington: The Delaware Heritage Press, 2001), 219.

50. "Suffrage Bill Now before Legislature," *Star*, March 9, 1913, 9; DESA Minutes, November 10, 1916, Ridgely Collection; Linda J. Lumsden, *Inez: The Life and Times of*

Inez Milholland (Bloomington: Indiana University Press, 2004), 152–63 (157); DuBois, *Suffrage*, 209–16.

51. Zanhiser and Fry, *Alice Paul*, 251; DuBois, *Harriot Stanton Blatch*, 177–81, 187–90; Fry, Mabel Vernon interview, Suffragist Oral History Project.

52. "Suffragists Meet to Honor a Woman," *EE*, December 27, 1916, 3; "Launch Delaware Suffrage Campaign," *MN*, January 8, 1917, 1, 2; Lumsden, *Inez*, 164–78 (178); Doris Stevens, *Jailed for Freedom* (New York: Liveright, 1920), 63. Lumsden speculates that Milholland may have been suffering from undiagnosed chronic leukemia. The Delaware CU poster's designer was Percy Van Eman Ivory, a member of the famed Howard Pyle studio in Wilmington, whose wife Elizabeth Post Schofield Ivory joined the CU when the couple moved to Wilmington. In later versions, the poster's caption read "Forward into Light!"

53. "Launch Delaware Suffrage Campaign," 1, 2; "Suffragists Open State Campaign," *EJ*, January 8, 1917, 10.

54. DESA Special Meeting Minutes, January 10, 1917; January 26, 1917; Ridgely Collection; "Women Plead for Right of Ballot," *MN*, February 17, 1917, 4; Florence Bayard Hilles, Letter to Editor, "Suffragists Hopeful," *Star*, February 4, 1917, 6. See Chapter 3 for a discussion of "preparedness."

55. "Launch Delaware Suffrage Campaign," 1, 2; "Militant 'Suffs' to Picket White House," *MN* January 10, 1917, 1; "Delaware Suffragists Leave for Picket Duty," *MN*, February 17, 1917, 12; Zahniser and Fry, *Alice Paul*, 252–56; Lumsden, *Inez*, 174–76; Agyemang and Inglis, "Naomi Schopfer Barrett (Bennett)," and Veronica Cantoran-Torres and Cameron Miles, "Biographical Sketch of Mary E. Brown," *OBD*, accessed online at https://documents.alexanderstreet.com/d/1008342639. Harriot Stanton Blatch had employed silent vigils during the 1915 New York referendum campaign.

56. Lunardini, *From Equal Suffrage to Equal Rights*, 110–11 (111); "Suffragists to Help," *MN*, February 7, 1917, 4; Delaware Equal Suffrage Association, Minutes, March 9, 1917, Ridgely Collection; "Mrs. Hilles Heads Woman's Party," *EE*, April 14, 1917, 3; "Suffrage Sentinels Arraigned by the Government," *The Suffragist* 5, no. 75 (June 30, 1917): 6–8. See also Franzen, *Anna Howard Shaw*, 170–71; and Zahniser and Fry, *Alice Paul*, 259–60.

57. DESA Minutes, July 27, September 27, November 22, 1917, Ridgely Collection.

Chapter 3

1. Ethel Pennewill Brown Leach, *DELAWARE AWAKE!* 1918, University Museums, University of Delaware, accessible at https://library-artstor-org.udel.idm.oclc.org/#/asset/SS34737_34737_8412066. See also Labert St. Clair, *The Story of the Liberty Loans* (Washington, D.C.: James William Bryan Press, 1919).

2. "'Delaware Awake' Given to College," Wilmington *Evening Journal*, May 14, 1918, 11 (hereafter *EJ*). Ethel Brown was a member of the famed Howard Pyle studio. See also Helen Kendrick Johnson, *Women and the Republic: A Survey of the Woman-Suffrage Movement in the United States and a Discussion of the Claims and Arguments of its Foremost Advocates* (1897; New York: Guidon Club, 1913), 79; and Kimberly Jensen, *Mobilizing Minerva: American Women in the First World War* (Urbana: University of Illinois Press, 2008), 20.

3. Lynn Dumenil, *The Second Line of Defense: American Women and World War I* (Chapel Hill: University of North Carolina Press, 2017), 15; Ellen Carol DuBois, *Suffrage: Women's Long Battle for the Vote* (New York: Simon & Schuster, 2020), 238–42.

4. "Colonization of Belgians," Wilmington *Morning News*, October 21, 1914, 6 (hereafter *MN*); "Red Cross Relief," *MN*, March 15, 1916, 5; "Work of the Red Cross Relief," *MN*, April 21, 1916, 5; "$3082 State Fund for Jews' Relief," *EJ*, January 28, 1916, 23; Wilmington New Century Club Papers, Accession #84.11, Box 16, Current Events Club Minutes, Volumes 1 & 2, 1916, Delaware Historical Society; Meghan Willis, "Biographical Sketch of Mabel Lloyd Fisher Ridgely," *Online Biographical Dictionary of the Woman Suffrage Movement in the United States*, eds. Thomas Dublin and Kathryn Kish Sklar (Alexandria, VA: Alexander Street, 2015–) (hereafter *OBD*), accessed on line at https://documents.alexanderstreet.com/d/1009656548; Anne M. Boylan, "Biographical Sketch of Winifred Morris," *OBD*, accessed online at https://documents. alexanderstreet.com/d/1009859942; and Janet Lindenmuth, "Biographical Sketch of Sallie Topkis Ginns," *OBD*, accessed online at https://documents.alexanderstreet. com/d/1010595688; Myron L. Lazarus, "Interview with Mrs. James N. Ginns (née Sallie T. Topkis)," n.d., MSS 179, Robert H. Richards, Jr., Delaware Oral History Collection, Special Collections Department, University of Delaware Library; Toni Young, *Becoming American, Remaining Jewish: The Story of Wilmington, Delaware's First Jewish Community, 1879–1924* (Newark: University of Delaware Press, 1999), 221–31.

5. "Knitting Socks Part of Women's Preparedness Training," *EJ*, May 26, 1916, 6; Advertisement for "Preparedness Chocolates," *EJ*, October 6, 1916, 10; Jensen, *Mobilizing Minerva*, 58–59; Elaine F. Weiss, *Fruits of Victory: The Women's Land Army of America in the Great War* (Dulles, VA: Potomac Books, 2008), 60–66. See also David M. Kennedy, *Over Here: The First World War and American Society* (New York: Oxford University Press, 1982), 30–35. The Women's Land Army enlisted young women, working together under supervision, to meet wartime demands for farm labor as well as to increase the food supply generally. In Delaware, it had a strong proponent in Winifred Robinson, dean of the Women's College in Newark. See "Expect Large Class at Women's College," *EJ*, September 9, 1918, 10.

6. "Prominent Women Join in Movement for Preparedness," *EJ*, November 9, 1915, 12; "General Wickersham Parade Marshal; Women to Take an Important Part in Preparedness Demonstration," Wilmington *Every Evening*, May 23, 1916, 2 (hereafter *EE*); "'Antis' Open War with Suffragists Over Club Issue," *EJ*, July 2, 1914, 1, 2; Anthony Higgins, ed., "Mary Wilson Thompson Memoir, Part Three" *Delaware History* 18, no. 3 (Spring-Summer 1979): 207–9. In 1914, the General Federation of Women's Clubs endorsed suffrage for the first time; the Delaware Federation declined to follow suit. See letter from the Delaware Federation's president, Ray H. Powell, to NAWSA, July 13, 1916, confirming that the federation had not yet endorsed suffrage, "Women's Suffrage Movement," Miscellaneous Clippings Collection, Delaware Historical Society.

7. "Links Preparedness with Patriotism," *EJ*, January 3, 1916, 12; "$5692.75 in Hand for Boy Scouts," *EJ*, March 3, 1916, 7; "Women's Day at Trinity A.M.E. Church," *Baltimore Afro-American*, April 1, 1916, 7; Chad L. Williams, *Torchbearers of Democracy: African American Soldiers in the World War I Era* (Chapel Hill: University of North Carolina Press, 2010), 5–8, 350; Jensen, *Mobilizing Minerva*, 37–39.

8. Mary Louise Degen, *The History of the Woman's Peace Party* (1939; New York: Garland, 1972), 151; "Formation of the Parade: Order in which Organizations Will

March Today," *New York Times*, May 13, 1916, 4; "Every Calling in the Line: Clergy, Doctors, Lawyers, Join with the Men of the Many Trades," *New York Times*, May 14, 1916, 1–3; "135,683 Paraded for Preparedness," *New York Times*, May 14, 1916, 1; "No Riders Allowed in Great Pageant," *EJ*, May 27, 1916, 2; "Thousands Cheer Marching Citizens," *MN*, June 12, 1916, 1, 2. On the San Francisco event, see Alexandra Nickliss, *Phoebe Apperson Hearst: A Life of Power and Politics* (Lincoln: University of Nebraska Press, 2018), 398–407.

9. "Preparedness Day Parade," Wilmington *Sunday Morning Star*, June 11, 1916, 1, 6 (title varies; hereafter *Star*); Caroline M. Cooper to Eleanor G. Karsten, 7 June 1916, Woman's Peace Party, Delaware Branch Correspondence, 1915–1918, Swarthmore College Library Special Collections.

10. Alice P. Smyth to Eleanor Karsten, 1 May 1916, Woman's Peace Party, Delaware Branch Correspondence; "Claims War Might Have Been Averted," *MN*, May 21, 1915, 6; "Woman's Peace Party," *EE*, February 27, 1915, 11; "Object to Military Training in Schools," *EJ*, January 17, 1917, 7; "Woman's Peace Party," *EE*, May 16, 1917, 7; "9,000 Marchers in Parade for Preparedness," *EE*, June 12, 1916, 2; "145,000 Parade in New York for Nation's Safety," *EE*, May 13, 1916, 1. See also Degen, *History of the Woman's Peace Party*, 166–68; Harriet Hyman Alonso, *Peace as a Women's Issue: A History of the U.S. Movement for World Peace and Women's Rights* (Syracuse, NY: Syracuse University Press, 1993), 68–78; Susan Zieger, "The Schoolhouse vs the Army: U.S. Teachers and the Campaign against Militarism in the Schools, 1914–1918," *Journal of Women's History* 15, no 2 (Summer 2003): 15–60; and Nicole Vion, "Biographical Sketch of Mary H. Askew Mather," *OBD*, accessed online at https://documents.alexanderstreet.com/d/1009860187, and Anne M. Boylan, "Biographical Sketch of Emma Worrell," *OBD*, accessed online at https://documents.alexanderstreet.com/d/1009859945.

11. "Links Preparedness with Patriotism," 1, 12; "Mrs. Henry B. Thompson," *EE*, June 10, 1916, 9; Dumenil, *Second Line of Defense*, 13–21.

12. "Every Citizen Should Parade Says Mr. Marvel," *EE*, June 6, 1916, 2; "Women to March This Afternoon in Big Parade," *EE*, June10, 1916, 2; "Labor Opposes the Preparedness Plan," *EJ*, June 7, 1916, 6; "9,000 Marchers in Parade for Preparedness," 2; Susan Goodier, *No Votes for Women: The New York State Anti-Suffrage Movement* (Urbana: University of Illinois Press, 2013), 10–12, 104; "Preparedness Day, *Star*, 6.

13. "Anti-Suffrage Notes," *EE*, March 11, 1916, 9; "Anti-Suffrage Convention in Nation's Capitol," *EE*, October 11, 1916, 9; "Anti-Suffragists for 'America First,'" *EE*, July 3, 1916, 10; Goodier, *No Votes for Women*, 109–13; Ellen Carol DuBois, *Harriot Stanton Blatch and the Winning of Woman Suffrage* (New Haven, CT: Yale University Press, 1997), 180–81, 234–38; Susan Goodier and Karen Pastorello, *Women Will Vote: Winning Suffrage in New York State* (Ithaca, NY: Cornell University Press, 2017), 171–82. For New York anti-suffragists' use of their voting rights to seek the repeal of woman suffrage, see Christopher Capozzola, *Uncle Sam Wants You: World War I and the Making of the Modern American Citizen* (New York: Oxford University Press, 2008), 107.

14. J. D. Zahniser and Amelia R. Fry, *Alice Paul: Claiming Power* (New York: Oxford University Press, 2014), 262–63 (263); Christine Lunardini, *From Equal Suffrage to Equal Rights: Alice Paul and the National Woman's Party, 1910–1928* (New York: New York University Press, 1988), 110–11; Dumenil, *Second Line of Defense*, 21–22; Alonso, *Peace as a Women's Issue*, 74–75; DuBois, *Suffrage*, 223–26.

15. "Woman's Party in Convention Here," *MN*, April 14, 1917, 10; Joan Hoff Wilson, "Rankin, Jeannette Pickering," *Notable American Women: The Modern Period*, eds. Barbara Sicherman and Carol Hurd Green (Cambridge, MA: Harvard University Press, 1980), 566–68.

16. Alice Paul to State NWP Chairmen, 8 February 1917, Alice Paul Papers, Digital Edition, Series II, Schlesinger Library, Radcliffe Institute, Harvard University; Dumenil, *Second Line of Defense*, 21, 34–37; Maud Wood Park, *Front Door Lobby* (Boston: Beacon Press, 1960), 62, 77–78; Alonso, *Peace as a Women's Issue*, 75; Capozzola, *Uncle Sam Wants You*, 103–6; DuBois, *Suffrage*, 223–24.

17. Alice Moore Dunbar-Nelson, "Mine Eyes Have Seen [1918]," in *First World War Plays*, ed. Mark Rawlinson (London: Bloomsbury, 2014), 59–70; W.E.B. Du Bois, "Close Ranks," *Crisis* 16 no. 3 (July 1918): 111; "Mrs. A.D. Nelson in Peace Work," *EJ*, July 2, 1928, 4; Melinda Plastas, *A Band of Noble Women: Racial Politics in the Women's Peace Movement* (Syracuse, NY: Syracuse University Press, 2011), 60–65.

18. Delaware Equal Suffrage Association Minutes, March 9, 1917, Ridgely Collection Delaware Public Archives, #9200 R09, 002 1 box (hereafter DESA Minutes); "Women Meet and Plan for Defense," *MN*, March 31, 1917, 2.

19. See, for example, "Anti-Suffrage Notes" and "Equal Suffrage Association Meeting," *EE*, March 14, 1917, 9.

20. "To the Women of Wilmington," *MN*, June 2, 1917, 11; Mary Wilson Thompson and Emily Bissell to the Editor, "Why Suffrage Should Not Be Forced on Women," *EE*, May 12, 1917, 4. See also Capozzola, *Uncle Sam Wants You*, 26–28, 86–95.

21. Rose Lippincott Hizar Duggin, letter to the editor, "When Suffragist Meets Anti-Suffragist," *EJ*, May 16, 1917, 3; "Local Suffrage Notes," *EJ*, June 29, 1917, 15; "State Suffragists against Pickets," *MN*, November 23, 1917, 7; Anne M. Boylan, "Biographical Sketch of Rose L. Hizar (Mrs. William G.) Duggin," *OBD*, accessed online at https://documents.alexanderstreet.com/d/1010111650; DESA Minutes, February 25, 1918, Ridgely Collection.

22. "Suffrage and Service—They Go Together," *The Woman Citizen* 2, no. 14 (March 2, 1918), 261; Anne M. Boylan, "Biographical Sketch of Mary Seward Phillips (Mrs. John R.) Eskridge," *OBD*, accessed online at https://documents.alexanderstreet.com/d/1010111651; DESA Minutes, March 25, 1918, and September 8, 1919, Ridgely Papers. A fifth Liberty Loan campaign launched in 1919 after the war's end.

23. The term "human conservation," coined by Progressive-era environmentalists, stressed the public health benefits of conserving natural resources, such as clean water and soil, in protecting people from environmental degradation.

24. "Delaware City," *MN*, May 14, 1917, 3; "Delaware City," *MN*, May 8, 1917, 3; "Earnest Women to Assist Nation," *MN*, July 10, 1917, 3; "Three Night Schools Ready for Pupils," *EJ*, November 13, 1917, 7; "Need Legislation to Aid Children," *MN*, February 23, 1918, 7; "Garrett Settlement Notes," *EJ*, June 8, 1918, 9; "Public School 22 Under Discussion," *EE*, November 27, 1917, 11; "Colored Clubwomen Hear Timely Talks," *EJ*, July 3, 1918, 14; "Women's Club Election," *EJ*, July 5, 1918, 19; Alice Dunbar-Nelson, "Negro Women in War Work," in Emmett J. Scott, *Scott's Official History of The American Negro in the World War* (Chicago: Homewood Press, 1919), 383. Elizabeth Williams Tyler, the Garrett Settlement's public nurse, was the sister of Suffrage Study Club member Caroline B. Williams; see Stephanie Clampitt, "Biography of

Caroline B. Williams," *OBD*, accessed online at https://documents.alexanderstreet.com/d/1009594393.

25. DESA Minutes, November 22 and November 30, 1917, Ridgely Collection; "State Suffragists Gather at Newport," *EJ*, November 22, 1917, 7; "State Suffragists against Pickets," *MN*, November 23, 1917, 7; DuBois, *Suffrage*, 243–45.

26. "Suffrage to Pass in House Today by President's Aid," *EE*, January 10, 1918, 1; "President Wilson Favors the Suffrage Amendment," *MN*, January 10, 1918, 1; DESA Minutes, Ridgely Collection: February 1, 1918 (asking donation); March 25, 1918 (library); April 29, 1918 (no funds spent); May 27, 1918 (Catt and Park visit); May 31, 1918 (Mabel Willard); June 24, 1918 (state fair decision); DuBois, *Suffrage*, 245–46.

27. Lunardini, *From Equal Suffrage to Equal Rights*, 110–14; Zahniser and Fry, *Alice Paul*, 254–62. One should not overdraw the contrasts between NWP picketing and NAWSA lobbying. The NWP conducted organized lobbying from the start, and continued to do so throughout the war. See, for example, the notes that party lobbyists compiled on Congress members' voting records: Congressional Voting Card Collection, https://nationalwomansparty.pastperfectonline.com/.

28. "Women are Prepared for Defense Work," *EJ*, April 2, 1917, 7; "208 Women Enroll for Home Defense," *EJ*, April 24, 1917, 12; "Register Women for Defense Work," *MN*, April 25, 1917, 5.

29. "Pickets in War Work," *New York Times*, May 6, 1918, 8; Maayme Agyemang and Maggie Inglis, "Biographical Sketch of Naomi Schopfer Barrett (Bennett)," *OBD*, accessed online at https://documents.alexanderstreet.com/d/1009054725; Gabriella DiMarco and Maeve Shields, "Biographical Sketch of Annie J. Magee [or McGee]," *OBD*, accessed online at https://documents.alexanderstreet.com/d/1009054724; Victoria Auer and Caroline Klinger, "Biographical Sketch of Catherine Boyle," *OBD*, accessed online at https://documents.alexanderstreet.com/d/1008342600; Anne M. Boylan, "Biographical Sketch of Annie Melvin Arniel," *OBD*, accessed online at https://documents.alexanderstreet.com/d/1009054733; and Colleen Hall, "Biographical Sketch of Adelina Piunti (DiSabatino)," *OBD*, accessed online at https://documents.alexanderstreet.com/d/1008342590. See also Capozzola, *Uncle Sam Wants You*, 85. In documents accompanying her 1918 passport application, available on Ancestry.com, Hilles listed the tattoo as a "distinguishing mark."

30. Zahniser and Fry, *Alice Paul*, 256–65 (256–57); "Anti-Suffrage Notes," *EE*, April 28, 1917, 9; "Anti-Suffrage Notes," *EE*, May 9, 1917, 7. See also excerpt from diary of Thomas W. Brahany, one of Wilson's secretaries, March 4, 1917, *The Papers of Woodrow Wilson*, ed. Arthur Link, et al., 69 vols. (Princeton, NJ: Princeton University Press, 1966–1994): 41: 329–30, describing initial White House staff reactions to the pickets. Carrie Chapman Catt to Alice Paul, 24 May 1917, National Woman's Party Records, Library of Congress, Box 49 Reel 33. See also Carrie Chapman Catt to Woodrow Wilson, 7 May 1917, *Papers of Woodrow Wilson*, 42:237; and Robert Booth Fowler, *Carrie Catt: Feminist Politician* (Boston: Northeastern University Press, 1986), 151–52.

31. Zahniser and Fry, *Alice Paul*, 269; Doris Stevens, *Jailed for Freedom* (New York: Boni and Liveright, 1920), 95–96, 100–3 (100, 103); Carol E. Hoffecker, "Delaware's Woman Suffrage Campaign," *Delaware History* 20, no. 3 (Spring-Summer 1983): 156–57; Madison Heitz, Mia Cimino, and Jessica Sharp, "Biographical Sketch of Florence Bayard Hilles," *OBD*, accessed online at https://documents.alexanderstreet.com/d/1008342612; "Suffragists May Get Jail Sentences," *EJ*, June 26, 1917, 13; "Jail

Experience Does Not Weaken Zeal for Suffrage," *EE*, June 30, 1917, 5. A copy of the pardon can be found in the Callery Collection of Bayard Family Papers, Box 62, Folder #12, Delaware Historical Society.

32. Zahniser and Fry, *Alice Paul*, 98–101, 279–97; "Miss Paul Removed to Prison Hospital: Transferred from Psychopathic Ward on a Stretcher, She Writes in Smuggled Note," *New York Times*, November 17, 1917, 11.

33. Zahniser and Fry, *Alice Paul*, 275–76, 280; DuBois, *Harriot Stanton Blatch*, 204–8; on Mabel Ridgely, see "$9,770,500 of Loan Sold by Women," *EJ*, November 7, 1918, 5.

34. "White House Picket Broken in Health," *Star*, November 11, 1917, 6; DESA Minutes, July 27, November 22, 1917, Ridgely Collection.

35. "Congressman Baer as a Cartoonist Protests against Occoquan," *The Suffragist* 5, no. 86 (September 15, 1917): cover; Zahniser and Fry, *Alice Paul*, 276, 286; Rosalyn Terborg-Penn, *African American Women in the Struggle for the Vote, 1850–1920* (Bloomington: Indiana University Press), 133–35.

36. Zahniser and Fry, *Alice Paul*, 286–97 (295, 287). Historians debate whether the prisoners' release came as the result of an agreement between Paul and Wilson; given existing sources, it is impossible to know. For the case for an agreement, see Sally Hunter Graham, "Woodrow Wilson, Alice Paul, and the Woman Suffrage Movement," *Political Science Quarterly* 98, no. 4 (1983–84): 676–78 (676).

37. Capozzola, *Uncle Sam Wants You*, 117–43; Alonso, *Peace as a Women's Issue*, 73–83; Jean Bethke Elshtain, *Jane Addams and the Dream of American Democracy: A Life* (New York: Basic Books, 2002), 206–9.

38. "Youth Arrested for Non-Registration," *EE*, June 16, 1917, 1; "First Delaware Slacker Arrested," *MN*, June 18, 1917, 2; "Court Rules Out Draft Act Attack," *EJ*, November 14, 1917, 13; "Donald Stephens Declared Slacker," *MN*, December 4, 1917, 1; "Donald Stephens Goes to Jail for Nine Months," *EE*, July 24, 1918, 1, 6 ; "Don Stephens at Liberty," *EJ*, March 10, 1919, 7; Donald Stephens Correspondence, Arden-Stephens Papers, Accession #1992.30, Box 9, Folder 12, Delaware Historical Society; Donald Stephens obituary, *MN*, January 22, 1971, 2. Donald Stephens's father, Frank, an ardent suffragist and war opponent, was arrested in 1918 for violating the Espionage Act, but acquitted at trial.

39. "Asks Citizens to Pledge Support for President," *EE*, March 3, 1917, 10; "Agency to Help Run Down Plotters: American Protective League Now Has Complete Organization in this State," *MN*, July 1, 1918, 1; "12 Held at Shore as Draft Dodgers," *EJ*, August 17, 1918, 9; "German Not Taught," *MN*, September 9, 1918, 1; "Women Would Burn Toys from Hunland," *EJ*, October 29, 1918, 8; "To Boost American-Made Goods Dec. 2–8," *EJ*, November 26, 1918, 6. See also Kennedy, *Over Here*, 52–82; and John A. Munroe, *The University of Delaware: A History* (Newark: University of Delaware, 1983), Chapter 7.

40. Kennedy, *Over Here*, 68–73; "Official Gazette Gives War News," *EE*, May 11, 1917, 2; "Four-Minute Men," *MN*, July 2, 1917, 4; "Camera News," *MN*, August 6, 1918, 7; "Let's Keep Those Docks Piled High!" *EE* August 17, 1918, 8; Sara Hunter Graham, *Woman Suffrage and the New Democracy* (New Haven, CT: Yale University Press, 1996), 108–10. See also Jonathan Auerbach, *Weapons of Democracy: Propaganda, Progressivism, and American Public Opinion* (Baltimore: Johns Hopkins University Press, 2015), 50–90; Alan Axelrod, *Selling the Great War: The Making of American Propaganda* (New York: Palgrave Macmillan, 2009), 77–157; and Kathleen Kennedy,

Disloyal Mothers and Scurrilous Citizens: Women and Subversion during World War I (Bloomington: Indiana University Press, 1999), 1–17.

41. Thompson and Bissell, Letter to the Editor, *EJ*, May 12, 1917, 11; W. David Lewis, "Bissell, Emily Perkins," *Notable American Women*, eds. Edward T. James, Janet Wilson James, and Paul S. Boyer, 3 vols. (Cambridge, MA: Harvard University Press, 1973), I: 152–53; Anthony Higgins, ed., "Mary Wilson Thompson Memoir (Part Three)," *Delaware History* 18, no. 3 (Spring-Summer 1979): 206–9. See also Priscilla Leonard [Emily Bissell], "The Working-Woman and Anti-Suffrage," *Harper's Bazaar* 43 (November 1909): 1169–70; and Capazzola, *Uncle Sam Wants You*," 103–6. Thompson's daughter, Elinor Thompson Douglas, remembered an "Italian chauffeur . . . my mother's maid, a Swiss governess, a chamber maid, a seamstress who lived in, and various others such as our black cook, butler, and laundress." Thompson Douglas, "Growing Up at Brookwood," *Delaware History* 18, no. 4 (Fall-Winter 1979): 267–73.

42. See the following articles, all in *MN*, "Domestic Help Scarce," July 20, 1918, 15; "Colored Women to do Men's Work," July 11, 1918, 4; July 26, 1918, 6; "Newark Notes of Real Interest; Negro Women Work on Railroad," September 26, 1918, 9; "Cooks in Demand," October 30, 1918, 5. See also Dunbar-Nelson, "Negro Women in War Work," 374–97; Judith Weisenfeld, *African American Women and Christian Activism: New York's Black YWCA, 1905–1945* (Cambridge, MA: Harvard University Press, 1997), 124–46; Dumenil, *Second Line of Defense*, 164–67, 176–81; and Carole C. Marks, *Farewell—We're Good and Gone: The Great Black Migration* (Bloomington: Indiana University Press, 1989).

43. Williams, *Torchbearers of Democracy*, 58–61 (59); Dunbar-Nelson, "Negro Women in War Work," 379–86 (380, 379); Jane Olcott, comp., *The Work of Colored Women* (New York: Colored Work Committee War Work Council, National Board, Young Women's Christian Association, n.d.), 11–23, 70–78; Addie Hunton and Kathryn M. Johnson, *Two Colored Women with the American Expeditionary Forces* (Brooklyn, NY: Brooklyn Eagle Press, 1920), photo of Hugo Williams, 84.

44. Plastas, *A Band of Noble Women*, 66; "Mrs. A.D. Nelson in Peace Work," *EJ*, July 2, 1928, 4.

45. "Colored Residents Show Patriotism; 6000 Men Women and Children March in Brilliant Night Pageant," *EJ*, June 15, 1918, 7; "5000 Wilmington Negroes Parade in Honor of Flag Day," *EE*, June 15, 1918, 12, 14; Editorial, "A Fine Display of Patriotism," *EJ*, June 15, 1918, 4.

46. Dunbar-Nelson, "Negro Women in War Work," 383–84, 376; Hannah Patterson letters to Alice Dunbar-Nelson, Box 6, Folders 155 and 156, Dunbar-Nelson Papers; Nikki Brown, *Private Politics and Public Voices: Black Women's Activism from World War I to the New Deal* (Bloomington: Indiana University Press, 2006), 33–56 (45, 46); William J. Breen, "Black Women and the Great War: Mobilization and Reform in the South," *Journal of Southern History* 44, no. 3 (August 1978): 421–40.

47. Florence Bayard Hilles to Phoebe Hearst, 29 January 1918, Hearst Collection, Bancroft Library, University of California, Berkeley, accessed online at https://oac. cdlib.org/ark:/13030/hb4q2nb2kc/?order=25&brand=oac4; DuBois, *Suffrage*, 242–48.

48. "Seek Support for Suffrage Measure," *MN*, January 18, 1918, 1, 2; Lunardini, *From Equal Suffrage to Equal Rights*, 142 (Wilson note to Wolcott); Zahniser and Fry, *Alice Paul*, 304; "Suffrage Pickets Win On Appeal," *New York Times*, March 5, 1918, 1.

49. Stevens, *Jailed for Freedom*, 259–70; "Pickets in War Work," 8; Florence Bayard Hilles, "A Suffragist Makes Munitions," *The Suffragist* 6, no. 19 (May 25, 1918): 7;

"Mrs. F.B. Hilles a Munitions Worker," *MN*, April 27, 1918, 5; "Mrs. F.B. Hilles Munition Worker at Bethlehem Plant," *EE*, April 26, 1918, 1, 3; "To Help Rebuild Towns in France," *EJ*, January 18, 1919, 2.

50. Eleanor Taylor, "Munition Workers Wait for Audience with the President," *The Suffragist* 6, no. 20 (June 1, 1918): 10–11; Gladys Greiner, "Maryland Munition Workers Appeal to President," *The Suffragist* 6, no. 22 (June 15, 1918): 7; "The Appeal of a Munition Worker," *The Suffragist* 6, no. 21 (June 8, 1918): 7. See also "New Jersey Munition Workers Appeal to the President," *The Suffragist* 6, no. 24 (June 29, 1918): 11, 14.

51. "Robert Brueire Says War Administration Needs Women," *The Suffragist* 6, no. 21 (June 8, 1918): 7.

52. Zahniser and Fry, *Alice Paul*, 304–7; "Loaded Shell for Country; Imprisoned as Suffrage Picket," *Star*, August 11, 1918, 6; Linda J. Lumsden, *Inez: The Life and Times of Inez Milholland* (Bloomington: Indiana University Press, 2004), 181.

53. "Wilson Makes Suffrage Appeal, But Senate Waits," *New York Times*, October 1, 1918, 1; "Gives Joy to Suffragists," *New York Times*, October 1, 1918, 13; "Suffrage Beaten By the Senate," *New York Times*, October 2, 1918, 1.

54. Zahniser and Fry, *Alice Paul*, 308–9 (308).

55. "Protest Arrest of Suffragists; Mrs. Florence Bayard Hilles Sees Disgrace in Having to Condemn Disfranchisement," *EJ*, August 10, 1918, 12. See also Hilles's comments on the "party in power," Letter to the Editor, "The Suffrage Amendment," *MN*, March 18, 1918, 4; and "Scores Democrats on Suffrage Stand," *EJ*, May 18, 1918, 16.

56. See Park, *Front Door Lobby*, 157–89; Eleanor Flexner, *Century of Struggle: The Woman's Rights Movement in the United States* (Cambridge, MA: Harvard University Press, 1959), 283–310; and DuBois, *Suffrage*, 245–50.

57. Melanie Grant, Victoria Bartlett, and Colleen Hall, "Biographical Sketch of Eva Halpern (Mrs. Albert) Robin," *OBD*, accessed online at https://documents.alexanderstreet.com/d/1010596148; autobiographical materials, Eva Robin Papers, ca. 1887–1959, Collection 1216, Box 1, folder 6, UCLA Library Department of Special Collections, Los Angeles, CA.

58. Grant, et al., "Eva Halpern Robin," and Ella Sargent, Taylor Curley, and Colleen Hall, "Biographical Sketch of Agnes Y. Downey," *OBD*, accessed online at https://documents.alexanderstreet.com/d/1010596167; DESA Minutes, May 30, June 29, 1917; February 1, March 25, May 27, June 24, October 28 (resolution), October 31, November 1, November 11, November 28, 1918, Ridgely Collection. See also Park, *Front Door Lobby*, 216; Flexner, *Century of Struggle*, 310–20; DuBois, *Suffrage*, 250.

59. "Present 'Votes' Cause to Unions," *MN*, September 12, 1918, 10; "To All Working Men," *MN*, November 4, 1918, 3; "The Real Question Which Confronts Delaware's Wage-Earners," *MN*, November 4, 1918, 10; DESA Minutes, October 31, 1918, Ridgely Collection; Graham, *Woman Suffrage and the New Democracy*, 119–22 (121); *History of Woman Suffrage*, eds. Elizabeth Cady Stanton, Susan B. Anthony, et al., 6 vols. (Rochester, NY: various, 1889–1922), V: 641 (hereafter *HWS*).

60. DESA Minutes, November 11, 1918, Ridgely Collection.

61. DESA Minutes, October 31, 1918 (Ball interview), Ridgely Collection; Graham, *Woman Suffrage and the New Democracy*, 122.

62. Flexner, *Century of Struggle*, 311; Graham, *Woman Suffrage and the New Democracy*, 122.

63. "Saulsbury's Defeat Should be Warning to Others, Mrs. Hilles Says," *EJ*, November 6, 1918, 1.

64. DESA Minutes, November 28, December 4, December 5, December 29, 1918, Ridgely Collection; "Woman Suffrage Leaders Campaign to Gain Support," *MN*, December 10, 1918, 6; Dumenil, *Second Line of Defense*, 256–57.

65. DuBois, *Suffrage*, 247–48.

66. "Suffragists Burn Words of Wilson," *EJ*, December 17, 1918, 15; Auer and Klinger, "Catherine Boyle," *OBD*; Flexner, *Century of Struggle*, 312–15.

67. DESA Minutes, January 6 and 10, 1919, Ridgely Collection.

68. Zahniser and Fry, *Alice Paul*, 311–12; "Wilmington Suffragist Arrested in Washington," *MN*, January 6, 1919, 1; "More Delaware Women Arrested," *EJ*, January 14, 1919, 1. See also Belinda A. Stillion Southard, *Militant Citizenship: Rhetorical Strategies of the National Woman's Party, 1913–1920* (College Station: Texas A&M University Press, 2011), 165–71.

69. "Mrs. Arniel Again Under Arrest," *EJ*, January 6, 1919, 6; "Wilmington Suffragist Sentenced to Prison," *MN*, January 7, 1919, 1; "Angry Crowds Chase Torch Bearing Suffs," *MN*, January 8, 1919, 6; "In the Name of Right and Justice," *The Suffragist 7*, no. 53 (January 25, 1919), 7–9; "Were Treated Well, Say Suffragists," *EJ*, January 21, 1919, 13; Boylan, "Annie Melvin Arniel"; Inglis, "Naomi Schopfer Barrett"; Hall, "Adelina Piunti"; DiMarco and Shields, "Annie McGee"; Auer and Klinger, "Catherine Boyle"; and Cantoran-Torres and Miles, "Mary E. Brown," *OBD*. For the Brown family's 1919 telegrams, see "Brown, Mary E. (1865–1948)," Social History Welfare Project, Virginia Commonwealth University Libraries, accessed online at https://socialwelfare.library. vcu.edu/woman-suffrage/brown-mary-e-suffragist/.

70. "Mrs. Anna M'Gee in Washington, Jail," *EJ*, January 22, 1919, 2; "Suffragists Hope for Wolcott's Aid," *EJ*, January 23, 1919, 7; "Farewell Luncheon Given Mrs. Hilles," *MN*, January 23, 1919, 3; "Suffragists Dine Mrs. W.S. Hilles," *EE*, January 23, 1919, 10. For the NWP list of women who served jail sentences, see "When You Vote, Remember These," *Equal Rights* 16, no. 29 (August 23, 1930): 228–30; a shorter list appears in Stevens, *Jailed for Freedom*, 354–71. On the bonding experiences of pickets, see Zahniser and Fry, *Alice Paul*, 258–59. On prison pins, see Susan Ware, *Why They Marched: Untold Stories of Women Who Fought for the Right to Vote* (Cambridge, MA: Harvard University Press, 2019), 237–39 (photo, 239).

71. "To Help Rebuild Towns in France: Mrs. Hilles Will Go over with American Committee," *EJ*, January 18, 1919, 2. On William Hilles's views, see Florence Bayard Hilles to Alice Paul and Lucy Burns, 15 May 1914, National Woman's Party Records, Library of Congress, Box I:17, Reel 10; and Florence Bayard Hilles to Phoebe Apperson Hearst, 16 January and 8 September 1915, Hearst Papers. On Hilles's and Vernon's views on the amendment's chances, see "Suffragists Hope for Wolcott's Aid," 7. Hilles's passport application, on which she listed her skills, including her French-speaking fluency and the ability to drive (specifically a "Cadillac"), can be found on Ancestry.com, *U.S. Passport Applications, 1795–1925* online at https://www.ancestrylibrary.com/imageviewer/collections/1174. On the American Committee for Devastated France, see "Anne Morgan's War: Rebuilding Devastated France, 1917–1924," The Morgan Library and Museum, New York, accessed online at https://www.themorgan.org/exhibitions/anne-morgans-war.

72. DESA Minutes, January 27 and February 3, 1919, Ridgely Collection; "Woman Suffrage Question Looms Up in Legislature," *MN*, January 22, 1919, 1; "Suffrage Plea

by Mrs. Victor DuPont," *EJ*, January 28, 1919, 16; "New Business in Senate Fails to Materialize," *MN*, January 21, 1919, 4 (Thompson letter).

73. Zanhiser and Fry, *Alice Paul*, 313–14; "The Demonstration of February 9," *The Suffragist* 7, no. 8 (February 22, 1919): 10–11; "Six Suffragettes Places under Arrest," *New York Times*, March 5, 1919, 3; "Believe Militants Balk Suffrage," *EJ*, February 11, 1919, 11 (Eva Robin statement).

74. Stevens, *Jailed for Freedom*, 348; Carrie Chapman Catt and Nettie Rogers Shuler, *Woman Suffrage and Politics: The Inner Story of the Woman Suffrage Movement* (New York: Scribner's, 1926), 339–42.

75. Dumenil, *Second Line of Defense*, 56–57 (56).

Chapter 4

1. The House of Representatives had provided the necessary two-thirds vote for ratification on January 10, 1918, then reasserted its support on May 21, 1919; the new Senate ratified on June 4, 1919. See Doris Stevens, *Jailed for Freedom* (New York: Boni and Liveright, 1920), 348. Delaware's Representative in the House, Caleb R. Layton, voted yea, while the state's two senators paired their votes: L. Heisler Ball, a newly elected Republican, voted yea; Josiah O. Wolcott, a Democrat and the first Delaware senator elected (1916) after the enactment of the Seventeenth Amendment, voted nay.

2. "May Call Special Session to Ratify Suffrage Bill," Wilmington *Morning News*, June 27, 1919, 7 (hereafter *MN*); "Delaware's Victory Luncheon," *The Woman Citizen* 4, no. 7 (July 19, 1919): 171. The best study of the ratification struggle in Delaware is Carol E. Hoffecker, "Delaware's Woman Suffrage Campaign," *Delaware History* 20, no. 3 (Spring-Summer 1983): 149–67. For general context, see Mary R. de Vou, "The Woman Suffrage Movement in Delaware," in *Delaware: A History of the First State*, eds. H. Clay Reed and Marion Björnson Reed, 2 vols. (New York: Lewis Historical Publishing Company, 1947), I: 349–70.

3. Elaine Weiss, *The Woman's Hour: The Great Fight to Win the Vote* (New York: Viking, 2018), 278–308.

4. Dawn Langan Teele, *Forging the Franchise: The Political Origins of the Women's Vote* (Princeton, NJ: Princeton University Press, 2018), 6, 31–33, 44; Carrie Chapman Catt and Nettie Rogers Shuler, *Woman Suffrage and Politics: The Inner Story of the Woman Suffrage Movement* (New York: Scribner's, 1926), 407–10.

5. "Suffragists Want Legislative Vote," Wilmington *Evening Journal*, June 11, 1919, 7 (hereafter *EJ*); "Doubt Favorable Vote by 1919 Legislature," *EJ*, June 27, 1919, 1. For the National Woman's Party's ratification efforts, see Inez Haynes Irwin, *The Story of the Woman's Party* (New York: Harcourt, Brace & Co., 1921), 418–76.

6. Etta J. Wilson, "Delaware's Educational Progress, 1917–1945," in Reed, *Delaware*, II: 691–93; Robert J. Taggart, *Private Philanthropy and Public Education: Pierre S. du Pont and the Delaware Schools, 1890–1940* (Newark: University of Delaware Press, 1988), 74–80; Taggart, "Pierre S. du Pont and the Great School Fight of 1919–1921," *Delaware History* 17, no. 3 (Spring 1977): 155–78; Richard B. Carter, *Clearing New Ground: The Life of John G. Townsend, Jr.* (Dover: Delaware Heritage Press, 2001), 243–73; John A. Munroe, *History of Delaware*, 3rd edition (Newark: University of Delaware Press, 1993), 198–202; Hoffecker, "Delaware's Woman Suffrage Campaign," 149–67.

Townsend had previously called a special session in 1918, at which the legislature ratified the Eighteenth (Prohibition) Amendment.

7. "Doubt Favorable Vote by 1919 Legislature," 1, 15; "Suffragists of State Celebrate Their Victory," Wilmington *Every Evening*, June 27, 1919, 14 (hereafter *EE*); Delaware Equal Suffrage Association Minutes, June 30, 1919, Ridgely Collection, Delaware Public Archives, #9200 R09, 002 1 box (hereafter DESA Minutes). On suffragist movement culture, see Sarah Hunter Graham, *Woman Suffrage and the New Democracy* (New Haven, CT: Yale University Press, 1996), 4.

8. DESA Minutes, July 1919, Ridgely Collection; Colleen Hall, "Biographical Sketch of Leah Burton (Paynter)," *Online Biographical Dictionary of the Women Suffrage Movement in the United States*, eds. Thomas Dublin and Kathryn Kish Sklar (Alexandria, VA: Alexander Street, 2015–) accessed online at https://documents.alexanderstreet.com/d/1010596163 (hereafter *OBD*). See also Melanie Grant, Victoria Bartlett, and Colleen Hall, "Biographical Sketch of Eva Halpern (Mrs. Albert) Robin," *OBD*, accessed online at https://documents.alexanderstreet.com/d/1010596148.

9. DESA Minutes, July 1919; July 28, 1919, Ridgely Collection; *History of Woman Suffrage*, ed. Ida Husted Harper (New York: National American Woman Suffrage Association, 1922), VI: 92–94 (hereafter *HWS*).

10. Jessie Hardy MacKaye, "Campaigning in Delaware with the Granddaughter of a Statesman," *The Suffragist* 7, no. 34 (August 23, 1919): 7; "Local Suffragists Hold Mass Meeting This Afternoon," *Star*, August 3, 1919, 11; "Women of Many Minds Ask Ballot," *EJ*, August 4, 1919, 7; "Mrs. Frederick Bringhurst," *Sunday Morning Star*, August 10, 1919, 22 (title varies; hereafter *Star*); "Pageant of the States to Aid Suffrage Cause," *EE*, August 7, 1919, 6; "Children Parade Tonight in Ratification Pageant," *MN*, August 9, 1919, 1; "As Work for Ratification Proceeds," *The Suffragist* 7 no. 31 (August 9, 1919): 8–9. The Majestic Theatre was located at Seventh and Market Streets.

11. Marie Lockwood to John G. Townsend, 12 August 1919, and Townsend to Lockwood, 16 August 1919; both in "Letters re Suffrage" file, John G. Townsend, Jr., Governor's Papers, RG 1307.7, Delaware Public Archives. Lockwood's letter appeared in *The Suffragist* 7, no. 34 (August 23, 1919): 7. See also Janet Lindenmuth, "Biographical Sketch of Marie Lockwood," *OBD*, accessed online at https://documents.alexanderstreet.com/d/1010595689.

12. "Suffrage Pageant," *EE*, August 11, 1919, 2; "Miss Lockwood Talks for Woman's Party," *EJ*, August 14, 1919, 1; "Doesn't Speak for All Suffragists," *EJ* August 15, 1919, 1; DESA Minutes, September 29, 1919, Ridgely Collection; "Equal Suffrage Board Meeting," *MN*, September 30, 1919, 7.

13. DESA Minutes, September 29, October 27, November 24, 1919, Ridgely Collection; "Suffragists in New Quarters," *EJ*, January 15, 1920, 7. See also Meghan Willis, "Biographical Sketch of Mabel Lloyd Fisher Ridgely, *OBD*, accessed online at https://documents.alexanderstreet.com/d/1009656548.

14. John G. Townsend, Jr. to Will Hays, 4 November 1919, Townsend Papers; Taggart, *Private Philanthropy and Public Education*, 86–88, 123; W.C. Jason quoted in Carol E. Hoffecker, *Democracy in Delaware: The Story of the First State's General Assembly* (Wilmington: Cedar Tree Books, 2004), 165.

15. "May Call Special Session to Ratify Suffrage Bill," *MN*, June 27, 1919, 7; "Woman's Party Plans Meeting Tomorrow," *EE*, August 2, 1919, 2; "Women of Many Minds Ask Ballot," 7; "Local Suffragists Hold Mass Meeting This Afternoon," *Star*,

August 3, 1919, 11; Alison Lewis, "Biographical Sketch of Alice Gertrude Baldwin," *OBD*, accessed online at https://documents.alexanderstreet.com/d/1009054793; Carol A. Scott, "Biographical Sketch of Blanche Williams Stubbs, *OBD*, accessed online at https://documents.alexanderstreet.com/d/1009054791.

16. William Tuttle, *Race Riot: Chicago in the Red Summer of 1919* (New York: Atheneum, 1978); "Want Doctor to Sell Property," *EJ*, November 26, 1919, 3; Chad L. Williams, *Torchbearers of Democracy: African American Soldiers in the World War I Era* (Chapel Hill: University of North Carolina Press, 2010), 246–60 (260). Wilmington's *Every Evening* was a particularly egregious purveyor of race-baiting material. See, for example, "Reds Among Negroes Shown by their Papers," December 11, 1919, 10, suggesting that Black soldiers sought "sex equality" by marrying French women; and an editorial, "The Race Riots in Washington," July 24, 1919, 4, blaming white racial rioting on Black male "assaults" on white women.

17. "In the Interest of Colored Girls," *Wilmington Daily Republican*, May 13, 1897, 2; "W.C.T.U. Institute," *EJ*, March 31, 1911, 2; "3 Days' Sessions of Women's Clubs," *EJ*, September 16, 1919, 3; "Colored Women's Federation," *EJ*, January 23, 1919, 2; "Ask Funds for Industrial Home," *EJ*, March 13, 1920, 7; "Plan Industrial Home for Colored Girls," *Sunday Morning Star*, March 28, 1920, 42; "Industrial School for Colored Girls," *EE*, May 29, 1920, 3; Elizabeth Lindsay Davis, *Lifting as they Climb* (1933; New York: G.K Hall, 1996), 120.

18. Hoffecker, "Delaware's Woman Suffrage Campaign," 163. See also Robyn Muncy, *Creating a Female Dominion in American Reform, 1890–1935* (New York: Oxford University Press, 1994).

19. "Doctors to Open Dry Law Fight in Legislature," *MN*, March 8, 1920, 1–2; "The Thirty-Sixth State," *The Woman Citizen* 4 (March 27, 1920): 1033; petitions and letters to John G. Townsend, Jr., Governor's Papers Regarding Suffrage, Delaware Public Archives; Carter, *John G. Townsend*, 266–74; "Anti-Suffragists Hurl Oral Bombs at Their Enemies," *EE*, March 20, 1920, 1–2; de Vou, "Woman Suffrage Movement in Delaware," 361–62; Maud Wood Park, *Front Door Lobby* (Boston: Beacon Press, 1960).

20. Hoffecker, "Delaware's Woman Suffrage Campaign," 163–64; "Nation Watching Delaware," *Philadelphia Inquirer*, March 25, 1920, 1; "In Doubtful Delaware," *Anaconda Standard*, March 28, 1920, 20; "Delaware Doubtful," *Miami Herald*, March 24, 1920, 1; "Delaware Suffrage Placed in Friendly Hands by Assembly," *Philadelphia Inquirer*, March 25, 1920, 1; "Delaware Fails of Being 36th Suffrage State," *Duluth News-Tribune*, April 2, 1920, 1; "Women Still Hope for Victory in Delaware," *Fort Wayne News Sentinel*, April 2, 1920, 13; "Suffrage Issue May be Voted on Today; Women Given Hearing," *MN*, March 26, 1920, 1.

21. "M'Adoo's Speech on Ratification Arouses Interest," *MN*, March 18, 1920, 1–2; "Dela. Center of Suffrage Fight," *EJ*, March 15, 1920, 3; "Battle in Court Threat of Antis," *MN*, March 12, 1920, 5; "Mrs. Carrie Chapman Catt," *EE* March 18, 1920, 9; "Lack Votes to Pass Suffrage," *EJ*, March 22, 1920, 7; de Vou, "Woman Suffrage Movement in Delaware," 363–64; "The Betsy Ross of Suffrage," *The Suffragist* 7, no. 28 (July 19, 1920): cover; Zahniser and Fry, *Alice Paul*, 317. Among well-known NWP organizers who spent time in Delaware were Anita Pollitzer, Elsie Hill, and Betty Gram.

22. "Mrs. Henry P. Scott," *EE*, March 13, 1920, 7; "Charge Steam Roller Methods Being Used to Get Ratification," *MN*, March 20, 1920, 1, 4; "Splendid Delaware," reprint from *Baltimore Sun*, *The Woman Patriot* 4, no. 15 (April 10, 1920): 3;

"Dauntless Delaware," *The Woman Patriot* 4, no. 23 (June 5, 1920): 1–2; "Merely Bidding for Votes," *The Woman Patriot* 4, no. 15 (April 10, 1920): cover. The Thompsons were Republicans; see Anthony Higgins, ed., "Mary Wilson Thompson Memoir (Part Three)," *Delaware History*, 18, no.3 (Spring-Summer 1979): 202–3. On Charlotte Rowe, see Susan Goodier, *No Votes for Women: The New York State Anti-Suffrage Movement* (Urbana: University of Illinois Press, 2013), 103–6; and Weiss, *The Woman's Hour*, 115–21.

23. Kimberly Jensen, *Mobilizing Minerva: American Women in the First World War* (Urbana: University of Illinois Press, 2008), 151–53.

24. "Suffrage Fight in and out of State Assembly," *EE*, March 23, 1920, 3; "Suffrage Issue May be Voted on Today; Women Given Hearing," *MN*, March 26, 1920, 1; Susan E. Marshall, *Splintered Sisterhood: Gender and Class in the Campaign against Woman Suffrage* (Madison: University of Wisconsin Press, 1997), 5, 93–140. On post-1917 changes to anti-suffrage rhetoric, see Thomas J. Jablonsky, *The Home, Heaven, and Mother Party: Female Anti-Suffragists in the United States, 1868–1920* (Brooklyn: Carlson, 1994), 98–100; Goodier, *No Votes for Women*, 124–26; and Marshall, *Splintered Sisterhood*, 205–8. See also Weiss, *The Woman's Hour*, 119–20; Alice Sheppard, *Cartooning for Suffrage* (Albuquerque: University of New Mexico Press, 1994); and Anne M. Boylan, *Women's Rights in the United States: A History in Documents* (New York: Oxford University Press, 2016), 144–57.

25. W. David Lewis, "Bissell, Emily Perkins," *Notable American Women*, eds. Edward T. James, Janet Wilson James and Paul S. Boyer, 3 vols. (Cambridge, MA: Harvard University Press, 1970), I: 152–53; James F. Louis, "Dodge, Josephine Marshall Jewell," ibid., I: 492–93; Jane Jerome Camhi, *Women Against Women: American Anti-Suffragism, 1880–1920* (Brooklyn: Carlson, 1994), 239–41; Willard Saulsbury Papers, University of Delaware Library Special Collections, MSS 331, Box 57, Folder 27 (Bissell correspondence), and Box 44, Folder 52 (Thompson telegram). See also Manuela Thurner, "Better Citizens without the Ballot: American Anti-Suffrage Women and their Rationale during the Progressive Era," *Journal of Women's History* 5, no. 1 (Spring 1993): 33–60.

26. Mary de Vou to H. Clay Reed, undated postscript to 1944 letter, H. Clay Reed Papers, MSS 0499, Box 4, Folder 66, University of Delaware Library Special Collections, Newark; Marshall, *Splintered Sisterhood*, 12; "Society Greets Young Debutante," *MN*, November 19, 1919, 5; May du Pont Saulsbury, *The Summer of 1919* (New York: Privately Printed, 1920); "Eugene du Pont's Wife Dies after 4–Year Illness," *MN*, November 23, 1954, 1, 3; "Miss Florence C. Hall," *EJ*, September 11, 1963, 16; "Elizabeth du Pont Bayard, 95, Widow of U.S. Sen. Bayard," *EJ*, September 15, 1975, 28; "Mrs. E. N. C. Lea Dies at Age of 84," *MN*, November 1, 1945, 1, 4; "Mrs. A. H. Pennewill Rites," *MN*, December 30, 1937, 4; "Mrs Thompson Rites Tomorrow," *MN*, April 3, 1947, 4.

27. Mary de Vou to H. Clay Reed, September 8, 1946, Reed Papers.

28. Anne Calvert Neely (Alice Paul's press assistant) to Mrs. Francis Nielson, 3 April 1920, National Woman's Party Records, Library of Congress, Microfilm Edition, Box I:118, Reel 78; "Women Confident of Ratification," "Fate of Amendment Involved in Doubt," and "Sees Hard Suffrage Battle in Delaware," all in *EE*, March 13, 1920, 2; "Antis Gain Strength Despite Appeals by Political Leaders," *MN*, March 17, 1920, 1–2; "Present Ratification Bill Today, Hearings Tomorrow," *MN*, March 24, 1920, 1–2; "Only Political Miracle Can Save Ratification as Battle Gets Warmer,"

MN, March 25, 1920, 1–2 (1); "Situation Shows No Signs of Change One Way or Other; Signers of the 'Round Robin' Defeat Pledge in the House Still Solid," *EE*, March 26, 1920, 1.

29. "Crux of Suffrage Issue," *EE*, March 13, 1920, 2; Editorial, "Features of the Special Session," *EE*, March 19, 1920, 4; "Think Suffrage Up to States," *EJ*, May 13, 1920, 1–2; "Layton-M'Nabb Combine to Defeat Ratification; Blame on Republicans," *EJ*, March 29, 1920, 1–2 (McNabb slurs); Alexander Keyssar, *The Right to Vote: The Contested History of Democracy in the United States* (New York: Basic Books, 2000), 217.

30. E.G.S., "Negro Women Unjustly Made Target by McNabb," *Star*, April 4, 1920, 5; Alanna Gordon, "Biographical Sketch of Emma Belle Gibson Sykes," *OBD*, accessed online at https://documents.alexanderstreet.com/d/1009054792. See also Deborah Gray White, *Too Heavy a Load: Black Women in Defense of Themselves* (New York: Norton, 1999), 104–6.

31. "Suffragists at Farewell Luncheon," *EJ*, March 11, 1915, 7; "To Organize City for Suffrage Cause," *EJ*, July 19, 1916, 1; "Women's Club Election," *EJ*, July 5, 1918, 19; "Urge Women to Support Suffrage," *EJ*, April 13, 1920, 7; "Suffrage Meeting Tonight," *EE*, April 13, 1920, 6; "Suffrage Meetings," *EE*, April 14, 1920, 6. See also Suzanne Lebsock, "Woman Suffrage and White Supremacy," in *Visible Women: New Essays on American Activism*, eds. Nancy A. Hewitt and Suzanne Lebsock (Urbana: University of Illinois Press, 1993), 62–100.

32. "Suffrage Plea by Mrs. Victor du Pont," *EJ*, January 28, 1919, 16; "Urge Lester to Vote for Suffrage," and "Smyrna Suffrage Meeting," both *EJ*, April 14, 1920, 21; "Smyrna Suffragists Discuss Amendment," *EE*, April 16, 1920, 6; Anne M. Boylan, "Biographical Sketch of Marjorie Willoughby Josephs Speakman," *OBD*, accessed online at https://documents.alexanderstreet.com/d/1009859944; Dora Kelly Lewis to Louise Lewis, Dover, 14 April 1920, Dora Kelly Lewis Correspondence, Historical Society of Pennsylvania, accessed online at http://digitalhistory.hsp.org/pafrm/doc/selected-dora-kelly-lewis-correspondence-july-4-1917–april-14-1920; Jill Zahniser, "Biographical Sketch of Dora Kelly Kuhn Lewis," *OBD*, accessed online at https://documents.alexanderstreet.com/d/1006939758. The *Smyrna Times* made no mention of the issue (April 14, 1920, 1; April 21, 1920, 1).

33. Lebsock, "Woman Suffrage and White Supremacy," 62–78; Zahniser and Fry, *Alice Paul*, 217–18; Graham, *Woman Suffrage and the New Democracy*, 23–25; Elna Green, *Southern Strategies: Southern Women and the Woman Suffrage Question* (Chapel Hill: University of North Carolina Press, 1997), 78–126; Aileen S. Kraditor, *The Ideas of the Woman Suffrage Movement, 1890–1920* (New York: Columbia University Press, 1965), 165–85; Rosalyn Terborg-Penn, "Discrimination against Afro-American Women in the Woman's Movement, 1830–1920," in *The Afro-American Woman: Struggles and Images*, eds. Sharon Harley and Rosalyn Terborg-Penn (Port Washington, NY: Kennikat Press, 1978), 17–27; Terborg-Penn, *African American Women in the Struggle for the Vote*, 107–35; Marjorie Spruill Wheeler, *New Women of the New South: The Leaders of the Woman Suffrage Movement in the Southern United States* (New York: Oxford University Press, 1993), 100–32.

34. Dora Kelly Lewis to Louise Lewis, Dover, 14 April 1920; Lebsock, "Woman Suffrage and White Supremacy," 77; "Triumphant Suffrage," *Baltimore Afro-American*, March 26, 1920, 4.

35. De Vou, "Woman Suffrage Movement in Delaware," 363; Hoffecker, "Delaware's Woman Suffrage Campaign," 158; Catt and Shuler, *Woman Suffrage and Politics*, 408; Carter, *Clearing New Ground*, 271–73; "A.I. du Pont Holds Key to Suffrage," *Philadelphia Inquirer*, April 4, 1920, 2.

36. The driver was probably Helena Hill Weed, who was in Delaware as an NWP strategist.

37. Hoffecker, "Delaware's Woman Suffrage Campaign," 164; "Suffrage Defeated in House by Vote of 22 to 9," *EJ*, April 1, 1920, 1, 7; "Line-up on Suffrage," *MN*, April 2, 1920, 1; "Suffragists 'Kidnap' Representative Hart to Ward Off Defeat," *MN*, April 1, 1920, 1. In her 1937 memoir, Mary Wilson Thompson repeated the kidnapping charge, putting Florence Bayard Hilles at the wheel of the "high-powered motor" speeding toward Hart's Townsend home. See Anthony Higgins, ed., "Mary Wilson Thompson Memoir (Part Four)," *Delaware History* 18, no. 4 (Fall-Winter 1979): 254.

38. "Suffrage Defeated in House by Vote of 22 to 9"; "Women Still Hope Delaware Will Grant Vote," *EJ*, April 2, 1920, 1; "Suffrage Seems Hopelessly Dead in Legislature," *EE*, April 2, 1920, 1, 21; "Virginia M. Scott Dies at Her Home," *MN*, July 27, 1942, 2.

39. "Mrs. Ridgely Gets Favorable Letters," *EJ*, April 7, 1920, 2; "Some Active Suffragists of Sussex," *Star*, April 18, 1920, 33; "Suffrage Issue Depends of Wish of Constituents," *MN*, April 6, 1920, 1; "Two Rallies Held in Georgetown Show Changing Sentiment," *Star*, April 4, 1920, 1; "Quiet at Dover with Suffrage in Background," *EJ*, April 6, 1920, 1; letter of Mrs. George W. Marshall, Milford, *EE*, April 16, 1920, 6; "Republican Leaders Keep Up Suffrage Fight," *EJ*, May 18, 1920, 1. Wilmington's *Every Evening* newspaper reported that anti-suffrage leader Mary Wilson Thompson had acquired a second "round robin" pledge from House members, obligating them "'not to vote for ratification at any time during the present session of the Legislature'": "No Vote Today on Suffrage Bill in Legislature," *EE*, April 9, 1920, 1. In her memoir, Mary Wilson Thompson put the number of signed pledges at eighteen. See Higgins, ed., "Mary Wilson Thompson Memoir (Part Four)," 255.

40. "De Valera Will Speak at Dover and Here Today," *MN*, April 6, 1920, 1; "DeValera Makes Suffrage Plea," *EJ*, May 18, 1920, 1, 12; "Dover Solons Resent Acts of Outsiders on Suffrage," *EJ*, May 19, 1920, 1, 7. See also Margaret Ward, "Suffrage First, above All Else! An Account of the Irish Suffrage Movement," *Feminist Review*, no. 10 (February 1982): 21–36.

41. "Forward Delaware!" *The Woman Citizen* 4, no. 41 (May 1, 1920): 1204; "Delaware's Second Chance," *The Suffragist* 8 (May 8, 1920): 53–55, 70–72; "Suffrage Cohorts Stormed Capital Battling for Votes," *EE*, April 20, 1920, 6; "Ovation for Suffrage When Convention Urges Ratification," *MN*, April 21, 1920, 1; de Vou, "Woman Suffrage Movement in Delaware," 366; Catt and Shuler, *Woman Suffrage and Politics*, 411–12.

42. "How Senators Voted on the Greatest Issue of the Day," *MN*, May 6, 1920, 1.

43. De Vou, "Woman Suffrage Movement in Delaware," 367 ("lock and key"); Catt and Shuler, *Woman Suffrage and Politics*, 412 ("stolen"); "Suffrage Fate Up to Meeting in Dover Today," *EJ*, May 17, 1920, 3; "State Senate to Adopt Suffrage This Afternoon," *EJ*, May 5, 1920, 1, 7; "M'Nabb Jarred by Women's Petition," *EJ*, May 6, 1920, 18; Constance J. Cooper, "Biographical Sketch of Jane White Pennewill," *OBD*, accessed online at https://documents.alexanderstreet.com/d/1010111668.

44. "McNabb Charges Bribery Attempt, Gives No Proof," *EJ*, May 7, 1920, 1, 7; *Star*, May 2, 1920, 1; "Wilson Asks Democrats to Support Suffrage," *EJ*, June 2, 1920, 1,

9; "House Votes Down Suffrage by 22 to 9," *EJ*, April 1, 1920, 7; "Suffrage Defeated without Reaching Floor of House," *MN*, June 3, 1920, 1–2; "Suffrage is Dead; No New House Vote," *EJ*, June 3, 1920, 1, 2; Hoffecker, "Delaware's Woman Suffrage Campaign," 166; de Vou, "Woman Suffrage Movement in Delaware," 367; "Delaware Again Defeats Suffrage," *The Woman Patriot* 4, no. 23 (June 5, 1920): 1; "Dauntless Delaware," 1–2; Higgins, ed., "Mary Wilson Thompson Memoir (Part Four)," 251–59 (257); Weiss, *The Woman's Hour*. The existing evidence does not bear out Mary de Vou's charge that House members tricked the pro-suffrage group by adjourning before a scheduled ratification vote.

45. "A. I. Du Pont Holds Key to Suffrage," *Philadelphia Inquirer*, April 4, 1920, 2.

46. "Suffrage Campaign Seeking to Impress Sussex Politicians: Fight Against Gov. Townsend for Delegate, Linked with Suffrage by Opposition," *Star*, April 11, 1920, 1–2; "Some Active Suffragists of Sussex," 33; Catt and Shuler, *Woman Suffrage and Politics*, 409–10; Carter, *Clearing New Ground*, 280–88.

47. "Women Still Hopeful Delaware Will Grant Vote," 1; "Suffrage Campaign Seeking to Impress Sussex Politicians: Fight Against Gov. Townsend for Delegate, Linked with Suffrage by Opposition," *Star*, April 11, 1920, 1; Carter, *Clearing New Ground*, 200–202; Hoffecker, *Democracy in Delaware*, 158–65.

48. Flexner, *Century of Struggle*, 296–98; Weiss, *The Woman's Hour*, 228–29. See letter to Sunday *Star* signed "Suffragist," April 4, 1920, 5, citing Democrats' thralldom "to the 'booze' interests" and downstate employers' fear that suffrage would be "a menace to their exploitation of women and children"; Carter, *Clearing New Ground*, 230; Munroe, *History of Delaware*, 160–66; "House Defeats Physicians' Bill By Close Vote," *MN*, April 20, 1920, 1; "Will War on the Wets," *MN*, April 20, 1920, 4. Changes to the suffrage-temperance nexus in New Castle County can readily be traced in the WCTU county branch's shifting concerns after 1918: Delaware WCTU, New Castle County Branch Minutes, Box 1, Folder 27, Delaware Historical Society.

49. Munroe, *History of Delaware*, 162. On legislators' assumptions about women voters, see Teele, *Forging the Franchise*, 31–37.

50. William W. Boyer and Edward C. Rutledge, *Delaware Politics and Government* (Lincoln: University of Nebraska Press, 2009), 54–56, 86; John A. Munroe, *History of Delaware*, 3rd edition (Newark: University of Delaware Press, 1993), 168. Population statistics from Reed, ed., *Delaware*, II: 976; David Ames, et al., "African American Population of Delaware," Center for Historic Architecture and Engineering, University of Delaware, 1991; Mary Wilson Thompson to John G. Townsend, Jr., January 23, 1920, Townsend Papers, Delaware Public Archives.

51. DESA Minutes, November 16, 1916, January 5, 1917, Ridgely Collection; "Milford and That Canvass," *EJ*, March 15, 1917, 4; "Antis Claim New Strength in Kent," *EE*, March 18, 1920, 6; *Star*, March 28, 1920, 2; "Look to Sussex for Suffrage Aid," *EJ*, April 12, 1920, 2; "Suffs Will Hold Street Meeting," *MN*, April 17, 1920, 12; "Legislature to Grant Suffrage Hearing," *EE*, March 15, 1920, 6; "Anti-Suffrage Meeting at Milford," *EE*, April 10, 1920, 12; "'Antis' to Strengthen Down State Work," *Star*, April 11, 1920, 17; "Anti-Suffrage at Middletown," *EE*, April 21, 1920, 20; "Smyrna Turns Out to Hear Antis," *EE*, April 24, 1920, 2; "Laurel Sentiment Strongly Against Equal Suffrage," *EE*, April 28, 1920, 2.

52. Cartoon, *MN*, May 7, 1920, 1; Taggart, "Pierre S. du Pont and the Great School Fight," 174–75; Weiss, *The Woman's Hour*, 309–24.

53. "Urges Free Ballot for Colored Women: Mrs. Alice Dunbar-Nelson Speaks for Enlightened Use of the Franchise," *Star*, August 22, 1920, 3; "Women at Booths to Register Early; Reveal Ages, Too," *EJ*, September 18, 1920, 1, 7; "Bridgeville Voters Hear G.O.P. Issues," *EJ*, October 30, 1920, 8; "Colored Women in Republican Club," *EJ*, September 8, 1920, 8; "Delaware League of Women Voters in Convention," *EE*, September 29, 1920, 1, 13; "Women Will Have But Two Days to Register," *Star*, August 15, 1920, 1, 6; "First to Register is Woman's Claim," *MN*, September 21, 1920, 3; "Blue Hen's Chickens Scratching up Politics," *The Woman Citizen* 5, no. 19 (October 9, 1920): 509, 512. See also Liette Gidlow, "Delegitimizing Democracy: 'Civic Slackers,' the Cultural Turn, and the Possibilities of Politics," *Journal of American History* 89, no. 3 (December 2002): 922–57.

54. "Drive Started on J. E. M'Nabb," *EJ*, October 23, 1920, 1, 11; "Where the Suffrage Issue Counted," *The Woman Citizen* 5, no. 25 (November 20, 1920): 682, 689; "After M'Nabb for Fight on Suffrage," *EJ*, October 16, 1920, 5; Cooper, "Jane White Pennewill,"; Anne M. Boylan, "Biographical Sketch of Mary Seward Phillips (Mrs. John R.) Eskridge," *OBD*, accessed online at https://documents.alexanderstreet.com/d/1010111651; and Constance J. Cooper, "Biographical Sketch of Anna Bathsheba Fisher (Mrs. Willard S.) Morse," *OBD*, accessed online at https://documents.alexanderstreet.com/d/1010111667. On Lloyd and Lord's alliance with McNabb, see "Mr. Townsend Would Step Aside to Pass Suffrage; Hart Balks at Vote Today," *EJ*, March 31, 1920, 1, 11.

55. Alice Dunbar-Nelson, "Race Prejudice in the Local Campaign," *Star*, October 17, 1920, 5; "Republican Speaker in Row at Dover," *EE*, October 14, 1920, 6; "Mrs. Terrell Protests," *EE*, October 15, 1920, 3; "Colored Women in Big Rally," *EJ*, October 15, 1920, 26. Terrell described the incident in her autobiography, *A Colored Woman in a White World* (Washington, DC: Ransdell, 1940), 349–54, terming it "the only unpleasant experience I have had during a political campaign" (350). For Isaacs's statement and his disingenuous response to criticisms of it, see "Democrats Swear Out Four Warrants," *EJ*, October 15, 1920, 10; and "Isaacs Replies to Warner on Election Cases," *EJ*, October 20, 1920, 1. During October, too, Dunbar-Nelson was dealing with a humiliating reprimand from Howard High School's principal, Ray Wooten, which eventually led to her dismissal from the post she had held for eighteen years; see *Give Us Each Day: The Diary of Alice Dunbar-Nelson*, ed. Gloria T. Hull (New York: Norton, 1984), 41–42.

56. Alice G. Baldwin to Portia M. Wiley, 14 November 1920, NAACP Papers, Library of Congress, microfilm edition, Part 12: Selected Branch Files, 1913–1939; Part B: The Northeast, Reel #1; "G.O.P. Women in Jubilee; Applaud M'Nabb's Defeat," *MN*, November 3, 1920, 1, 13; "Where the Suffrage Issue Counted: In Delaware," *Woman Citizen* 5, no. 25 (November 20, 1920): 682, 689; Alison Lewis, "Alice Gertrude Baldwin," *OBD*, accessed online at https://documents.alexanderstreet.com/d/1009054793"; Cooper, "Jane White Pennewill"; Cooper, "Anna Fisher Morse"; and Boylan "Mary Seward Phillips (Mrs. John R.) Eskridge," *OBD*.

57. "47,084 Register to Vote in City, 19,763 Women," *MN*, October 18, 1920, 1; "Republicans See Victory in Delaware," *EJ*, November 1, 1920, 1, 9; "Record Vote is Polled in City; Women Rush Booths," *EJ*, November 2, 1920, 1, 14; Editorial, "Women's Part in the Election," *EE*, November 10, 1920, 4; Keyssar, *The Right To Vote*, 168–71; Christina Wolbrecht and J. Kevin Corder, *A Century of Votes for Women: American*

Elections Since Suffrage (New York: Cambridge University Press, 2020), 61–87; Higgins, ed., "Mary Wilson Thompson Memoir (Part Four)," 251.

58. "Repubs Favor Clean Election," *EJ*, October 9, 1920, 1, 2; "Democratic Women Start Organization," *EE*, July 21, 1922, 2; Anne M. Boylan, "Biographical Sketch of Annie Melvin Arniel," *OBD*, accessed online at https://documents.alexanderstreet.com/d/1009054733; Boylan, "Margaret Burton White Houston"; Boylan, "Mary Seward Phillips (Mrs. John R.) Eskridge"; Anne M. Boylan, "Biographical Sketch of Anna May Beauchamp Reynolds," *OBD*, accessed online at https://documents.alexanderstreet.com/d/1009859943; Willis, "Mabel Lloyd Fisher Ridgely"; and Boylan, "Marjorie Willoughby Josephs Speakman." Speakman later served on the National Council of Republican Women, and in the 1950s, as a presidential appointee, became the only woman member of the National Council of Consultants to the Small Business Administration.

Epilogue

1. NAACP Papers, Library of Congress, microfilm edition, Voting Rights Campaigns, Part 4, Reel #2; Paula Giddings, *When and Where I Enter: The Impact of Black Women on Race and Sex in America* (New York: William Morrow, 1984), 166; Lynn Dumenil, *The Second Line of Defense: American Women and World War I* (Chapel Hill: University of North Carolina Press, 2017), 263; Liette Gidlow, "More than Double: African American Women and the Rise of a 'Women's Vote,'" *Journal of Women's History* 32, no. 1 (Spring 2020): 58. On African American women's participation in the League of Women Voters, see Evelyn Brooks Higginbotham, "Clubwomen and Electoral Politics in the 1920s," in *African American Women and the Vote, 1837–1965*, eds. Ann D. Gordon and Bettye Collier-Thomas (Amherst: University of Massachusetts Press, 1997), 144–50.

2. See William Pickens, "The Woman Voter Hits the Color Line," *The Nation* 111 (October 6, 1920): 372–73.

3. "City Charter Gains Support," *Evening Journal* (hereafter *EJ*), February 9, 1921, 1, 3; "Colored Women for New Charter," *Morning News* (hereafter *MN*), February 9, 1921, 11; "Washington Letter," *New York Age*, February 19, 1921, 2; Ella Rush Murray, "The Woman's Party and the Violation of the 19th Amendment," *The Nation* 112 (February 16, 1921): 257–58; Freda Kirchwey, "Alice Paul Pulls the Strings," *The Nation* 112 (March 2, 1921): 332–33; *The Crisis* 21 (April 1921): 260; "Miss Vernon Given Ovation," *MN*, February 17, 1921, 2; "Women Going to Washington," *Every Evening* (hereafter *EE*), May 20, 1922, 6; "Colored Clubwomen Advocate New Laws," *EJ*, January 19, 1923, 22; Giddings, *When and Where I Enter*, 166–70; Nancy F. Cott, *The Grounding of Modern Feminism* (New Haven, CT: Yale University Press, 1987), 68–70.

4. "Memorial to Suffragists," *EJ*, January 26, 1921, 5; Giddings, *When and Where I Enter*, 168–69 (168); Lisa Tetrault, *The Myth of Seneca Falls: Memory and the Women's Suffrage Movement, 1848–1898* (Chapel Hill: University of North Carolina Press, 2014), 187–90. The "portrait monument," as it was later dubbed, was quickly relegated to the crypt below the Capitol Rotunda. For coverage of the controversy over its representational exclusions, see "A Black Group Assails Statue of Suffragists," *The New York Times*, March 9, 1997, 8.

5. "Explains Clash over Dr. Banton," *EJ*, April 14, 1921, 10; "Colored Women Urge Dr. Banton's Election," *MN*, June 2, 1921, 7; "Dedication of Girls' School," *EJ*, December

Notes 215

6, 1924, 15; "School Gifts Appreciated," *EJ*, October 26, 1922, 11; "Negro Women Must Be Emancipators of Race," *EE*, October 16, 1922, 5; "Ask State to Bar Ku Klux," *EJ*, August 5, 1921, 1, 16; "Appropriations to Run State for Two Years Now in Legislature," *EJ*, March 15, 1923, 10; "Colored Clubwomen Advocate New Laws," *EJ*, January 19, 1923, 22; "Delaware N.A.A.C.P Opposes Ku Klux Meeting in Wilmington," Chicago *Broad Ax*, August 18, 1923, 2; "Negroes Oppose Klan Meeting," *EJ*, August 3, 1923, 21; "Clash Over Use of City Playfields," *EJ*, August 4, 1927, 1, 11; "Industrial School Needs More Funds," *Sunday Morning Star*, February 24, 1929, 5 (hereafter *Star*); Carol A. Scott, "Biographical Sketch of Blanche Williams Stubbs," *Online Biographical Dictionary of the Women Suffrage Movement in the United States*, eds. Thomas Dublin and Kathryn Kish Sklar (Alexandria, VA: Alexander Street, 2015-) (hereafter *OBD*), accessed online at https://documents.alexanderstreet.com/d/1009054791; Annette Woolard-Provine, *Integrating Delaware: The Reddings of Wilmington* (Newark: University of Delaware Press, 2004), 86; *Report of the Industrial School for Colored Girls of Delaware at Marshallton, Delaware, December, 1928* (Wilmington, n.p., 1929), 3–4.

6. Christina Wolbrecht and J. Kevin Corder, *A Century of Votes for Women: American Elections since Suffrage* (New York: Cambridge University Press, 2020), 69–85 (85); *Star*, October 17, 1920, 21; "Lay Plans for Liberal Party," *EJ*, April 13, 1922, 10; "Progressive Party Opens Headquarters," *MN*, September 6, 1924, 4; "Elizabeth Stirlith Runs as Elector for Progressive Party," *EE*, September 15, 1924, 1; Janet Lindenmuth, "Biographical Sketch of Elizabeth Bussier Stirlith," *OBD*, https://documents.alexanderstreet.com/d/1010595690.

7. Gidlow, "More Than Double," 53–54.

8. "Negro Women Must be Emancipators of Race; Federation Told Vote against Dr. Layton is Step in This Direction," *EE*, October 26, 1922, 5; "Republicans Carry Wilmington by 1700; Layton Badly Cut," *MN*, November 8, 1922, 17; "Raps Some as Party Traitors," *EJ*, October 18, 1924, 3; Melinda Plastas, *A Band of Noble Women: Racial Politics in the Women's Peace Movement* (Syracuse, NY: Syracuse University Press, 2011), 65–67; Lisa Materson, *For the Freedom of Her Race: Black Women and Electoral Politics in Illinois, 1877–1932* (Chapel Hill: University of North Carolina Press, 2009), 127–33, 183–84.

9. "Mrs. Henry Ridgely Describes League of Women Voters," *EE*, October 19, 1921, 1; "Rivalry in Children, Not Armaments, Urged on Women," *MN*, October 21, 1921, 5; "Women's Legislative Committee to Meet," *EE*, April 25, 1923, 20; "Women Ask for Legislation," *EJ*, February 24, 1925, 10; "Women to Urge Passage of Bills by Legislature," *MN*, March 16, 1929, 1; "Justly Indignant," *EJ*, April 21, 1923, 4, quoting an *EE* editorial. In the 1915 case of *Mackenzie v. Hare*, the Supreme Court had upheld a federal law taking away the citizenship of American-born women who married men with foreign citizenship (American-born men who married women with foreign citizenship were not affected). The highest-profile Delawarean who lost her citizenship due to the federal law was Alice du Pont Ortiz. See "Admit 44 More to Citizenship," *EJ*, June 10, 1926, 5. The Joint Legislative Committee was modeled on the Women's Joint Congressional Committee, a national organization coordinating lobbying in Congress. See Jan Doolittle Wilson, *The Women's Joint Congressional Committee and the Politics of Maternalism, 1920–1930* (Urbana: University of Illinois Press, 2007).

10. "Club Women to Co-Operate," *EJ*, December 5, 1928, 24; "Club Women to Investigate One Man Car Plan; Better Housing also Subject," *EJ*, January 2, 1929, 14.

11. Cott, *Grounding of Modern Feminism*, 247–63; Kirsten Marie Delegard, *Battling Miss Bolsheviki: The Origins of Female Conservatism in the United States* (Philadelphia: University of Pennsylvania Press, 2012).

12. 2. "Birth Rates and Infant Mortality Rates, 1929," *Public Health Reports* 45, no. 45 (November 7, 1930): 2757, "Baby Bill Assailed," *MN*, April 26, 1921, 6; "An Appeal to the Senate," *The Woman Patriot* 10 (December 1, 1926): 1; *Congressional Record*, 69th Congress, 2nd Session, 68 (January 8, 1927): 1285; "Statement of Anti's Campaign Expenses," *EE*, June 30, 1920, 9; Anthony Higgins, ed., "Mary Wilson Thompson Memoir" (Part Four), *Delaware History* 18, no. 4 (Fall-Winter 1979): 251. See also Anne M. Boylan, *Women's Rights in the United States: A History in Documents* (New York: Oxford University Press, 2016), 183–84.

13. "First Woman Jurist [Juror] for Court Here," *MN*, April 4, 1921, 12; "Miss Smith First Woman Notary," *EJ*, January 18, 1921, 10; "Miss Sybil Ursula Ward," *MN*, March 24, 1923, 7; "Woman on Federal Jury," *MN*, September 14, 1921, 1; "Husband, Wife Now Attorneys," *Journal-Every Evening*, November 22, 1941, 3; William P. Frank, "The Year Cabinet Was Created," *EJ*, January 4, 1971, 21.

14. "Women at Memorial," *EJ*, December 7, 1929, 13; "Wilmington Women to Attend Memorial," *MN*, December 7, 1929, 7; "Belmont Funeral a National Tribute," *New York Times*, February 13, 1933, 17. See also Joan Marie Johnson, *Funding Feminism: Monied Women, Philanthropy, and the Women's Movement, 1870–1967* (Chapel Hill: University of North Carolina Press, 2017), 67–69.

15. "Annie S. McGee Jackson," *Equal Rights* 20 (May 12, 1934): 20; "Mary E. Brown Rites; Pioneer Suffragette," *Journal-Every Evening*, December 28, 1948, 21; "Militant Suffrage Worker Suicide," *Star*, February 10, 1924, 1; "Gas Fatal to Mrs. Arniel," *EJ*, February 11, 1924, 18.

16. Tetrault, *The Myth of Seneca Falls*, 190–92; Cott, *Grounding of Modern Feminism*, 75–79; Amy Aronson, *Crystal Eastman: A Revolutionary Life* (New York: Oxford University Press, 2020), 225–30; Kirchwey, "Alice Paul Pulls the Strings"; "Negro Women Appeal Against Ku Klux Klan," *EE*, October 12, 1923, 4. According to Cott, "two months after the [1921] convention, the NWP had 151 paid members" (72).

17. Carol E. Hoffecker, *Corporate Capital: Wilmington in the Twentieth Century* (Philadelphia: Temple University Press, 1983), 65–105; Madison Heitz, Mia Cimino, and Jessica Sharp, "Biographical Sketch of Florence Bayard Hilles," *OBD*, accessed online at https://documents.alexanderstreet.com/d/1008342612. On the Birth Control League, see "Birth Control Clinic Soon to Open in City," *EJ*, July 7, 1931, 1, 24; and First Unitarian Society of Wilmington Records, Box 3, folder 8, Delaware Historical Society.

18. "Bill is Backed by M'Dowell," *MN*, February 9, 1955, 34; "Mrs. W.S. Hilles, Noted Suffragist," *New York Times*, June 12, 1954, 15; Boylan, *Women's Rights in the United States*, 167–71, 194, 241–46. See also Marjorie Julian Spruill, *Divided We Stand: The Battle over Women's Rights and Family Values that Polarized American Politics* (New York: Bloomsbury, 2017).

19. William W. Boyer and Edward C. Rutledge, *Delaware Politics and Government* (Lincoln: University of Nebraska Press, 2009), 86; Suzanne Moore, "Have We Forgotten the Equal Rights Amendment?" Wilmington *News-Journal*, March 8, 2016, A8; Carl Heckert, "Equal Rights Amendment Caps almost 50 Years of Work," ibid., January 28, 2019, A11.

Bibliography

Manuscript Collections

Delaware Historical Society, Wilmington
Arden-Stephens Collection.
Bayard Family Papers, Callery Collection
First Unitarian Society of Wilmington. Records.
Helen Garrett Scrapbook
Florence Bayard Hilles Papers.
New Century Club of Wilmington Records.
Emalea Pusey Warner Papers.
Woman's Christian Temperance Union Papers.
Woman's Suffrage Movement. Miscellaneous Clippings Collection.
Thelma Young Papers.

Delaware Public Archives, Dover
Ridgely Family Papers, including Delaware Equal Suffrage Association
    Minutes, 1916–1919.
John G. Townsend, Jr., Governor's Papers.

University of Delaware Archives, Newark
Delaware Women's College Papers.

University of Delaware Library Special Collections, Newark
Alice Dunbar-Nelson Papers.
Alice Dunbar-Nelson Scrapbooks.
Henry Clay Reed Papers.
Willard Saulsbury Papers.

Library of Congress, Washington, D.C.
National American Woman Suffrage Association (NAWSA) Records.
   Microfilm edition.
National Association for the Advancement of Colored People (NAACP)
   Papers. Microfilm edition.
National Woman's Party (NWP) Records. Microfilm and Digital editions.

Bancroft Library, University of California, Berkeley
Phoebe Apperson Hearst Letters to Florence Bayard Hilles. Digital edition,
   https://oac.cdlib.org/ark:/13030/hb0r29n68n/?order=15&brand=oac4.

UCLA Library Department of Special Collections, Los Angeles, CA
Eva Halpern Robin Papers.

Historical Society of Pennsylvania, Philadelphia
Dora Kelly Lewis Correspondence, accessible at http://digitalhistory.
   hsp.org/pafrm/doc selected-dora-kelly-lewis-correspondence-
   july-4-1917–april-14-1920.

*Schlesinger Library, Radcliffe Institute for Advanced Study, Harvard University,
   Cambridge, MA*
Papers of Maud Wood Park in the Woman's Rights Collection, 1870–1960,
   Subseries C. Suffrage and Women's Rights. Digital Materials.
   https://hollisarchives.lib.harvard.edu/repositories/8/archival_objects/2621256.

Swarthmore College, Swarthmore, PA
Woman's Peace Party, Delaware Branch Correspondence, 1915–1918.

Published Primary Sources

Anthony, Susan B., et al. *History of Woman Suffrage.* 6 vols. New York: National
   American Woman Suffrage Association. 1889–1922.
Buhle, Paul and Mari Jo Buhle. *The Concise History of Woman Suffrage: Selec-
   tions from the History of Woman Suffrage.* Urbana: University of Illinois
   Press, 2005.
Catt, Carrie Chapman and Nettie Rogers Shuler. *Woman Suffrage and Politics:
   The Inner Story of the Suffrage Movement.* New York: Scribner's, 1926.
Davis, Elizabeth Lindsay. *Lifting as They Climb.* 1933; New York: G.K. Hall, &
   Co., 1966.
*Debates and Proceedings of the Constitutional Convention of the State of Dela-
   ware . . . Commencing December 1, 1896.* 5 vols. Milford: Milford Chronicle
   Publishing Co., 1958.
Dunbar-Nelson, Alice. "Negro Women in War Work." In Emmett J. Scott,
   Scott's Official History of The American Negro in the World War. Chicago:
   Homewood Press, 1919.
Gordon, Ann, et al., eds. *The Selected Papers of Elizabeth Cady Stanton and*

Susan B. Anthony. 6 vols. New Brunswick, NJ: Rutgers University Press, 1997–2013.

Higgins, Anthony, ed. "Mary Wilson Thompson Memoir (Part Three)." *Delaware History* 18, no. 3 (Spring-Summer 1979): 194–217.

———, ed. "Mary Wilson Thompson Memoir (Part Four)." *Delaware History* 18, no. 4 (Fall-Winter 1979): 238–66.

Hull, Gloria T., ed. *Give Us Each Day: The Diary of Alice Dunbar-Nelson.* New York: Norton, 1984.

Hunton, Addie, and Kathryn M. Johnson. *Two Colored Women with the American Expeditionary Forces.* Brooklyn: Brooklyn Eagle Press, 1920.

Irwin, Inez Haynes. *The Story of The Woman's Party.* New York: Harcourt, Brace, & Co., 1921.

Johnson, Helen Kendrick. *Women and the Republic: A Survey of the Woman-Suffrage Movement in the United States and a Discussion of the Claims and Arguments of its Foremost Advocates.* 1897; New York: Guidon Club, 1913.

Leonard, Priscilla [Emily Bissell]. "The Working-Woman and Anti-Suffrage." *Harper's Bazaar* 43 (November 1909): 1169–70.

Link, Arthur, et al., eds. *The Papers of Woodrow Wilson,* 69 vols. Princeton, NJ: Princeton University Press, 1966–1994.

National American Woman Suffrage Association. *Victory, How Women Won It: A Centennial Symposium, 1840–1940.* New York: H.W. Wilson, 1940.

Olcott, Jane. *The Work of Colored Women.* Colored Work Committee War Work Council, National Board, Young Women's Christian Associations (sic), New York City, n.d.

Park, Maud Wood. *Front Door Lobby.* Boston: Beacon, 1960.

Report of the Industrial School for Colored Girls at Marshallton, Delaware, December 1928.

Wilmington: n.p., 1929.

Root, Grace C. *Women and Repeal.* New York: Harper, 1934.

Saulsbury, May du Pont. *The Summer of 1919.* New York: Privately Printed, 1920.

St. Clair, Labert. *The Story of the Liberty Loans.* Washington, D.C.: James William Bryan Press, 1919.

Steckel, Minnie. "The Alabama Business Woman as Citizen." *Alabama College Bulletin,* 30:1 (July 1937): 11–63.

Stevens, Doris. *Jailed for Freedom.* New York: Boni and Liveright, 1920.

Terrell, Mary Church. *A Colored Woman in a White World.* Washington, D.C.: Ransdell, Inc., 1940.

———. *The Progress of Colored Women: An Address Delivered before the National American Woman Suffrage Association.* Washington, D.C.: Smith Brothers, 1898.

WCTU of Delaware. *Annual Reports* (title varies). 1887–1931.

YWCA of Wilmington. *Yearbooks* and *Annual Reports.* 1901–1936.

Interviews

Ginns, Sallie Topkis. Interview by Myron L. Lazarus, n.d. Robert H. Richards, Jr. Oral History Collection. MSS 179. University of Delaware Library Special Collections, Newark.

Paul, Alice. Interview by Amelia R. Fry. Suffragists Oral History Project. Bancroft Library. University of California, Berkeley. https://oac.cdlib.org/ark:/13030/kt6f59n89c/?brand=oac4.

Stirlith, Frank. Interview January 12 and 14, 1960, Box 1, Reel, 27, Eleutherian Mills-Hagley Foundation oral history interviews on the history of the DuPont Company Powder Yard [accession #1970.370]. Hagley Museum and Library, Wilmington, DE. http://digital.hagley.org/islandora/object/islandora:2033695#page/1/mode/1up.

Vernon, Mabel. Interview by Amelia R. Fry. Suffragists Oral History Project. Bancroft Library. University of California at Berkeley. http://bancroft.berkeley.edu/ROHO/projects/suffragist/.

Secondary Works: Print

Adams, Betty Livingston. *Black Women's Christian Activism: Seeking Social Justice in a Northern Suburb.* New York: New York University Press, 2016.

Adams, Katherine H. and Michael L. Keene. *Alice Paul and the American Suffrage Campaign.* Urbana: University of Illinois Press, 2008.

Alonso, Harriet Hyman. *Peace as a Women's Issue: A History of the U.S. Movement for World Peace and Women's Rights.* Syracuse, NY: Syracuse University Press, 1993.

Aronson, Amy. *Crystal Eastman: A Revolutionary Life.* New York: Oxford University Press, 2020.

Auerbach, Jonathan. *Weapons of Democracy: Propaganda, Progressivism, and American Public Opinion.* Baltimore: Johns Hopkins University Press, 2015.

Axelrod, Alan. *Selling the Great War: The Making of American Propaganda.* New York: Palgrave Macmillan, 2009.

Baker, Jean, ed. *Votes for Women: The Struggle for Suffrage Revisited.* New York: Oxford University Press, 2002.

Blair, Karen. *The Clubwoman as Feminist: True Womanhood Redefined, 1868–1914.* New York: Holmes & Meier, 1980.

Boyer, William W. and Edward C. Rutledge. *Delaware Politics and Government.* Lincoln: University of Nebraska Press, 2009.

Boylan, Anne M. *Women's Rights in the United States: A History in Documents.* New York: Oxford University Press, 2016.

———. "Claiming Visibility: Women in Public/Public Women in the United States, 1865–1910." In *Becoming Visible: Women in View in Late Nineteenth-Century America.* Edited by Janet Floyd, Alison Eastman and R. J. Ellis. Amsterdam: Rodopi, 2010.

———. "Delaware's African American Suffragists. Introduction." *Delaware History* 35, no. 2 (Fall-Winter 2019–2020): 106–16.

Bredbenner, Candice. *A Nationality of Her Own: Women, Marriage, and the Law of Citizenship*. Berkeley: University of California Press, 2002.

Breen, William J. "Black Women and the Great War: Mobilization and Reform in the South," *Journal of Southern History* 44:3 (August 1978): 421–40.

Brown, Nikki. *Private Politics and Public Voices: Black Women's Activism from World War I to the New Deal*. Bloomington: Indiana University Press, 2006.

Camhi, Jane Jerome. *Women Against Women: American Anti-Suffragism, 1880–1920*. Brooklyn: Carlson, 1994.

Capozzola, Christopher. *Uncle Sam Wants You: World War I and the Making of the Modern American Citizen*. New York: Oxford University Press, 2008.

Carter, Richard. *Clearing New Ground: The Life of John G. Townsend, Jr.* Wilmington: Delaware Heritage Press, 2001.

Chapman, Mary. *Making Noise, Making News: Suffrage Print Culture and U.S. Modernism*. New York: Oxford University Press, 2014.

Cooper, Brittney C. *Beyond Respectability: The Intellectual Thought of Race Women*. Urbana: University of Illinois Press, 2017.

Corder, J. Kevin, and Christina Wolbrecht. *Counting Women's Ballots: Female Voters from Suffrage Through the New Deal*. New York: Cambridge University Press, 2016.

Cott, Nancy F. *The Grounding of Modern Feminism*. New Haven, CT: Yale University Press, 1987.

———. "Marriage and Women's Citizenship in the United States, 1830–1934." *American Historical Review* 103, no. 5 (December 1998): 1440–75.

de Vou, Mary R. "The Woman Suffrage Movement in Delaware." In *Delaware: A History of the First State*. Edited by H. Clay Reed and Marion Björnson Reed. New York: Lewis Publishing Company, 1947.

Degen, Mary Louise. *The History of the Woman's Peace Party*. 1939; New York: Garland, 1972.

Delegard, Kirsten Marie. *Battling Miss Bolsheviki: The Origins of Female Conservatism in the United States*. Philadelphia: University of Pennsylvania Press, 2012.

Downey, Dennis B. "'Mercy Master, Mercy': Racial Politics and the Lynching of George White," *Delaware History* 30 (Spring/Summer 2003): 189–210.

Dublin, Thomas and Angela Scheuerer. "Why Did African American Women Join the Woman's Christian Temperance Union, 1880 to 1900?" *Women and Social Movements in the United States*. https://documents.alexanderstreet.com/c/1000636143.

DuBois, Ellen Carol. *Harriot Stanton Blatch and the Winning of Woman Suffrage*. New Haven, CT: Yale University Press, 1999.

———. *Suffrage: Women's Long Battle for the Vote*. New York: Simon and Schuster, 2020.

Dudden, Faye. *Fighting Chance: The Struggle over Woman Suffrage and Black Suffrage in Reconstruction America*. New York: Oxford University Press, 2011.

Dumenil, Lynn. *The Second Line of Defense: American Women and World War I*. Chapel Hill: University of North Carolina Press, 2017.

Edwards, Rebecca. *Angels in the Machinery: Gender in American Party Politics from the Civil War to the Progressive Era*. New York: Oxford University Press, 1997.

Elshtain, Jean Bethke. *Jane Addams and the Dream of American Democracy: A Life*. New York: Basic Books, 2002.

Evans, Richard. *The Feminists: Women's Emancipation Movements in Europe, America, and Australia, 1840–1920*. London: Croom Helm, 1977.

Flexner, Eleanor. *Century of Struggle: The Woman's Rights Movement in the United States*. Cambridge, MA: Harvard University Press, 1959.

Fowler, Robert Booth. *Carrie Catt: Feminist Politician*. Boston: Northeastern University Press, 1986.

Franzen, Trisha. *Anna Howard Shaw: The Work of Woman Suffrage*. Urbana: University of Illinois Press, 2014.

Gallagher, Julie A. *Black Women and Politics in New York City*. Urbana: University of Illinois Press, 2012.

Garvey, Ellen Gruber. "Alice Moore Dunbar-Nelson: The View from Her Scrapbook." *Legacy* 33, no. 2 (2016): 310–35.

Giddings, Paula. *When and Where I Enter: The Impact of Black Women on Race and Sex in America*. New York: William Morrow, 1984.

Gidlow, Liette. *The Big Vote: Gender, Consumer Culture, and the Politics of Exclusion, 1890s-1920s*. Baltimore: Johns Hopkins University Press, 2004.

———. "The Sequel: The Fifteenth Amendment, the Nineteenth Amendment, and Southern Black Women's Struggle to Vote." *Journal of the Gilded Age & Progressive Era* 17, no. 3 (July 2018): 433–49.

———. "Delegitimizing Democracy: 'Civic Slackers,' the Cultural Turn, and the Possibilities of Politics." *Journal of American History* 89, no. 3 (December 2002): 922–57.

———. "More Than Double: African American Women and the Rise of a 'Women's Vote.'" *Journal of Women's History* 32, no. 1 (Spring 2020): 52–61.

Giele, Janet Zollinger. *Two Paths to Women's Equality: Temperance, Suffrage, and the Origins of Modern Feminism*. New York: Twayne, 1995.

Gilmore, Glenda E. *Gender and Jim Crow: Women and the Politics of White Supremacy in North Carolina, 1890–1920*. Chapel Hill: University of North Carolina Press, 1996.

Ginzberg, Lori D. *Elizabeth Cady Stanton: An American Life*. New York: Hill and Wang, 2009.

———. *Untidy Origins: A Story of Woman's Rights in Antebellum New York*. Chapel Hill: University of North Carolina Press, 2005.

———. "Radical Imaginings: The View from Atop a Slippery Slope." *Journal of Women's History* 32, no. 1 (Spring 2020): 14–22.

Goodier, Susan. *No Votes for Women: The New York State Anti-Suffrage Movement.* Urbana: University of Illinois Press, 2013.

——— and Karen Pastorello, *Women Will Vote: Winning Suffrage in New York State.* Ithaca, NY: Cornell University Press, 2017.

Gordon, Ann D., and Bettye Collier-Thomas, eds. *African American Women and the Vote, 1837–1965.* Amherst: University of Massachusetts Press, 1997.

Gordon, Linda. "Black and White Visions of Welfare: Women's Welfare Activism, 1890–1945." *Journal of American History* 91 (September 1991): 559–90.

Graham, Sally Hunter. "Woodrow Wilson, Alice Paul, and the Woman Suffrage Movement," *Political Science Quarterly* 98, no. 4 (1983–1984): 665–79.

Graham, Sara Hunter. *Woman Suffrage and the New Democracy.* New Haven, CT: Yale University Press, 1996.

Green, Elna C. *Southern Strategies: Southern Women and the Woman Suffrage Question.* Chapel Hill: University of North Carolina Press, 1997.

Harley, Sharon, and Rosalyn Terborg-Penn, eds. *The Afro-American Woman: Struggles and Images.* Port Washington, NY: Kennikat Press, 1978.

Hicks, Cheryl D. *Talk With You Like a Woman: African American Women, Justice, and Reform in New York, 1890–1935.* Chapel Hill: University of North Carolina Press, 2010.

Hobbs, Allyson. *A Chosen Exile: A History of Racial Passing in American Life.* Cambridge, MA: Harvard University Press, 2014.

Hoffecker, Carol E. *Beneath Thy Guiding Hand: A History of Women at the University of Delaware.* Newark: University of Delaware, 1994.

———. *Corporate Capital: Wilmington in the Twentieth Century.* Philadelphia: University of Pennsylvania Press, 1983.

———. "Delaware's Woman Suffrage Campaign." *Delaware History* 20, no.3 (1983): 149–67.

———. *Democracy in Delaware: The Story of the First State's General Assembly.* Wilmington: Cedar Tree Books, 2004.

Hull, Gloria [Akasha]. *Color, Sex and Poetry: Three Women Writers of the Harlem Renaissance.* Bloomington: Indiana University Press, 1987.

"Interchange: Women's Suffrage, the Nineteenth Amendment, and the Right to Vote." *Journal of American History* 106, no. 3 (December 2019): 662–94.

Irving, Helen. *Citizenship, Alienage, and the Modern Constitutional State: A Gendered History.* Cambridge: Cambridge University Press, 2016.

Jablonsky, Thomas J. *The Home, Heaven, and Mother Party: Female Anti-Suffragists in the United States, 1868–1920.* Brooklyn: Carlson, 1994.

Jensen, Kimberly. *Mobilizing Minerva: American Women in the First World War.* Urbana: University of Illinois Press, 2008.

Johnson, Joan Marie. *Funding Feminism: Monied Women, Philanthropy, and the Women's Movement, 1870–1967*. Chapel Hill: University of North Carolina Press, 2017.

Kennedy, David M. *Over Here: The First World War and American Society*. New York: Oxford University Press, 1982.

Kennedy, Kathleen. *Disloyal Mothers and Scurrilous Citizens: Women and Subversion during World War I*. Bloomington: Indiana University Press, 1999.

Keyssar, Alexander. *The Right to Vote: The Contested History of Democracy in the United States*. New York: Basic Books, 2000.

Kousser, J. Morgan. *The Shaping of Southern Politics: Suffrage Restriction and the Establishment of the One-Party South, 1880–1910*. New Haven, CT: Yale University Press, 1974.

Kraditor, Aileen. *The Ideas of the Woman Suffrage Movement, 1890–1920*. New York: Columbia University Press, 1965.

Lebsock, Suzanne. "Woman Suffrage and White Supremacy: A Virginia Case Study." In *Visible Women: New Essays on American Activism*, edited Nancy A. Hewitt and Suzanne Lebsock. Urbana: University of Illinois Press, 1993.

Lemay, Kate Clarke, ed. *Votes for Women! A Portrait of Persistence*. Princeton, NJ: Princeton University Press for the Smithsonian Institution, 2019.

Lindsey, Treva. *Colored No More: Reinventing Black Womanhood in Washington, D.C.* Urbana: University of Illinois Press, 2017.

Lumsden, Linda J. *Inez: The Life and Times of Inez Milholland*. Bloomington: Indiana University Press, 2004.

Lunardini, Christine A. *From Equal Suffrage to Equal Rights: Alice Paul and the National Woman's Party, 1910–1928*. New York: New York University Press, 1988.

Marks, Carole C. *Farewell—We're Good and Gone: The Great Black Migration*. Bloomington: Indiana University Press, 1989.

Marshall, Susan. *Splintered Sisterhood: Gender and Class in the Campaign against Woman Suffrage*. Madison: University of Wisconsin Press, 1997.

Marth, Andrea. "The Fruits of Jim Crow: The Edgewood Sanatorium and African American Institution Building in Wilmington, Delaware, 1900–1940." MA Thesis, University of Delaware, 1994.

Materson, Lisa. *For the Freedom of Her Race: Black Women and Electoral Politics in Illinois, 1877–1932*. Chapel Hill: University of North Carolina Press, 2009.

Mayhall, Laura Nym. *The Militant Suffrage Movement: Citizenship and Resistance in Britain, 1860–1930*. New York: Oxford University Press, 2003.

Mead, Rebecca. *How the Vote Was Won: Woman Suffrage in the Western United States, 1868–1914*. New York: New York University Press, 2004.

McMillan, Sally G. *Lucy Stone: An Unapologetic Life*. New York: Oxford University Press, 2015.

Mjagkij, Nina and Margaret Spratt, eds. *Men and Women Adrift: Tthe YMCA and the YWCA in the City*. New York: New York University Press, 1997.

Munroe, John A. *History of Delaware*, 3rd Edition. Newark: University of Delaware Press, 1993.

———. *The University of Delaware: A History.* Newark: The University of Delaware, 1983, available at https://www1.udel.edu/Archives/books/munroe/index.html.

Nickliss, Alexandra. *Phoebe Apperson Hearst: A Life of Power and Politics.* Lincoln: University of Nebraska Press, 2018.

Orleck, Annelise. *Common Sense and a Little Fire: Women and Working-Class Politics in the United States, 1900–1965.* Chapel Hill: University of North Carolina Press, 1995.

Pierson, Laura M. *The Young Women's Christian Association of Wilmington, Delaware: "That They Might Live More Abundantly," History, 1895–1945.* Wilmington: YWCA, 1945.

Plastas, Melinda. *A Band of Noble Women: Racial Politics in the Women's Peace Movement.* Syracuse, NY: Syracuse University Press, 2011.

Reed, H. Clay and Marion Björnson Reed, eds. *Delaware: A History of the First State,* 2 vols. New York: Lewis Publishing Co., 1947.

Rhodes, Jane. *Mary Ann Shadd Cary: The Black Press and Protest in the Nineteenth Century.* Bloomington: Indiana University Press, 1999.

Robertson, Nancy Marie. *Christian Sisterhood, Race Relations and the YWCA, 1906–46.* Urbana: University of Illinois Press, 2007.

Salem, Dorothy B. *To Better Our World: Black Women in Organized Reform, 1890–1920.* Brooklyn: Carlson Publishing, 1990.

Santangelo, Lauren C. *Suffrage and the City: New York Women Battle for the Ballot.* New York: Oxford University Press, 2019.

Scharff, Virginia. *Taking the Wheel: Women and the Coming of the Motor Age.* New York: Free Press, 1991.

Schechter, Patricia. *Ida B. Wells-Barnett and American Reform, 1880–1930.* Chapel Hill: University of North Carolina Press, 2001.

Scott, Anne Firor. *Natural Allies: Women's Associations in American History.* Urbana: University of Illinois Press, 1991.

Sewell, Jessica Ellen. *Women and the Everyday City: Public Space in San Francisco, 1890–1915.* Minneapolis: University of Minnesota Press, 2011.

Shaw, Stephanie J. *What a Woman Ought to Be and to Do: Black Professional Women Workers during the Jim Crow Era.* Chicago: University of Chicago Press, 1996.

Sheppard, Alice. *Cartooning for Suffrage.* Albuquerque: University of New Mexico Press, 1994.

Spruill, Marjorie Julian. *Divided We Stand: The Battle over Women's Rights and Family Values That Divided America.* New York: Bloomsbury, 2017.

Stanislow, Gail. "Domestic Feminism in Wilmington: The New Century Club, 1889–1917." *Delaware History* 22, no. 3 (Spring 1987): 158–85.

Stillion Southard, Belinda A. *Militant Citizenship: Rhetorical Strategies of the*

National Woman's Party, 1913–1920. College Station: Texas A&M University Press, 2011.

Taggart, Robert J. *Private Philanthropy and Public Education: Pierre S. du Pont and the Delaware Schools, 1890–1940.* Newark: University of Delaware Press, 1988.

———. "Pierre S. du Pont and the Great School Fight of 1919–1921." *Delaware History* 17, no. 3 (1978): 155–78.

Taylor, Mark. "Utopia by Taxation: Frank Stephens and the Single Tax Community of Arden, Delaware." *Pennsylvania Magazine of History and Biography* 126, no. 2 (April 2002): 305–25.

Teele, Dawn Langan. *Forging the Franchise: The Political Origins of the Women's Vote.* Princeton, NJ: Princeton University Press, 2018.

Tetrault, Lisa. *The Myth of Seneca Falls: Memory and the Women's Suffrage Movement, 1848–1898.* Chapel Hill: University of North Carolina Press, 2014.

Terborg-Penn, Rosalyn. *African American Women in the Struggle for the Vote, 1850–1920.* Bloomington: Indiana University Press, 1998.

Thurner, Manuela. "Better Citizens without the Ballot: American Anti-Suffrage Women and their Rationale during the Progressive Era." *Journal of Women's History* 5 (Spring 1993): 33–60.

Tuttle, William. *Race Riot: Chicago in the Red Summer of 1919.* New York: Atheneum, 1978.

Van Voris, Jacqueline. *Carrie Chapman Catt: A Public Life.* New York: Feminist Press, 1987.

Ward, Margaret. "'Suffrage First, Above All Else!' An Account of the Irish Suffrage Movement." *Feminist Review* no. 10 (Summer 1982): 21–36.

Weisenfeld, Judith. *African American Women and Christian Activism: New York's Black YWCA, 1905–1945.* Cambridge, MA: Harvard University Press, 1997.

Weiss, Elaine F. *Fruits of Victory: The Women's Land Army of America in the Great War.* Dulles, VA: Potomac Books, 2008.

———. *The Woman's Hour: The Great Fight to Win the Vote.* New York: Viking, 2018.

Wellman, Judith. *The Road to Seneca Falls.* Urbana: University of Illinois Press, 2004.

Wheeler, Marjorie Spruill. *New Women of the New South: The Leaders of the Woman Suffrage Movement in the Southern States.* New York: Oxford University Press, 1993.

White, Deborah Gray. *Too Heavy a Load: Black Women in Defense of Themselves.* New York: Norton, 1999.

Wilkerson-Freeman, Sarah. "Alabama White Women, the Poll Tax, and V.O. Key's Master Narrative of Southern Politics," *Journal of Southern History* 68, no. 2 (May 2002): 333–74.

Williams, Chad Lewis. *Torchbearers of Democracy: African American Soldiers in the World War I Era*. Chapel Hill: University of North Carolina Press, 2010.

Wilson, Jan Doolittle. *The Women's Joint Congressional Committee and the Politics of Maternalism, 1920–1930*. Urbana: University of Illinois Press, 2007.

Wolbrecht, Christina, and Kevin J. Corder. *A Century of Votes for Women: American Elections Since Suffrage*. New York: Cambridge University Press, 2020.

Woolard-Provine, Annette. *Integrating Delaware: The Reddings of Wilmington*. Newark: University of Delaware Press, 2004.

Young, Toni. *Becoming American, Remaining Jewish: The Story of Wilmington, Delaware's First Jewish Community, 1879–1924*. Newark: University of Delaware Press, 1999.

Zahniser, J. D. and Amelia R. Fry. *Alice Paul: Claiming Power*. New York: Oxford University Press, 2014.

Zieger, Susan. "The Schoolhouse vs the Army: U.S. Teachers and the Campaign against Militarism in the Schools, 1914–1918." *Journal of Women's History* 15, no 2 (Summer 2003): 15–60.

Secondary Works: Digital

American National Biography. New York: Oxford University Press, https://www-anb-org.udel.idm.oclc.org/.

Delaware State University. "History." https://www.desu.edu/about/history.

Online Biographical Dictionary of the Woman Suffrage Movement in the United States, eds. Thomas Dublin and Kathryn Kish Sklar. Alexandria, VA: Alexander Street, 2015–present. https://documents.alexanderstreet.com/VOTESforWOMEN.

"Brown, Mary E. (1865–1948)." Social History Welfare Project, Virginia Commonwealth University Libraries. https://socialwelfare.library.vcu.edu/woman-suffrage/brown-mary-e-suffragist/.

Index

Dunbar, Paul Laurence, 23, 27, 60
du Pont, Alfred I., 147–48, 151
du Pont, Henry A., 55, 67
du Pont, Josephine Anderson, 4, 65, 72, 140
du Pont, Pierre S., 123, 128–29, 148
du Pont, T. Coleman, 125, 148
Dyer Anti-Lynching Bill, 162

E. I. DuPont de Nemours Company, 51
Elections: 1916, 33, 63, 66–68; 1918, 82, 108,
    112; 1920, 152–57; 1922, 162–63; 1924 and
    1928, 163
emancipation, 11, 13, 23
Equal Rights Amendment (ERA), 5, 167–69
Equal Suffrage Study Club, 2, 4, 10, 34, 58,
    62; and Delaware Federation of Colored
    Women's Clubs, 130; and First World
    War, 75, 88, 89, 100–102; founders of,
    29; members' activism, 58–59; 138–40;
    and NAACP, 29–30; and 1920 election,
    152; in suffrage parade, 37. *See also*
    Suffragists, Black
Eskridge, Mary Phillips, 74, 87–88, 154, 156
Evening Journal, Wilmington, 56–57,
    58–59, 138, 144, 145, 155–56, 164

Federation of Christian Workers,
    Wilmington, 23, 27, 28–29, 45
First World War: Black Delawareans
    and, 75, 78–81, 100–103, 138–39, 154;
    censorship during, 97, 99; ends, 111;
    in Europe, 41, 63, 71; Liberty Loan
    program, 74–76, 86; patriotism and
    loyalty, 92, 97–98, 99; "preparedness,"
    76–82; protests during, 79; suffrage
    and, 75, 82–97; women workers and,
    91–92, 100, 102–103, 104, 116
Fox, Ida, 153

Garrett, Helen, 28, 166
Garrett Settlement House. *See* Thomas
    Garrett Settlement House
Garrett, Thomas, 2, 10–11, 12, 13
General Federation of Women's Clubs, 21,
    198n6
Georgetown New Century Club, 21
gerrymandering, 19, 149–50, 169
Ginns, Sallie Topkis, 64, 77, 104, 113, 126

Hamilton, Fannie Hopkins, 6, 26, 29
Harper, Frances Ellen Watkins, 13

Hart, Walter, 142–43
Hearst, Phoebe Apperson, 42, 65, 103
Hill, Elsie, 48–49
Hilles, Florence Bayard, 4, 46, 52–53, 165;
    arrest of, 71, 93; and Black suffragists,
    60, 62, 139–41, 160; and CU/NWP,
    42–43, 47–49, 64–66, 71, 103, 117, 133,
    137, 142–43, 166–68; and Democratic
    Party, 41–42, 93, 108; and DESA, 37, 40,
    43, 52, 64–65, 69–70, 72, 96, 108; family
    background of, 41–43; and First World
    War, 91–92, 104–5; in France, 117–18,
    126, 205n71; racial views of, 57–58,
    140–41, 160; suffrage tattoo of, 92; and
    Woodrow Wilson, 69, 93
Hilles, Katherine Lee Bayard, 126, 136
Hilles, William S., 42, 117, 166
Hoffecker, Carol E., 1, 141, 146
Hopkins, John O., 6, 29, 81, 102
Houston, Margaret White, 3, 18–21, 124–25,
    144, 156, 185n15
Houston, Robert Griffith, 20
Howard School, The, 22–23, 26, 81, 129,
    213n55
Howard University, Washington, D.C., 14,
    22, 39
Hughes, Charles Evans, 68

Industrial School for Colored Girls, 27,
    130, 161
Ivory, Percy Van Eman, 197n52

Jason, W. C., 128
Johnson, Ella Weldin, 16
Jones, Rosalie Gardiner, 33–34

Kearney, Belle, 30
Kent, Margaret, 18
Kilbreth, Mary, 133, 164–65
Kruse, Edwina, 26, 29, 102, 130
Ku Klux Klan, 30, 161, 163

Layton, Caleb R., 110, 147, 162–63, 206n1
Layton, Daniel, 147–48
Lea, Eliza Corbit, 85, 136
League of Colored Republican Women,
    152, 160–61
League of Women Voters, 152, 157, 159, 163,
    164, 165
Lewis, Dora Kelly, 132, 140–41
Lockwood, Belva, 16–17

About the Author

Anne M. Boylan is Professor Emerita of History and Women and Gender Studies at the University of Delaware. A social historian of the United States, she researches and writes on women's history, social and cultural history, voluntary associations, and religion. She is the author of numerous scholarly articles and four books: *Sunday School: The Formation of An American Institution, 1790–1880* (Yale, 1988); *The Origins of Women's Activism: New York and Boston, 1797–1840* (UNC, 2002); *Women's Rights in the United States: A History in Documents* (Oxford, 2016); and *Votes for Delaware Women* (Delaware, 2021). Boylan has been the recipient of fellowships and grants from, among others, the National Endowment for the Humanities and the Radcliffe Institute at Harvard University, and has been inducted into the Society of American Historians. She served as state coordinator for the entries for Delaware suffragists included in the *Online Biographical Dictionary of the Woman Suffrage Movement in the United States.*